THE BIG BOOK OF BOAT CANVAS

THE BIG BOOK OF BOAT CANVAS

Karen S. Lipe
illustrations by Cynthia Taylor Dax

International Marine
Camden, Maine

Published by International Marine

10 9 8 7 6 5 4 3 2

Library of Congress Cataloging-in-Publication Data

Lipe, Karen.
  The big book of boat canvas.

  1. Marine canvas work. I. Title.
VM531.L56 1988   623.8'62   87-36919
ISBN 0-915160-35-8

Questions regarding the content of this book should be addressed to:

International Marine Publishing
P.O. Box 220
Camden, ME 04843

Typeset by Camden Type 'n Graphics, Camden, Maine
Printed and bound by Rand McNally, Taunton, Massachusetts
Designed by Janet Patterson
Production Coordinator: Janet Robbins
Editors: Cynthia Bourgeault, Jonathan Eaton, Barbara Hatch,
        David Oppenheim

Photo Credits

Front cover, top to bottom: Don A. Bamford; Bob Lipe; Chris
    Cunningham; Jeff Debevec photo, courtesy Marine Textiles, Wayzata,
    MN (Fabrication by Needle Loft, Seabrook, TX; fabric is Sunbrella, Glen
    Raven Mills, Burlington, NC).
Back cover: Matthew Walker; courtesy Industrial Fabrics
    Association International, St. Paul, MN.
Text: p. 63, 67, Don A. Bamford; p. 113, Christine Charbonneau, Howes
    & Charbonneau Sailmakers, South Yarmouth, MA; p. 123, Jeanne
    Milburn, The Canvas Company, Seattle, WA; p. 138, Chris Cunningham;
    p. 150, 157, The Coverloft, Annapolis, MD.
Other photos courtesy Bob Lipe; Carol Ricketts of The Coverloft;
    Christopher Ford of Yacht Canvas; and Pat Means of Nautical Curtains
    and Cushions.

Dedication

This book is for all those people who have worked with me and whose contributions to my knowledge of this subject are immeasurable.

Contents

Acknowledgments

Thanks to all the clients and coworkers who have contributed to my experience in canvasworking. Special thanks to Cynthia Taylor Dax for her expert artistic ability and infinite patience and willingness to work with me, and to Rich Stewart, whose editorial, technical, and emotional support is always valued. Thanks to Jim Kraft for his early contributions in the art department. Bob Lipe has been especially helpful with photography, editorial comment, and moral support. Carol Ricketts of The Coverloft, Christopher Ford of Yacht Canvas, and Pat Means of Nautical Curtains and Cushions have contributed pictures of various projects as has the Industrial Fabrics Association International. Thanks to all of you. Through all of the shapes this book has assumed, many editorial people have been helpful. Thanks specifically to Jon Eaton, Cynthia Bourgeault, Jim Gilbert, and Steve Doherty. And thanks to all the rest of you who worked toward the completion and production of this work. There is strong evidence of your skills here, and I appreciate your time and your energy.

Introduction

The use of the word "canvas" to describe all fabric work aboard boats started centuries ago when bosuns made everything from sails to clothes out of canvas. We still use the term to mean anything aboard a boat made of fabric, even though very little today is actually made out of cotton canvas.

The purpose of this book is to provide clear and simple instructions for a variety of "canvas" projects for your boat. Canvas work is one of the crafts that mariners have pursued for centuries, and for the boat owner, it can provide real satisfaction. Not only does it reduce the cost of outfitting—which can be considerable for some custom-made canvas items—but it provides you with the type of canvas equipment that exactly suits your cruising requirements and precisely fits your boat. The projects described here not only contribute to your comfort and safety aboard; they also, in many cases, will protect your boat so as to reduce maintenance. While the projects in this book have been designed and laid out primarily for sailboats, a considerable number of them are equally applicable to powerboats.

This present book represents a thorough revision of my two earlier books, *Boat Canvas from Cover to Cover* and *More Boat Canvas*, combined with a whole new section on interior canvas work. More than a dozen new below-decks projects are included, designed to help you create a gracious yet functional cruising space. Throughout these chapters the term "canvas" is used quite loosely indeed, with recommended materials ranging from vinyl to velvet and including a variety of synthetic blends. In addition to the specific projects, I've included a chapter on design and color considerations to help you make design choices that are right for your cruising style.

As in my two previous books, the instructions are accompanied by detailed illustrations and photographs. Before you begin any project, I strongly recommend that you read through the entire book first to get a feeling for the subject. Most of the projects involve simple sewing techniques that are easy to master with a bit of practice, even if you've never done any sewing before. But they do take careful planning, layout, cutting, and assembly to produce the kind of finished project you will be proud of.

Planning is the key to success. Go at it in steps: (1) Choose a project. (2) List the required materials. (3) Diagram your assembly parts. (4) Purchase materials. (5) Label all parts (include dimensions, reinforcement positions, etc.). (6) Note special instructions that will help you visualize the steps and avoid errors. (7) Then begin the work.

Since this is a how-to book, you will be taken through each project step by step to completion. If you make a mistake or get tired, put the project aside for the day until you are fresh and ready to go at it again. Remember the old carpenter's adage: "Measure twice, cut once."

Half the success of your project lies in having the confidence to begin. Using the stages listed above, wade right in! After a few projects, once you've mastered the basic canvas-working skills, you'll probably find yourself designing projects of your own.

Enjoy yourself.

Karen S. Lipe
Annapolis, Maryland

PART ONE

A
Few
Fundamentals

1
The Sewing Machine

The projects in this book are designed to be sewn with a domestic sewing machine. Commercial machines will sew through more thicknesses at a higher speed than domestic machines. However, most of us do not require a fast machine, and most projects will not involve thicknesses that a good domestic machine cannot sew through.

It should be noted, however, that a sewing machine is a complex mechanism. Care should be taken to keep the machine well oiled and in proper adjustment, especially when it is used to sew heavy fabrics. Many domestic machines sew lightweight fabric for years without being oiled properly, but oil your machine faithfully when using heavy fabric.

An oiling diagram is normally included in your machine manual. If not, get one from your dealer or manufacturer. The oil can be purchased from any sewing machine dealer. Oiling may look complicated, but it's simple enough if you approach it a step at a time. Start at the needle side of the machine and work to the right. Place a few drops of sewing machine oil in each oil port. Be sure to run the machine sufficiently to work the oil into all moving parts. After oiling, use some scrap material to run several rows of stitching, so that if any oil escapes at first, it will not soil good fabric.

Check the teeth in the pressure plate. These feed the material through the machine, and after much use they may become dull and less effective. Worn teeth can be replaced for a few dollars. Many machine models allow you to raise and lower these teeth; if you raise them slightly higher than the normal sewing height, heavy fabrics will feed through more smoothly. Don't forget to lower the teeth again before sewing lighter fabrics.

Tension

The upper tension and bobbin tension must be equally balanced when sewing or the stitches will not be strong and even. The bobbin tension is adjusted with a tiny screw on the bobbin case. This adjustment should be made only after the upper tension has been adjusted, using the knob on the tension wheel. Note your owner's manual.

Proper stitch tension is shown in Fig-

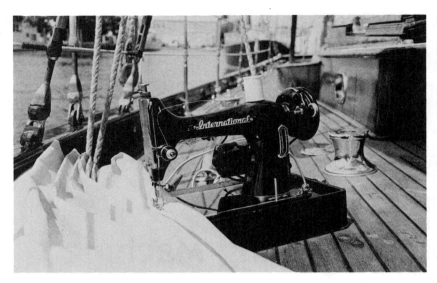

Figure 1–1.
Proper stitch tension.

Figure 1–2.
Upper tension too loose.

Figure 1–3.
Upper tension too tight.

ure 1–1. When the upper tension is too loose, the stitches look like those in Figure 1–2, and when the upper tension is too tight they look like those in Figure 1–3.

Be patient when adjusting the tension. Trial and error is the only method. The stitch tension is important and may need changing with each different type of fabric you use.

Needles and Thread

Heavy fabric should be sewn with number 16 or number 18 needles. The large needles pack more power and break less easily than small ones, and they also will accommodate larger thread. Try to use a good, all-purpose, cotton-wrapped polyester thread such as Coats & Clark Dual Duty. It is strong, sun resistant, and stretchable, and will last longer outdoors than Dacron thread. Heavy-duty polyester thread is another option, but it will cause you more tension problems than the all-purpose thread.

2
Tools and Hardware
for Canvas Work

Canvas work requires a handful of basic tools, plus a few specialty items, all pictured in Figure 2–1.

Scissors should be sharp and made of good steel or aluminum. Cloth edges that are cut well provide easier sewing.

A *ripper* is used for ripping out mistakes. It should be sharp, and it should be treated with respect. Used properly, it will rip a seam nicely in a short time. Used carelessly, it will rip material and skin.

Measuring tape and ruler, for measuring before you cut the cloth. (Remember the old carpenter's adage: "Measure twice; cut once.")

Grommet tool and die will be needed for setting grommets and can be purchased at good hardware or marine stores. A grommet set includes a hole cutter, base die, and grommet setter; each setter fits only one size of grommet. Numbers 2 and 3 are good, all-around grommet sizes.

To set a grommet, start by cutting a hole wherever required in the material, using the hole cutter and a hammer. Use a piece of hardwood or lead as a backing block (using masonry or a harder metal will cause the cutting edge of the hole cutter to chip and dull).

Place the male half of the grommet, flange down, on the base die, and place the hole in the cloth over the male end of this grommet half. Put the female half of the grommet over the cloth. Center the grommet setter in the hole of the base die (Figure 2–4), and tap the setter lightly with the hammer. Increase the strength of your hammer blows until the grommet is set. If the grommet can be twisted in the cloth, it is too loose. Repeat the setting procedure if necessary.

Plain grommets work well on two to four thicknesses of canvas; spur grommets work better when more layers are involved. The small setter and die that are usually found in a grommet kit will not last very long, but for putting in fewer than a dozen grommets, a kit is sufficient.

For setting snaps, a *snap setter* of some sort is essential. The small snap-setting kit shown in Figure 2–5 is made by Dot Fasteners. Punch a hole in the cloth

*Figure 2–1.
Necessary tools for canvas
work. From top to bottom:
scissors, ripper, hammer for
setting grommets, snap
attachment for Vise Grips,
Vise Grips (with snap-
installing attachments),
grommet set, snap setter kit,
measuring tape, and ruler.*

*Figure 2–2.
Male and female halves of a
grommet (above), and three
grommet types (below).*

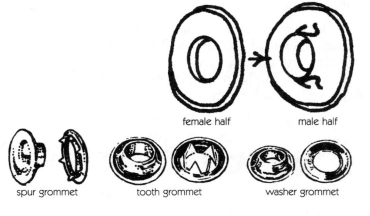

female half   male half

spur grommet   tooth grommet   washer grommet

using a ripper, leather punch, or nail; then place the male end of the snap (which often resembles a button) on the rubber disk. Place the hole in the fabric over the male post of the snap. The female end of the snap is placed on top of the fabric and the male fitting.

There are other options as well. A spool of thread can be used to set the snap if you do not have the dowel shown. More efficient snap setters such as the Vise-Grip set shown in Figure 2–1 are also available. However, the Vise-Grip set retails for about $40 and is usually not worth the investment unless you know you are going to do a great deal of snap setting.

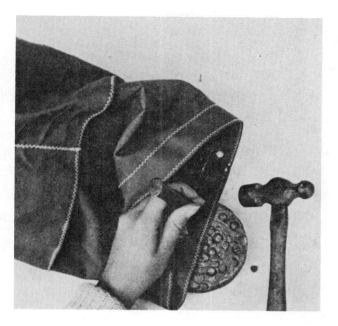

Figure 2–3.
Cutting the hole for a grommet.

Figure 2–4.
Setting the grommet.

Fasteners

Figure 2–6 shows the types of snaps and grommets available and most often used for fasteners. Dot Fasteners manufactures the majority of them, and they are sold by most marine hardware stores. The various snap fittings displayed in the photograph should be used for their intended purposes. There are a number of possible combinations available to fit each situation. (If you are attaching snaps at corresponding positions on a boat and cover, first attach the half that will be on the boat.)

Figure 2–5.
Setting a snap.

Figure 2–6.
Types of fasteners. Twist
fasteners, or turnbuttons, are
shown at the bottom.

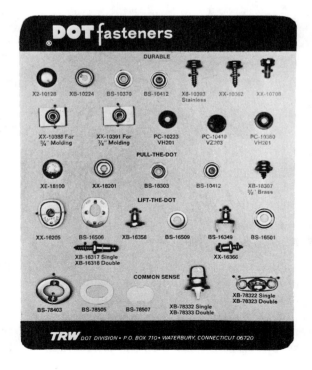

Twist fasteners (bottom row of the photograph) don't mix well with salt water because they can foul and become unturnable. However, if there will be considerable strain on the fastening, a snap will not hold. If you do not wish to use grommets and lacing, the twist fastener is a good alternative. It can be installed easily with a pair of pliers.

Zippers

Whenever possible I recommend that YKK Delrin zippers be used for exterior projects. Their large teeth make them stronger than a dressmaker's zipper, and they will resist deterioration due to weather. There are two sizes—number 5 and number 10. The number 5 is lighter than the 10 and can be used for interior and exterior cushions and light covers. Use the number 10 for dodgers, Biminis, awnings, sailcovers, and covers that will be under strain. This product can be purchased as one continuous length of zipper called a chain that you cut to your desired length, attaching a separate slider, or it can be purchased in precut lengths called jacket zippers. The latter are constructed with bottom stops, allowing you to unzip them without the slider coming off one side. Use jacket zippers whenever an opening must be free top and bottom.

These zippers can be purchased at most canvas shops and fabric stores.

3
Sewing Terminology
and Techniques

Using the Sewing Machine

For success in canvas work, you should be familiar with the sewing machine you are using. If you are not, practice on scraps of cloth with this manual in hand. Learn what each knob and lever on the machine does. Here are a few universal terms that will help.

Tension, as discussed in Chapter 1, is most important. It is controlled by the upper tension knob and a screw on the bobbin case. If the material doesn't feed smoothly, skipping stitches, or if stitches are loose (as described in Chapter 1), adjust the tension. Always adjust tension with the presser foot down.

Pressure is created by the presser foot. This foot holds the fabric firmly while the machine is stitching. Regulate the pressure so that material feeds smoothly. Pressure is too tight if the fabric puckers or drags or is too thick to go under the foot; it's too loose if the fabric slips or stops feeding.

Backstitching is usually done with a reverse lever or knob. This is a method of locking the stitching so that it will not ravel at the beginning or end of each seam. You should lock all your seams at the beginning and end by this method. If your machine has no reverse, stitch an inch at the beginning of the seam, bring the needle to its highest position with the hand-wheel, raise the presser foot, move the material back to its beginning position (without cutting the threads), and stitch again over the first stitching.

Staystitching is a line of stitching in a flat piece of fabric that keeps the fabric from stretching or raveling.

Topstitching is stitching on the right side of the fabric, close to the seam.

A *seam* is made whenever you sew two or more pieces of fabric together. The *seam allowance* is the amount of fabric allowed between the stitching line and the edge of the material. In all of the following chapters a 1/2-inch seam allowance is recommended.

Two basic seams are used throughout

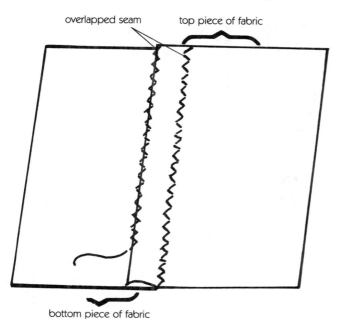

overlapped seam   top piece of fabric

bottom piece of fabric

Figure 3–1. An overlap seam finished with two rows of zigzag stitching.

this book—*overlap* and *flat-felled.* An overlap seam (Figure 3–1) is used when two selvage edges (factory-finished edges that will not ravel) are stitched together. When the edges to be joined are not finished, a flat-felled seam is used, and the seam allowance is finished with a line of *straight* (Figure 3–2) or *zigzag* (Figure 3–3) stitching to the underside of the material.

Zigzag stitching is used not only to bind raw edges, but also to stitch overlap seams and to sew knits. It is very strong, and will stretch rather than breaking as the fabric gives under tension.

Pin basting is done by placing pins perpendicular to the seam line to hold pieces of cloth together while stitching them.

Darting is a method of removing a triangular area of cloth, called a dart, without cutting away the material. It is most often used in canvas work to take the fullness out of hems or to remove excess cloth in covers. Begin stitching at the widest end of the dart and taper the stitching down to zero so that the dart will lie flat.

A *hem* is the finished edge. You should allow for 1½ to 2 inches of material for hems. Selvage edges (the factory-bound edge of the material) can be turned up the amount of the allowed hem al-

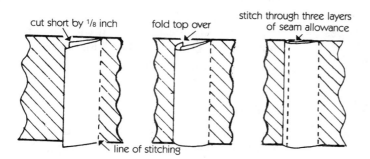

cut short by ⅛ inch   fold top over   stitch through three layers of seam allowance

line of stitching

Figure 3–2.
A flat-felled seam with the top seam allowance folded under and secured with a straight line of stitching.

Figure 3–3.
A flat-felled seam with the
raw edges finished in a line of
zigzag stitching.

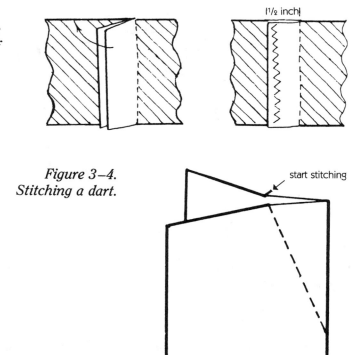

Figure 3–4.
Stitching a dart.

lowance and stitched (Figure 3–5). How-ever, raw edges that will ravel should be turned under ¼ inch and then turned un-der again 1¼ inch or 1¾ inches to finish the hem (Figure 3–6). This is known as a *double-rubbed hem*. Since most fastenings are mounted in the hem area, it is impor-tant to leave enough width in the hem to accommodate the fastener. If no fastener is needed, hems can be narrower.

A *casing* is similar to a hem, except that the two ends are left open to receive a batten, length of line, shock cord, or cur-tain rod.

Tabling is folded-over reinforcing ma-terial sewn along the corners and edges.

Stitching a Seam from Start to Finish

Thread your machine. Turn the hand-wheel to raise the needle to its highest point so that the thread will not slip out of the needle as stitching starts. (This should also be done at the end of every seam to prevent knotting on the underside of the

material.) Draw the needle and bobbin threads under the raised presser foot. Place the fabric under the raised presser foot with the seam edge on the right, and the bulk of the fabric on the left of the needle. Enough fabric should lie on the machine to prevent dragging. Lower the presser foot.

Start the machine with the foot pedal or knee lever. (You may have to turn the handwheel a quarter-turn to get the ma-chine started.) Stitch an inch and then backstitch an inch. Run the machine for-ward at an even speed, reducing speed as you come to the end of the seam. Back-stitch an inch. Stop the machine. Raise the needle to its highest point, lift the presser foot, draw out the fabric 4 or 5 inches from the needle, and clip the threads with scis-sors close to the fabric.

Guiding the Fabric

Most material can be directed under the needle by holding it with both hands in front of the presser foot. With heavy mate-

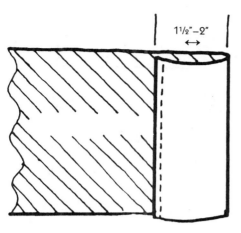

Figure 3–5.
Hemming a selvage edge.

1½"–2"

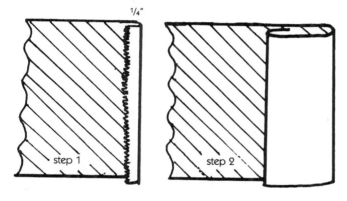

¼"

step 1   step 2

Figure 3–6.
Finishing a raw edge with a double-rubbed hem.

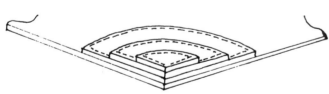

Figure 3–7.
Reinforcing a corner.

rial and very light material, you may want to have your left hand behind the presser foot to guide the material and your right hand in front of the presser foot. Heavy or slippery fabrics may need to be pulled lightly to help the feeder move the cloth through. You must coordinate this gentle pulling with the speed at which you are running the needle. If you begin breaking needles or enlarging stitches, you are pulling the material too hard. Frequent breaking of needles will damage the pressure plate on your machine. For very thick layers of canvas, you may have to make the

first few stitches by rotating the hand-wheel with your right hand.

Reinforcing Stress Points

Stress may be caused by strain from weight, wind, or stretching when an item is in use. Reinforcing stress points can be done in a number of ways. The most common method is the extra patch. (Turn under the raw edges and stitch it in place.) Since your grommets should be placed only in two or more layers of cloth (such as in a hem), place a patch 1¼ times the size of the grommet wherever a grommet is to

Figure 3–8.
Reinforcing a slash.

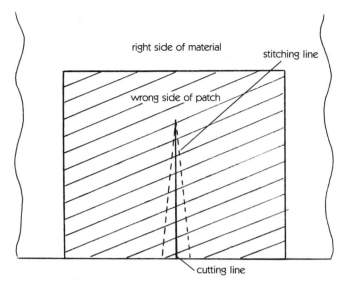

Figure 3–9.
Reinforcing a cutout, step 1.

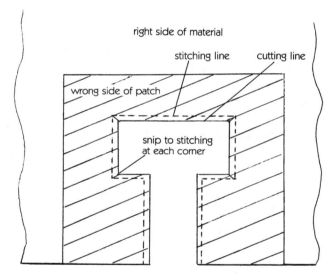

Figure 3–10.
Reinforcing a cutout,
step 2. Turn patch under
and topstitch.

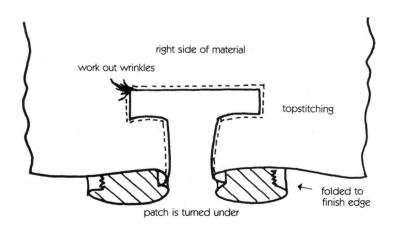

be set in a single layer of fabric. If extra-heavy strain will be applied, as happens at the corner of a winter awning, several patches of different sizes should be sewn, one on top of another (Figure 3–7).

Reinforcing Slashes or Cutouts

When a slash or cutout must be made to accommodate any protrusions such as shrouds, stanchions, cleats, masts, etc., the reinforcement patch can also finish the raw edge of the cloth. Cut a patch 1½ times the length and width of the slash or cutout. Pin this patch to the material, right sides together. (See "Right Side vs. Wrong Side" below. In this instance, the "right" side of the patch is the face that will show when the reinforcement is finished.) Draw the desired slash or cutout on the patch. Stitch in a triangle around the slash (Figure 3–8) and parallel to the cutting line for a cutout (Figure 3–9). Cut, taking out as much of the unnecessary cloth as

possible. However, don't cut any closer than ⅛ inch from the stitching. In the corners, cut diagonally right up to the stitching.

Turn the patch to the inside and work out all wrinkles. If the cloth pulls, you have not clipped the corners close enough. On the outside, topstitch around the edge of the slash or cutout (Figure 3–10).

On the inside, fold under the raw edges of the patch and stitch to the main piece of cloth (Figure 3–11).

Turning Corners

Whenever you must turn a corner, follow this procedure: Sew up to the corner of the stitching line. Rotate the needle through the fabric exactly at the corner. Slash the seam allowance almost to the needle. Lift the presser foot and rotate the cloth 90 degrees. Lower the presser foot and begin stitching again (Figure 3–12).

To make a gradual curve, make several

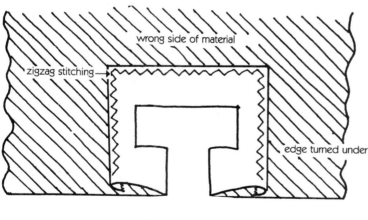

Figure 3–11.
Reinforcing a cutout,
step 3. Hemming the
patch.

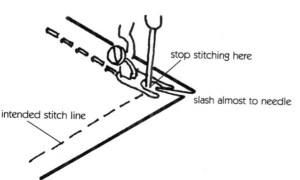

Figure 3–12.
Turning a corner.

*Figure 3–13.
Stitching a curve.*

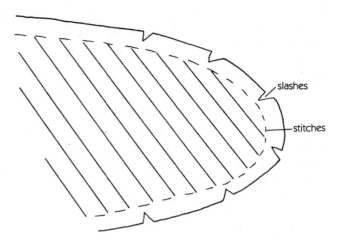

slashes

stitches

slashes in the seam allowance of the fabric as you stitch the curve (Figure 3–13).

Right Side vs. Wrong Side

Often I will refer to the *right* or *wrong* side of the material. The right side is the finished side, which you want to show when the project is completed. Canvas cloth does not usually have a right and a wrong side to it. The right and wrong side in this case is decided by the side on which you choose to turn the hems, place the seam allowance, etc. As long as you are consistent throughout the project, right side and wrong side won't be confusing, but every time you begin to sew a seam or hem be sure to check the material to make sure you are not switching sides.

PART TWO

Topside Projects

4
Color Considerations

The fabric color you choose will either enhance your boat's lines or draw attention to her worst features. Take a look at some older, more traditionally designed yachts. Choose fast, beautiful designs such as *Ticonderoga* or *Escapade*. Look at the old houseboats Trumpy or Elco used to build. See how their lines add to their beauty. Compare your own boat with them and determine where she is too tall, too boxy, too fat, too round, or just right. Now try to

use the color and shape of your exterior canvas to heighten the beauty of your boat.

Notice in Figure 4–1 how the color of the sail cover and dodger tends to change the appearance of the boat. In the first picture, where the canvas is white and matches the hull and deck, the eye tends to follow the lines of the caprail and cove stripe of the boottop. In the second picture, the color of the sail cover and dodger contrasts with the white hull, accentuat-

Figure 4–1.
Color contrasts for sailboats.

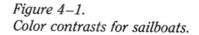
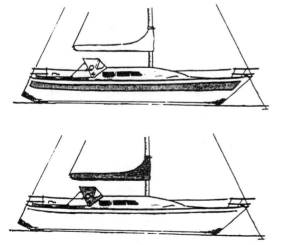
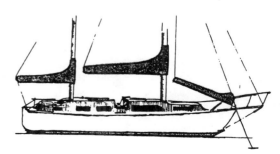

Figure 4–2.
Color contrasts for power yachts.

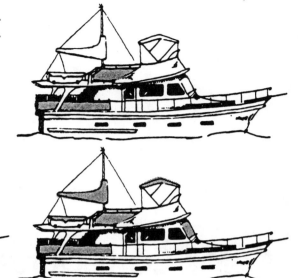

ing the length of the boat. A low-profile dodger can add to this effect, but a tall one will add to the sense of freeboard. On some boats with a colored cove or boot stripe, the appearance of length can be augmented by using a colored sail cover.

Also consider whether you want to draw attention to the canvas or whether you would rather have it blend into the hull and not be very noticeable. I prefer a white dodger with a white deck. The dodger then appears as an extension of the house rather than an addition. Winch covers may look nice to you standing upright, dark blue against white. Or perhaps you

would rather not see them. Varnished hatches covered with brown covers will look much the same as they do uncovered. Hatches covered with yellow covers will give the appearance of yellow squares in the deck.

Power yachts can also be enhanced by the height of their Biminis, the length of their weather cloths or the color of their bridge covers (Figure 4–2). Do you want your navy top to look like a hardtop extension of the overhead or do you want it to add to the aftward sweep of the bridge lines? Careful consideration of color can change the entire boat's appearance.

5
Fabric for
Exterior Projects

The fabric you choose for each project is an important consideration that will affect the project's longevity and aesthetic value. Some materials are more easily sewn than others, some are more durable or mildew resistant than others, and some are more easily folded and stowed. Thus, the entire project must be weighed against the individual properties of each fabric before choosing the best one for a particular job. Throughout this book, I have taken the liberty of suggesting fabrics that I would choose for various projects and have listed the fabrics in my own order of preference.

Traditional canvas is made of pure cotton thread and was once the exclusive material for sails, sail covers, and seat covers. Today we have many types of synthetic "canvas," which are grouped with cotton canvas because their weaves, textures, and uses are similar.

Untreated Canvas

Untreated canvas is soft, woven material that can be purchased in weights ranging from 8 to 24 ounces per square yard. The weight of the cloth will determine to a great extent its strength, as there are more threads per square foot in heavier cloth. There is a limit, however, to how heavy a material you can choose for certain projects. For instance, a sun canopy that is likely to be put up and taken down many times during a cruise cannot be easily stowed or handled if it is made of cloth heavier than 10 ounces. On the other hand, a cover that is used for protecting the boat from ice and snow could be made of 13- to 18-ounce cloth, because it is usually only handled twice a year, is not stowed on the boat in most cases, and will withstand the forces of the wind much better than lighter canvas. It is worth noting that any canvas heavier than 13 ounces will be difficult to sew on a domestic machine. However, you will rarely need canvas any heavier than this.

You will find untreated canvas available in widths of 31 inches and 36 inches for general purposes, and as wide as 120 inches for covering decks or making large awnings. It retails for about $4 per yard for 31-inch, 10-ounce canvas, rising in price for greater width and weight. The low

Fabrics for Exterior Canvas Work

FABRIC	WIDTH (IN INCHES)	WATER-REPELLENT	WATER-PROOF	STRETCH	ROTS IN SUNLIGHT	MILDEW RESISTANT
Canvas	31, 36, 42	Yes	Yes	2%	Yes	No
Treated Canvas	31, 36, 42	Yes	Yes	2%	In time	Yes
Acrylic Canvas	31, 46, 60	Yes	Yes	No	Eventually	Yes
Dacron	31, 45	Yes	No	No	Yes, quickly	Yes
Nylon	36, 45	Yes	No	Yes	In time	Yes
Spinnaker Cloth	40	Yes	No	Yes	In time	Yes
Vinyl Glass	20 gauge	Yes	Yes	Yes	Yes	Yes
	30 gauge	Yes	Yes	No	Yes	Yes
	40 gauge	Yes	Yes	No	Yes	Yes
Reinforced Vinyl	30, 60	Yes	Yes	Yes	Eventually	Yes
Textilene	60	Yes	No	No	Eventually	Yes

price is the only reason for using untreated canvas, now that so many other materials are available. It will mildew if allowed to get wet, will fade if dyed, and is not particularly resistant to sunshine.

Treated Canvas

There are many brands of treated canvas, some of the more popular being Vivatex, Graniteville, Terrasol, and Permasol. All of these are cotton canvas treated with a mildew-resistant coating. There is a small difference in price, but basically the difference among the brands is in the colors available. Vivatex, the best-known treated canvas, usually comes only in natural colors: pearl gray, which is really a pale green; colorless, which is a natural off-white with a slight brown fleck; and khaki, a golden tan. The traditionalist will probably choose one of these three colors. Permasol and Graniteville come in a variety of colors and patterns and seem to hold up as well as Vivatex. Terrasol comes only in natural colors. Treated canvas will last from five to seven years or more with heavy use, provided it is kept reasonably dry and clean. I have covers made of Vivatex that are 15 years old and have had heavy use for the last six years. The cloth is still in good condition, but the stitching has needed replacing.

Treated canvas retails for $10 to $15 a yard. It usually comes in 31-inch and 36-inch widths and 8.98- and 10.38-ounce weights. Just a dollar more a yard, it is much superior to untreated canvas for most marine uses. It will shrink when wet, up to 2 percent of the cloth's original size. This usually has no effect on anything you make with it. However, when making something you wish to fit drum-tight at all times, you must allow for this shrinkage and make the item 1 percent larger than the required size.

Acrylic Canvas

Acrylic canvas is a synthetic fabric with the look, weight and feel of cotton canvas. It works well for all outdoor covers, awnings, winter covers, and sailcovers and is also an alternative to vinyl for cockpit cushions. There are many companies manufacturing acrylic canvas, and their products seem to be of comparable quality. Sunbrella and Yachtcrylic have been on the market the longest. Argonaut, Diklon Super Wide, and Sun Master also are acrylic fabrics. They are available in a wide range of colors, and all of them are very resistant to ultraviolet light and fading. Red acrylic is the only exception; it turns pink in time. Acrylic canvas is very stable, water resistant, breathable, and easy to work with while sewing. Its only drawback is its high price. One yard of 46-inch-wide acrylic will cost $14.50.

Dacron (Terylene)

Dacron is the synthetic fiber of which most sails are made. It is tremendously strong and water resistant. It also resists mildew well but is very susceptible to damage by sunlight. Although people recommend making awnings of lightweight Dacron, I would strongly advise making only sails of it and keeping them covered at all possible times; Dacron rots quickly in the sun and does not make a good awning or anything else that must withstand long hours of sunlight. It comes in varying widths and runs from $6.50 to $11 a yard, depending on weight.

Spinnaker Cloth or Nylon Sailcloth

Nylon is somewhat less susceptible to the sun's rays than Dacron, but it will stretch, whereas Dacron will not. It is very lightweight, and therefore many people will choose it to make sail bags, ditty bags, and awnings. These are appropriate uses if you reinforce the strain positions well and don't mind the incessant crinkling noise that the nylon makes in the wind. Nylon is the most difficult of all woven cover materials to sew on because it tends to slide around when being sewn. Neither Dacron nor nylon breathes as well as canvas does. Nylon sells for $6 to $8 per yard and comes in various widths and colors.

Vinyl Glass

Vinyl glass, also called isinglass after the old-fashioned natural material, is used primarily in dodgers and hatch covers where vision is important. It comes in several grades. Vinyl glass sold off a roll is far inferior to glass sold by the sheet. Look for double-polished vinyl glass as your first choice because it will give less of a fishbowl effect. The most common vinyl-glass weight is 20 gauge. Forty-gauge vinyl is actually two layers of 20-gauge glass laminated together. It is used only in large enclosures since it is not as flexible as 20-gauge glass. In the past few years, 30-gauge glass has also become available. I recommend it over the 40-gauge for large enclosures on power yachts because it provides clearer vision and is easier to handle. For almost all other applications 20-gauge glass will suffice.

Reinforced Vinyl

Weblon, Facilon, Herculite, Structural, and Temperlux are all brands of reinforced vinyl. Some are reinforced with Dacron, some with polyester. I prefer the polyester reinforcing because it does not break down as quickly in the sunlight and tends to be a bit more stable. Some people prefer reinforced vinyl to acrylic, but I don't. Vinyl does clean more easily, but because it tends to shrink and stretch with heat and cold, it will not achieve quite as nice a fit. Since it doesn't breathe, don't use it on instruments, outboard motors, or anything else that could be harmed by trapped moisture. Price: $11 a yard.

Textilene

Textilene is relatively new on the market and is used primarily for cockpit cushions. It is a very strong, stable, open-weave vinyl that is also water resistant in the sense that it will not absorb water. However, since it is an open-weave fabric, it will not keep water out. It is a possible choice for sheet bags and those projects meant only to organize rather than to keep items dry.

6
Canvas Bucket, Ditty Bag, or Rigger's Bag

The ditty bag, a favorite of sailors since square-rigger days, is a cylindrical bag made of cloth with literally hundreds of uses. A simple ditty bag with drawstring closure will conveniently hold anything from clothespins to spare parts. Make it larger, and you have a sail or laundry bag. Put a metal or wooden hoop in the top and give it a rope handle, and you have a rigger's bag that will not only stand up by itself, but also carry various rigger's tools when someone has to go aloft. It will also serve as a canvas bucket.

Materials Needed
- canvas (Vivatex, Yachtcrylic, Permasol, spinnaker cloth, or sailcloth)

For ditty or sail bag:
- length of line to match the circumference, plus 4 inches
- 1 or 2 grommets

For canvas bucket:
- wooden, metal, or plastic hoop to match the circumference of the bucket
- 4 grommets

- 6 feet of 1/2-inch line for handle
- circular piece of plywood to match the circumference of the bucket (optional)

For rigger's bag:
- 1 circular piece of 1/4-inch or 1/8-inch line for drawstring, if required
- 2 grommets
- 6 feet of 1/2-inch line for handle
- circular piece of plywood to match the circumference of the bag (optional)

Construction

Step 1. Decide on the size bag you need. An average ditty bag might have a diameter of 5 inches and a height of 8 inches. A rigger's bag should be larger, say 10 inches in diameter and 15 inches high. Select the size that suits your purposes.

Step 2. Cut one or two circular pieces of canvas the diameter of the bag. This can be done easily with a ruler. For instance, if the diameter is 10 inches, place the ruler on the cloth. Mark the center at

Figure 6–1.
Marking a circle.

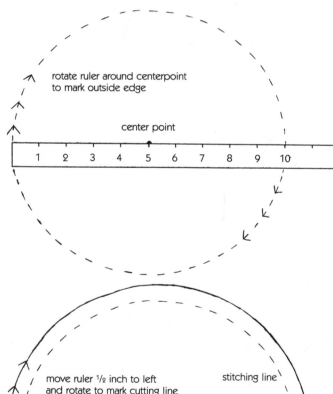

rotate ruler around centerpoint
to mark outside edge

center point

1 2 3 4 5 6 7 8 9 10

Figure 6–2.
Marking the cutting line.

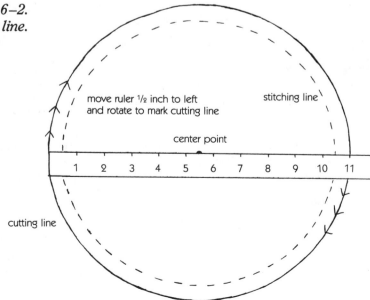

move ruler ½ inch to left
and rotate to mark cutting line

stitching line

center point

1 2 3 4 5 6 7 8 9 10 11

cutting line

5 inches and the limits of the diameter at 0 and 10 inches. Rotate the ruler, keeping the center mark at 5 inches, and continue to mark the outer edges at 0 inches and 10 inches (Figure 6–1). This should give you an accurate circle for the finished size. Remember that you must have 1/2-inch seam allowance. Place the center mark at 5½ inches and the limits of the diameter at 0 and 11 inches, and mark as before. This will give you your cutting line.

For small ditty bags, one circle is sufficient. Bags that will carry heavier gear should have a double bottom. Cut another circle to match the first.

Step 3.   To calculate the length measurement of the main piece of cloth, first figure the circumference of the circle by multiplying the diameter of the circle by π (3.14). (For example, 10 inches x 3.14 = 31.40 inches, or about a 31½-inch circumference.)

Step 4.   Add 1 inch to the circumference for seam allowance (1/2 inch at each end) to get the total length measurement of the main piece of cloth (31½ + 1 = 32½ inches).

Step 5.   Decide on the height of the bag. Add 1½ inches for the hem and 1/2 inch for the seam allowance at the bottom. (15 + 1½ + 1/2 = 17 inches).

Step 6.   Cut the main piece of cloth. Our example will have a height of 17 inches and a length of 32½ inches.

Step 7.   If pockets are desired, cut one or two strips of cloth to be sewn onto the main piece. The length should be the same as that of the main piece, and the height should be a bit over half the height of the bag. For the example bag, the pocket strips should be cut 32½ inches by 8 inches. Don't forget to add 1/2 inch for the hem on the top of the pocket strip and 1/2 inch for the bottom seam allowance. If you want pockets on both the inside and the outside, hem the top edge of each pocket strip and pin the two pocket strips to the main piece, one on each side. Line up the bottom edges of all three pieces and sew vertical lines of stitching as shown in Figure 6–3. If only one strip of pockets is required, follow the same procedure, using only one strip of cloth. Reinforce the pockets by stitching over the first stitching twice more. If you wish to add a design done with embroidery, ink, paint, or cloth on one of the pockets, do the design before sewing the pocket strip to the main piece.

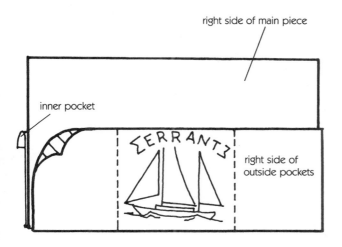

right side of main piece

inner pocket

ƧERRANTƷ

right side of
outside pockets

*Figure 6–3.
Layout of
pockets.*

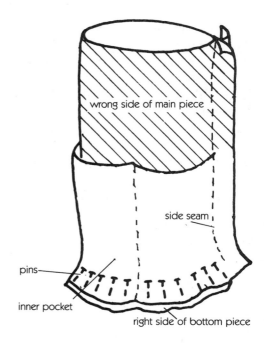

Figure 6–4.
Stitching the side seam.

wrong side of main piece

side seam

pins

inner pocket

right side of bottom piece

Step 8. Fold the main piece of cloth in half, right sides together, forming the side seam. Stitch this seam ½ inch from the edge of the cloth (Figure 6–4).

Step 9. If two thicknesses of bottom will be used, stitch the two bottoms together, wrong sides facing, close to the edge of the material.

Step 10. Place the bottom piece in the bottom of the main piece, right sides together. Pin the bottom in place, with the pins perpendicular to the seam line (Figure 6–4). The sewing machine needle will sew over pins that are placed perpendicular to the seam line, but will have difficulty sewing over pins placed parallel to the seam line.

Step 11. Sew the bottom in place by stitching ½ inch from the edge of the material. Reinforce this seam by stitching

Figure 6–5.
Recommended orientation of pins for pin basting.

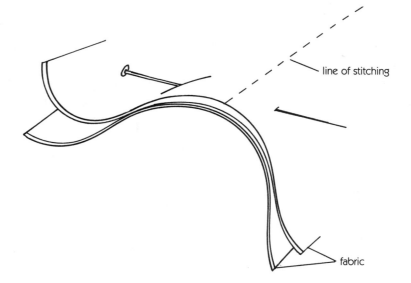

line of stitching

fabric

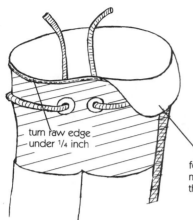

Figure 6-6.
Rolling the line casing. This drawing shows the bag inside out, but the easiest way to stitch the casing is with the bag right side out, rolling the casing to the inside. If you want the drawstring to cinch from the inside of the bag, as you might in a small ditty bag, set the grommets in the turned-down lip.

turn raw edge under 1/4 inch

fold over to make line casing, then stitch

Figure 6-7.
Rigger's bag.

again. Zigzag the edge of the bottom if possible. Turn the bag right side out.

Step 12.   Place the grommets for the drawstring. In a small bag, where small line will be used, one grommet is sufficient. In a heavier bag, distribute the weight evenly by using two grommets on each side.

Ditty or sail bag: Set the grommets 1 inch from the top edge of the bag. Turn the top down 1/4 inch to hide the raw edge. Fold the new top edge down so that it just covers the lower edge of the grommet, and stitch. Put the drawstring through the grommet or grommets, and roll the material over it to make the line casing. Stitch

the hem down, being careful not to catch the line with the needle (Figure 6-6).

Rigger's bag or canvas bucket: Fold 1/2 inch of cloth down around the top edge and stitch. Fold the cloth down over the hoop, add 1 inch, and stitch. Set grommets through both thicknesses of cloth in the hem area, below the hoop (Figure 6-7). If extra-heavy gear is to be carried, reinforce the grommets by placing an extra patch of material under the grommet before setting it. You may also want to cut a plywood bottom the exact circumference of the bottom of the bag. Sand the rough edges, and place the bottom in the bag. Splice on rope handles as you choose or knot them as shown in Figure 6-7.

7
A Simple Duffel Bag

This simple duffel bag is a handy traveling companion or storage bag for diving gear, laundry, out-of-season or specialty clothes, or special equipment. The design given here is plain but can be customized with pockets, different straps, and materials to fit your needs.

Materials Needed

- cloth (acrylic canvas, treated canvas, spinnaker cloth, heavy cotton duck, or Cordura, a woven nylon fabric backed with neoprene)

For the simple duffel:

- 1 piece of cloth 32 inches by 37 inches for main piece
- 2 circles 10 inches in diameter for the two ends
- 1 strip of nylon webbing 2 or 2½ inches by 38 inches for a long handle
- 1 strip of nylon webbing 2 or 2½ inches by 11 inches for a short handle
- 1 zipper 34 inches long, preferably heavy-duty Delrin 10-D

Construction

Step 1. Cut the cloth to the above measurements or to your own size requirements. Remember, you will need extra cloth for pockets. Don't forget to allow for ½-inch seams.

Step 2. Handles: Cut nylon webbing for the handles. If your duffel is to be a different size than the one described here, remember that the long and short handles should match the length and end-circle diameter, respectively, of the duffel. Burn each end of webbing with a match or lighter to prevent raveling.

Step 3. Top End: Lay the short handle across one circular piece of cloth. Stitch across both ends of the handle, close to the edge. Reinforce first stitching twice on each end (Figure 7–2).

Step 4. Long Handle: Place the handle 4 inches away from the long edge of the main piece of cloth. Stitch across each end of the long handle, close to the edges of the main piece of cloth. After reinforcing the stitching three more times, sew a triangu-

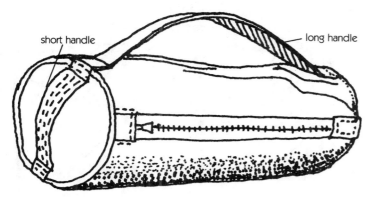

Figure 7–1.
Duffel bag.

short handle

long handle

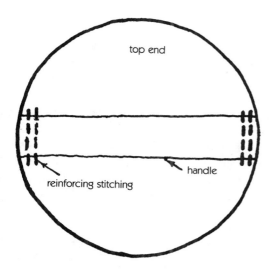

Figure 7–2.
Handle for the top end.

top end

handle

reinforcing stitching

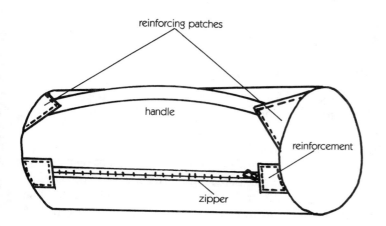

Figure 7–3.
Installing the long handle and the zipper.

reinforcing patches

handle

reinforcement

zipper

Figure 7–4.
Installing the end pieces.

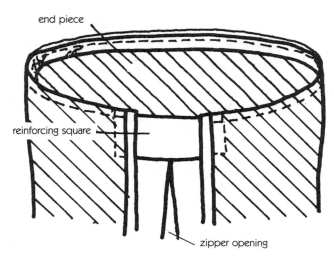

lar reinforcing patch over both ends of the handle.

Step 5. Zipper: Fold under ½ inch on both edges of the 37-inch side of the cloth, and stitch close to the folded edge. Work with the zipper facing up, and lay the folded edge of the fabric on top of the zipper tape. The right side of the fabric should be facing you. Using the zipper foot of the sewing machine, sew one side of the zipper to the 37-inch side of the main piece. Be sure to center the zipper in the middle of the 37-inch side. With the zipper closed, place the zipper tape under the other 37-inch side and stitch, again using the zipper foot. You should now have a tube of cloth held together with a zipper. Sew both sides of the zipper with another row of stitching.

Step 6. Reinforcing Squares: Turn the tube right side out. Cut four 3-by-3-inch pieces of cloth from scraps of the material. Place a pair of squares right sides together. Stitch three sides together, leaving the fourth side open for turning the square right side out. Turn the square right side out, and repeat the procedure with the remaining pair of squares. Sew the completed squares at each end of the zipper by placing the raw edge of the

square patch even with the raw edge of the main piece at either end. Then stitch the sides of each square parallel to the zipper and across the raw end. Be careful not to catch the zipper chain. Also, be careful not to pull the two sides of the main piece too close together. Not only will these squares reinforce the ends of the zipper, but they will complete the tube created by the main piece of cloth as well (Figure 7–3).

Step 7. For the ends, open the zipper and turn the duffel inside out. Pin the ends of the duffel into the tube, right sides together. Place the pins perpendicular to the seam line. Doublestitch both ends into the tube (Figure 7–4). Zigzag the raw edge if possible. The raw ends of the handles will be inside the seam. Turn right side out.

Customizing

Design the inside or outside pocket before you begin to sew the duffel together. Remember to do all the sewing you can on each individual piece before assembling the duffel. Rope or webbed handles can be used instead of cloth handles if you prefer. Refer to Chapter 2 if you choose to use grommets to hold the line or snaps to shut the pockets.

8
Ready Bags
and Sea Sausages

One of the problems every sailor faces is what to do with all those sails. Here are two suggestions: a sea sausage and a ready bag. Both allow you to stow a headsail on deck and protect it from the weather. A sea sausage is useful if you're sailing short-handed and want a quick place to store a headsail in a storm or when changing headsails at sea. The ready bag is designed for stowing the sails on deck when you're not sailing. Both bags should be made of breathable material and should be strong enough to withstand a breaking wave that comes over the bow.

Sea Sausages

I call this bag a sea sausage because it looks like a long sausage tied to the lifeline. It is essentially a rectangular piece of fabric that bundles up a genoa and holds it securely to the lifeline when the sail is not in use. When a headsail change is needed, the first step is to lay the sea sausage flat on the foredeck. The genoa is then dropped and flaked on top of the sausage. When the sail is completely on deck, it is a simple matter to wrap it using the sail stops se-

cured to the sausage, and secure the tiedown lines to the lifeline or stanchions. If your vessel has two forestays, you can leave this sail hanked on the starboard stay, loosen the port sea sausage, and raise a smaller or larger genoa on the port stay.

Materials Needed

- acrylic canvas
- nylon webbing for the sail stops
- nylon webbing for tiedowns to secure the sea sausage to the boat

Measuring

With the headsail on the forestay, allow the sail to flake itself down as it normally falls to the deck. Pull once on the clew of the sail so that it stretches out along the caprail of the boat. Measure the length of the sail from the headstay to the clew. This will be the length of the bag. Measure the circumference of the flaked sail at the fore and aft ends. These measurements will be the approximate widths of the sausage. Adding an extra inch or two to the width makes it easier to stow sails in a rough sea.

33

Measure the distance between the stanchions to locate the positions of the tie-down straps. They will provide stronger tiedown points than the lifeline.

Construction

Step 1.   Measure out the canvas and draw the shape of the sea sausage onto the fabric.

Step 2.   Add 2 inches all around for hems. Mark three or four points on one edge, preferably at positions where stanchions will adjoin the sausage in use. A sail stop will be stitched across the outside face of the fabric at each of these points (Figure 8–2), so mark a stitching line across the width of the fabric at each point. Mark down about one-quarter of the width of the fabric, again on the outside face, to show

Figure 8–1.
Sea sausage.

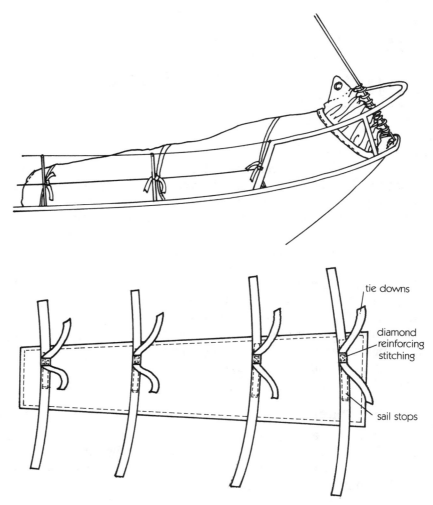

tie downs

diamond reinforcing stitching

sail stops

Figure 8–2.
Layout for the sea sausage. In the boxed diamond pattern used to stitch the tiedown lines over the sail stops, you stitch the perimeter of the box first, and then the X in the middle, without breaking the thread. Thus, you end up stitching over two segments twice.

where the nylon-webbing tiedowns will be stitched over the sail stops.

Step 3.   Cut out the fabric and the needed webbing. Burn the ends of the webbing to prevent raveling. Cut sail stops 36 inches longer than the width of the sea sausage where each stop is to be attached.

Step 4.   Hem all edges of the fabric by folding the fabric over twice (an inch for each fold) and stitching once next to the fold and once next to the edge (in effect, a double-rubbed hem).

Step 5.   Place the sail stops in position and stitch them to the outside face of the sausage with a box pattern of straight stitches, ending the box 4 to 8 inches shy of either sausage edge. Stitch back and forth two or three times across the ends of each box.

Stitch the tiedowns to their marked positions on top of the sail stops using a reinforced diamond stitch pattern (Figure 8–2).

Ready Bags

A ready bag has a zipper on top that allows the bag to lie flat when open and a zipper in front that allows it to close around the headstay (Figure 8–3). A ready bag will keep the sun off the sail far better than a sea sausage, so if protection from the sun is a serious consideration, the ready bag is the preferred option. While a ready bag allows you to stow the headsails on their stays with a minimum of effort, it will not make handling the sails at sea any easier than if you were bagging them.

Materials Needed

- acrylic canvas, 1 large piece (or 2 smaller pieces sewn together) to form the cylindrical tube, 1 smaller piece to form the circular end
- 2 zippers (including at least one jacket type)
- grommets for drainage
- nylon webbing
- vinyl binding

Measuring

With the sail on the stay, flake it out along the deck. Then, starting at the clew, loosely roll it up toward the headstay. When you have a roll whose height is about level with the hanks on the stay, measure the length from the stay, top and

Figure 8–3.
Ready bag.

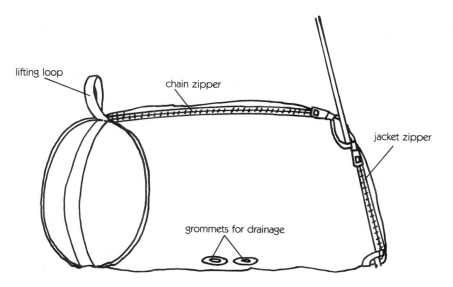

lifting loop

chain zipper

jacket zipper

grommets for drainage

Figure 8–4.
Measuring for
the main piece.

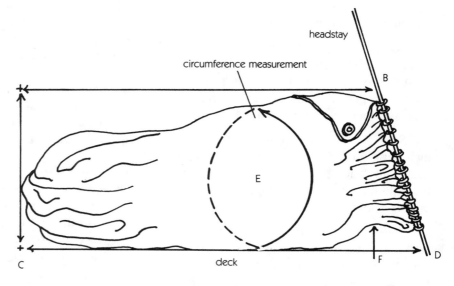

bottom (A-B, C-D), and the circumference of the sail at its largest point (E). Measure the distance between the bottom of the headstay and the point on the deck directly beneath B (F-D) (Figure 8–4).

Construction

Step 1.   Mark out the single piece of fabric that will form the top, bottom and sides. If your fabric is not wide enough, stitch two pieces together. (Refer to Chapter 3, Sewing Techniques.) Be sure to mark the angle for the headstay (Figure 8–5).

Step 2.   Add ½-inch seam allowance to all edges of the main piece.

Step 3.   Cut out the main piece and attach drainage grommets (Figure 8–5).

Step 4.   Cut a circle to fit the circumference of the bag (E), plus ½-inch for seam allowance. (The diameter of this circle is E divided by 3.14, plus 1 inch.)

Step 5.   Put a zipper in the top of the ready bag by first folding over the ½-inch seam allowances on each side so that the edges are finished, then topstitching the zipper in place. Place the slider on the zip-

Figure 8–5.
Marking for the main piece.

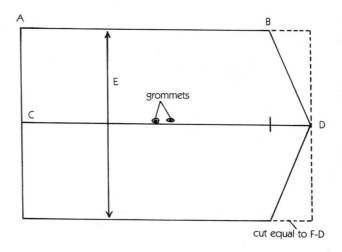

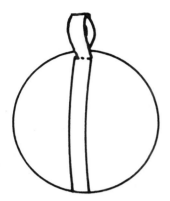

Figure 8–6.
Stitching the lifting loop to the
end of the ready bag.

per so that when the zipper is closed the slider is at the headstay.

Step 6.   Stitch webbing down the middle of the round piece that will be used for the end of the bag. Make a loop at the top edge. Stop the stitching 1 inch away from the edge of the circle (Figure 8–6).

Step 7.   With right sides together, place the circle in the end of the bag, and pin it in place.

Step 8.   Stitch the circle in place. Stitch over the end of the zipper twice. Be careful not to catch the end of the webbing loop in this stitching.

Step 9.   Again turn the bag right side

out. Place the jacket zipper in the front (headstay) edge by first turning under the 1/2-inch seam allowance in the bag. Top-stitch the zipper in place.

Step 10.   Use vinyl binding to bind the hole that is created in the bag for the headstay. (See Figure 15–14). Stop off the zippers at the same time as in Chapter 7, Step 6.

Open the bag completely. Slide the bag under the rolled-up sail. Pull up the sides, and zip up the top zipper. Bring the front of the bag around the headstay, and zip up the front zipper. Hook the jib halyard to the loop, and lift the bag off the deck.

9
Spar Bag

When you carry a sailing dinghy aboard, it is usually helpful to contain the mast, boom, running rigging, and possibly the sail all together in one bag. I recommend that such a bag be made of an acrylic-fiber canvas or cotton canvas, because it should be water resistant and yet be able to breathe. It is usually necessary to tie this bag on deck somewhere, because most boats don't have below-deck storage for anything of this length. Whatever tiedown system you devise (and I'll have my own suggestion to offer), the first requirement is that it be strong. A grommet and line attached to one layer of fabric won't do. In all the stories I've heard of things being washed away at sea, spar bags are the most common losses. Once the gear is in the bag, it constitutes a fair amount of weight, thereby creating lateral resistance to any waves that might come aboard. Each tiedown must be reinforced and the line allowed to wrap around the outside of the entire bag to distribute the load evenly.

Materials Needed

- ½ yard more acrylic than the length of your spar

- webbing or line for tiedowns
- 2 number 1 grommets
- number 4 (⅛-inch-diameter) Dacron line for drawstring

Construction

Step 1. Place your mast, boom, running rigging, and sail next to each other in the most compact arrangement possible. Measure the maximum length. Add 6 inches to this measurement for the total length of fabric necessary for the main piece. Measure the largest circumference the gear offers. Add 1½ inches to this measurement for the total width of the main piece (Figure 9–2).

Step 2. Cut a piece of fabric this length and width.

Cut a circle for one end of the bag. (To determine the diameter, divide the width of the main piece (excluding seam allowance) by 3.14 and then add 1 inch for seam allowances.)

Step 3. Pick one end of the piece of fabric to be the top, or open end, of the spar bag. Mark off a line 1½ inches from

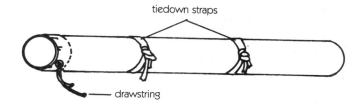

tiedown straps

drawstring

Figure 9–1.
Spar bag.

the edge of the top. Mark off ½ inch along the bottom and side edges for your stitching line.

Step 4.   Choose the positioning of your tiedown system. The positions should line up with something strong, i.e., stanchions, grabrail, or coaming hardware. If you can't decide where you want to tie the bag, put a tiedown 8 inches in from each end and one or two in the middle, depending on the length of the bag. Use either Dacron or nylon webbing because these are soft enough to tie. If you decide to use three tiedowns, cut three pieces of webbing three times the circumference of the bag. Position these pieces on the outside of the flat piece of fabric, and stitch the middle of the webbing to the center of the bag

sing reinforcing patches and a boxed diamond stitch.

Step 5.   With right sides together, stitch the side of the bag with a straight stitch. Don't stitch over the webbing for your tiedown system. Pin the round end to the main piece, right sides together. Doublestitch (Figure 9–3). Turn bag right side out. Set a number 1 grommet on either side of the side seam in the top of the bag for the drawstring. Place a piece of webbing under each grommet for extra reinforcement.

Step 6.   Fold the fabric on the 1½-inch line (or to cover the grommets). Fold the edge of the fabric ¼ inch under to make a casing with a finished edge. Take

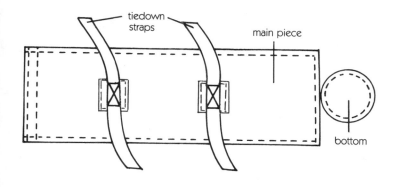

tiedown straps

main piece

bottom

Figure 9–2.
Cutting pieces for the spar bag.

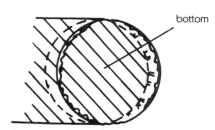

bottom

Figure 9–3.
Stitching the bottom.

Figure 9–4.
Installing the drawstring.

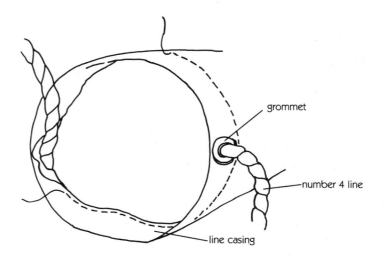

number 4 line and tuck it inside this fold. Allow each end of the line to pass through the grommets (Figure 9–4).

Step 7. Being careful not to stitch through the line, stitch the casing down. You may need to use a zipper foot to get past the grommets.

Step 8. Knot both ends of the line together with a figure-eight or overhand knot so that it won't pull back through the grommets.

Step 9. Slide your sailing rig into the bag, cinch up the drawstring, and tie securely to the boat.

10
Life Jacket Bag

Life jackets are Coast Guard-required for all boats. They are also items that, for obvious safety reasons, should be kept near at hand. Because of the materials they are made of, jackets rot easily from exposure to sunlight, heavy weather, and moisture. Most of the time, people keep them stashed in a cockpit or bridge locker where they tend to get wet and dirty, or covered up with gear. When an emergency arises, the life jacket is hard to get at and is often so tangled up in its own straps that a person struggling in the water will find it useless. A solution to all of these problems is a life jacket bag that lives on deck and holds four to six life jackets, keeping them dry, clean, untangled, and ready for use at a moment's notice. A good stowing area on most sailboats is aft on the lazarette deck or on the stern pulpit. Power yachtsmen often stow jackets on the flying bridge, secured to a seat locker or aft railing. Before you construct the bag, determine where you will want to store it so you can decide what kind of fastening system you'll require.

Materials Needed

- reinforced vinyl (I recommend reinforced vinyl for this project because you want the bag to be waterproof. Vinyl fabric will only leak where the needle makes a hole. You can seal those holes with silicone sealer.)
- Velcro or buckles
- line or webbing

Construction

Step 1. Decide how many life jackets you want the bag to hold. Neatly wrap each life jacket so each strap can be easily loosened. Put the jackets in a pile. You may have to tie them together so they will stay in some semblance of a bundle while you measure them. Imagine they fill a rectangular space.

Step 2. Measure the width, height, and length of your imaginary rectangle. If you've tied the jackets in a tight bundle, add 1 inch to each measurement. If you've

Figure 10–1.
Life jacket bag.

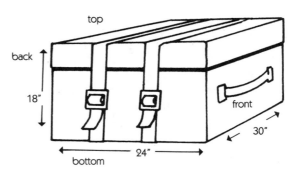

tied them loosely and feel you could easily put the life jackets into the bag, then use the exact measurements.

Step 3.   Add ¹/₂-inch seam allowance to all edges you must stitch together and 1¹/₂ inches to each edge you must hem. The bag should be made with one piece forming the front, bottom, back, and top, with enough fabric for a 4-inch overlap. For instance, if your bag is to be 30 by 24 by 18 inches, as in Figure 10–2, the main piece of fabric will have all of the measurements laid out on the drawing. The side pieces should be the measurement of the bag, 24 inches by 18 inches, with a 4-inch

flap to tuck under the top piece for further water protection.

Step 4.   Add ¹/₂-inch seam allowance all around the three sides, and add 1¹/₂ inches to the edge of the 4-inch flap.

Step 5.   Cut two pieces of fabric for the end flaps of the top to overlap the sides of the bag (in this case, 4 inches by 24 inches with ¹/₂-inch seam allowance on three sides and 1¹/₂-inch hem allowance on the bottom side).

Step 6.   Cut out all of these pieces and mark the seam allowances and the corners as shown in Figure 10–2.

Figure 10–2.
Pieces for the life jacket bag.

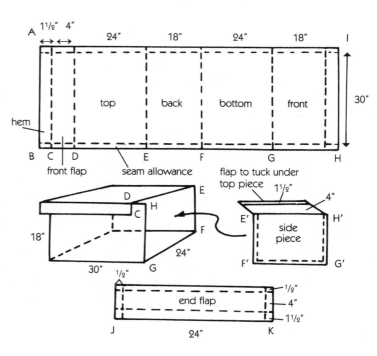

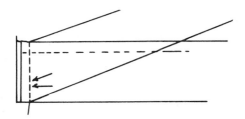

Figure 10–3.
Stitching the ends of the
overhang.

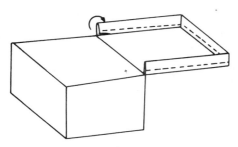

Figure 10–4.
Hemming the overhang.

Step 7.   Mark and stitch the fastening system to the back or bottom of the bag. (See ahead.)

Step 8.   Stitch the hem in the main piece of fabric at positions H–I and A–B.

Step 9.   Stitch the hem of the end flaps along edge J–K. On one flap turn under the short seam allowance at J and stitch it as a hem. Do the same to the other end flap at K.

Step 10.   Turn under the hem of the side pieces. With right sides together, match the corners of the side pieces to the main piece: E to E', F to F', G to G', H to H'. Sew along the H–G, G–F, and F–E edges.

Step 11.   Stitch the end flaps to the top of the main piece along edge D–E, placing the ends so that the short hemmed edge of each flap meets the top at E.

Step 12.   Stitch the edges of the front 4-inch overlap to the front edges of the end flaps, working with right sides together (Figure 10–3).

Step 13.   Hem the edge of the overlap on the front and side edges (Figure 10–4).

Fastening System

I prefer to have my life jackets firmly secured on deck. You may prefer to have them in a bag in the lazarette or in the seat locker. Use your own circumstances to design a fastening system. One system I suggest serves as a means of keeping the bag closed and attached to the boat. Two 2-inch nylon webbing straps are stitched with a boxed diamond pattern to the bottom of the bag. Buckles are then attached to the straps so they can be cinched up tight, or Velcro can be substituted as a fastener. Sew light lines to the straps at two or three places along the bottom so you can tie the bag to the lifelines, pulpit, or grabrail. An alternative to placing these lines on the webbing is to stitch light lines into the four corners of the bottom seam of the bag. Whatever system you design must allow for quick access to the life jackets and be able to withstand the force of a wave coming aboard. Use reinforcing patches wherever you think additional strength might be needed.

11
Sheet Bags, Tool Bags, and Lazarette Shelves

There are many small items that need to be stored in big lockers on boats. And there are many ways you can use small canvas bags or envelopes to create small storage spaces for small items. To me, there is nothing more frustrating than going into a typical seat or lazarette locker to find a line, opening the lid, and looking at two awning poles, one deck brush, four life jackets, one bucket, one charcoal grill, and a trash can all tied together in some disorganized mess with the docklines. Considering that most boats today are built with cockpit lockers that two people can stand in, there's no need for the mess.

Lazarette Shelf

A simple shelf can be built out of fabric and installed with a couple of eyeplates and line to help subdivide a huge locker, thereby creating some usable space (Figure 11–1).

Materials Needed
- acrylic canvas
- 3/4-inch elastic Dacron tape
- 4 grommets

- 4 eyeplates
- light line

Step 1. Measure the space you want the shelf to cover.

Step 2. Cut a piece of fabric this shape.

Step 3. Add 1$\frac{1}{2}$ inches hem allowance.

Step 4. Hem all four edges. If you are going to place much weight on the shelf, tuck Dacron tape inside the hem for reinforcement.

Step 5. Set a grommet in each corner.

Step 6. Install eyeplates in the locker at the height the shelf will be. Tie the shelf in with light line.

Sheet Bags

Another way to clean up the deck of a boat is to stow the lines neatly when they aren't being used. A sheet bag is easy to make and will keep the deck lines neatly coiled when

44

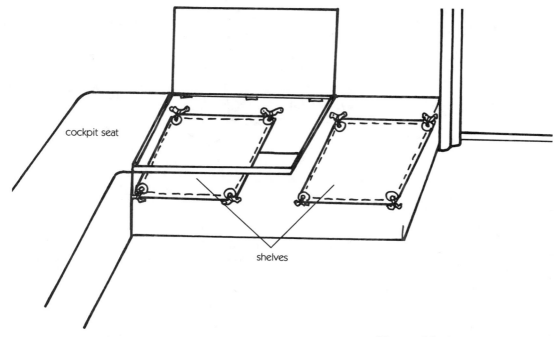

Figure 11–1.
Shelf placement in lazarette
or cockpit locker.

they aren't needed. It is important to plan where you will mount each sheet bag. You don't want to obstruct a convenient leaning place or create an area that will trip you up when maneuvering in the cockpit. Sometimes it's best to have the bags a little less handy rather than have them form an obstruction. Usually you'll want to mount the bag close to the winch or the cleat from which the line is handled. Figure 11–3 shows a sheet bag for the spinnaker

halyard mounted on the side of the house rather than aft. This way the backrest provided by the house is not obstructed.

Sheet bags can also be used around the mast to store halyards and in the lockers to stow all kinds of gear. You may want one just inside the companionway to store your sail stops. They are also useful for storing winch handles, navigation equipment, cleaning equipment—and your suntan oil and sunglasses.

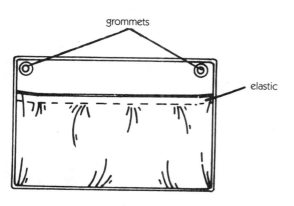

Figure 11–2.
Sheet bag.

*Figure 11–3.
Sheet bag on side of
house.*

Materials Needed

- acrylic canvas
- fasteners (grommets, turn buttons, Lift-the-Dots, or snaps)
- ³/₄-inch elastic band
- Dacron tape

Construction

Step 1. Coil your sheet or halyard in the coil size you are likely to use. Lay the coil flat on a table and squash it to form a hank. Measure its maximum length and width. This should be the approximate size of the sheet bag. Since the front piece of the bag will allow more room than a flat piece of canvas, don't make the bag as big

as the measurements indicate. For example, if your line measures 22 inches by 8 inches, you might make the bag 18 inches by 7 inches.

Step 2. Mark and cut two pieces of fabric to form the back and the front. The back should be cut to the length that you need, but add 5 inches to your width measurement. For example, if your bag is to measure 18 inches by 7 inches, cut the back piece 18 inches by 12 inches. The 5-inch difference will allow the back to be taller than the front and still accommodate a 2-inch double-rubbed hem in the top. Cut the front piece to the desired length plus 4 inches, and to the desired width

*Figure 11–4.
Pieces for a sheet bag.*

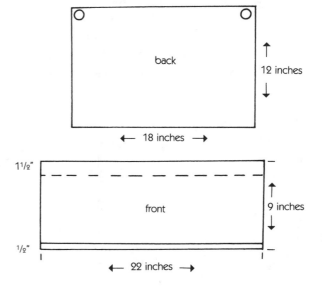

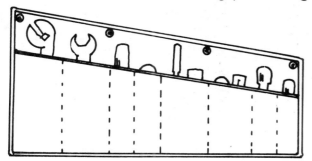

Figure 11–5.
Tool bag.

plus 2 inches. On our example bag, the front piece would measure 22 inches by 9 inches (Figure 11–4).

Step 3.   Stitch a 1-inch casing in the top edge of the front piece by folding over the fabric on the 1½-inch line, folding the raw edge under, and stitching down. Thread ¾-inch elastic tape through this casing, and stitch down one end. Pull the elastic through so the front piece is gathered up to be the same length on the top as the back piece. Anchor the tape in place.

Step 4.   Hem the top edge of the back piece. If the line is particularly heavy, put Dacron tape in the hem for extra reinforcement.

Step 5.   Place the wrong side of the front on the right side of the back, lining up the two bottom corners. Stitch the sides and bottom of the bag together.

Step 6.   Bind the bag on the sides and bottom edges with vinyl binding (Figure 15–14).

Step 7.   If the bag is heavy, use turn buttons or Lift-the-Dots for fasteners. Lighter line can be held with snaps. If the bag is more than 8 inches long or is heavy, place a fastener in each corner and one or more in the middle of the bag.

Tool Bag

For tools often used on deck, why not make a canvas tool roll? I recommend that you use cotton canvas, which is absorbent and can be soaked with oil to prevent rusting. This type of tool roll can be hung in a locker for your favorite screwdrivers, pliers, crescent wrench, deck key, flashlight, etc.

Materials Needed

- canvas
- grommets, snaps, turn buttons, or Lift-the-Dots

Construction

Step 1.   Lay out the tools you want the bag to hold. Measure the space they occupy and the maximum height. Be sure the mounting area is large enough.

Step 2.   Cut one piece of fabric this size. Cut another piece of fabric the same length but at least 3 inches shorter in height.

Step 3.   Bind the top edge of the short piece with vinyl binding.

Step 4.   Stitch the short piece to the long piece, lining up the bottom edges.

Step 5.   Lay the tools on top of the bag, and draw a line between each one with chalk. Stitch through the top and bottom piece on these lines to form compartments (Figure 11–5).

Step 6.   Bind all four sides with vinyl binding (Figure 15–14).

Step 7.   Set fasteners in the top edge and hang.

12
Sailboard Bag

Those of you traveling in the tropics often carry sailboards on deck. If you want to keep all your sailboard gear intact and out of the sun during a passage, or when not in use, make a cover for it. If you travel from beach to beach, you may also want to put the board, boom, and mast in one place to make them easy to handle and to protect them from road grime.

The design suggested here contains the board, boom, skeg, and daggerboard. It doesn't contain the mast, because the mast is not as easily damaged and can be more easily stored on its own. One obvious possibility is to add loops to the side of the bag through which to slide the mast.

As with most other heavy gear you might carry on deck, you should think about where you are going to carry it and how you're going to fasten it down. A sailboard is sufficiently heavy that it must be tied to the shrouds or lifelines. The safest solution is to sew on loop handles, as in a duffle bag, through which a sturdy tiedown line can be threaded to lash the sailboard to the boat. Do not depend on small tiedown lines to take the weight of the board.

Materials Needed

- acrylic canvas
- zipper the length of the bag
- webbing

Design and Measurements

If you lay your sailboard on the floor with the boom, skeg, and daggerboard on top of it in their desired positions, the shape of your bag becomes apparent. Place a piece of paper under the board, and place the boom on top of the board in its most compact fashion. Trace the resulting shape. This will be the bottom of the bag. From the line you've drawn on the paper, measure over the top of the board with a flexible tape measure at 1-foot intervals from bow to stern. Mark these measurements at each station on the pattern. These will be the measurements of the top. The top will be a bit larger than the bottom, but it should be the same shape.

On another piece of paper, trace the shape of the daggerboard and skeg. Cut out these shapes and see if both items can be placed in one pocket or if they need separate ones. If one fits within the space

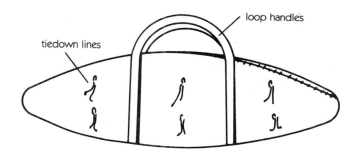

Figure 12–1.
Sailboard bag.

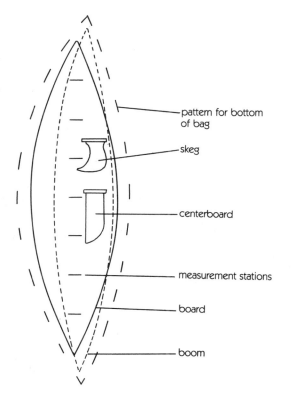

tiedown lines

loop handles

pattern for bottom
of bag

skeg

centerboard

measurement stations

board

boom

Figure 12–2.
Making the pattern. The
top-piece pattern (not shown
here) *is expanded as necessary*
from the bottom pattern,
measuring symmetrically
outward either side of the
centerline at 1-foot intervals
bow to stern. The top pattern
is cut out first; after it is
transferred to the fabric, it is
trimmed back to the outline of
the bottom pattern.

of the other, one pocket will probably do. Again, measure over the top of these pieces to determine the size of the pocket, which will be inside the finished bag. The sailboard bag will act as the bottom of the pocket, and the front piece may need some extra length.

Decide how to rig your fastening system. If you are using loop handles made of webbing, as shown in Figure 12–1, mark these positions on your pattern.

Returning to the bottom pattern, expand its outline symmetrically around the fore-and-aft centerline, using the meas-

urements of the top piece, to get a top pattern. Cut out the top pattern and trace its shape on the fabric. Then cut back the top pattern to the pattern for the bottom and trace this shape on the fabric.

On one side of the top, position the pattern for your skeg and daggerboard. Most sailboards come with a bag for the sail. You may choose to slide this bag into the sailboard bag before zipping it up, or you may wish to make a special pocket in the top of the bag for the sail. If so, measure the sail to see what size the pocket should be. Add 1/2-inch seam allowance to

Figure 12–3.
Pieces of the sailboard bag.

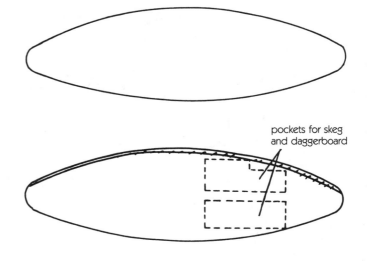

pockets for skeg
and daggerboard

Figure 12–4.
Putting in the zipper.

zipper teeth

zipper tape

stitch line

fabric folded over 1/2"

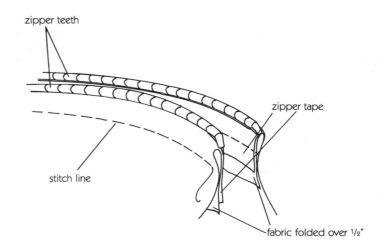

Figure 12–5.
Stitching on the pockets.

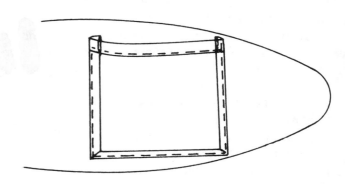

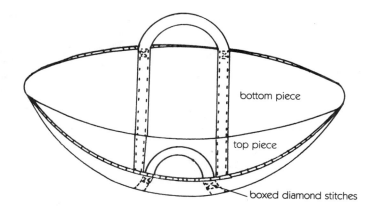

bottom piece

top piece

boxed diamond stitches

Figure 12–6.
Stitching on the handles.
The bag is shown
unzipped and inside out.

all edges of the pieces and 1½ inches for hemmed edges.

Construction

Step 1.   Cut out all the pieces (Figure 12–2).

Step 2.   Fold over ½ inch of fabric on one edge of the top piece where the zipper will be stitched.

Step 3.   Under this folded edge, stitch one side of a piece of zipper chain that is the same length as the top piece. Along the matching edge stitch the other half of the zipper to the bottom of the bag (Figure 12–4).

Step 4.   With right sides together, place the top and bottom of the bag to-gether. You may see that there is more fabric at the edge of the top than at the edge of the bottom. If necessary, pin these two pieces together before stitching them.

Step 5.   Stitch nylon webbing for handles as shown in Figure 12–6.

Step 6.   Hem the pockets for the sail, daggerboard, and skeg. Fold under ½ inch all around the three remaining sides. Pin or staple them to the predetermined position on the inside face of the top of the bag. Topstitch them in place (Figure 12–5).

Step 7.   For extra support, sew vinyl binding or webbing over the seam allowance where the zipper comes through the fabric.

13
Bicycle Bag

Those of you carrying bicycles aboard are probably aware of the constant maintenance they require when exposed to a marine environment. A cover will alleviate that problem tremendously. Usually what is easiest also works best, so try a bag that simply slips over the top of your bike and cinches up on the bottom with a drawstring. The bag should be somewhat fitted so it won't hang all over the deck. Also, you should be able to tie the bag, with the bike enclosed, directly to the shrouds, lifelines, or stern railing. Do not depend on the strength of the fabric to hold the bike aboard.

Materials Needed
- acrylic canvas
- line
- grommets

Measuring and Stitching

Step 1.   If you fill in the adjoining diagrams with the measurements of your bike, you will find you have all the dimen-

*Figure 13–1.
Bicycle bag.*

drawstring

Figure 13–2A.
Height and length measurements.

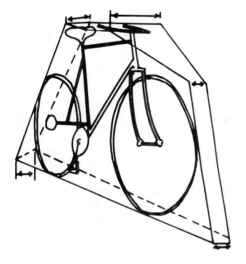

Figure 13–2B.
Depth measurements.

sions you will need (Figures 13–2A and 13–2B).

Step 2. Measure these pieces out on the fabric and cut them out. Be sure to add 1/2-inch seam allowances to the sides and top edges and a 1 1/2-inch hem allowance to the bottom edge.

Step 3. With right sides together, stitch the middle band to the sides.

Step 4. Turn the cover right side out, and place a grommet in the hem.

Step 5. Roll the fabric on the 1 1/2-inch line and stitch the casing in. Before stitching, lay a piece of 1/4-inch line in the casing, allowing the ends of the line to extend through the grommet.

Step 6. If necessary, place two large grommets on either side of the cover, exactly opposite each other, and align them with the frame of the bike. You can pass a line through these grommets to tie the bike (not just the cover) to the boat.

14
Building an Awning

An awning, or canopy, can save the cruising boat on a layover or the little-used boat from hours of finish-devouring sunlight, rain, and snow. It can also increase the amount of living space and create privacy. However, since an awning is designed to fly over a boom and be supported by the boat's standing rigging, it cannot be used while underway. (An awning should not rest on the boom, or both awning and sail cover will chafe.)

Figure 14–2 shows some basic awning layouts. Choose one of these, or customize to suit your needs. For instance, part of the awning might be used as a cockpit canopy that is easy to put up, take down, and stow. This canopy will protect the cockpit from too much sun and lower the temperature below decks. A winter-storage or long-layover cover can be attached to the cockpit canopy to form a full boat cover. Side curtains can be designed to create privacy in the cockpit, or to keep out the glare of the sun.

There are two basic methods of supporting an awning: with ropes or with battens. A roped awning is stronger; if

properly constructed and secured, it can be left up in a 60-knot gale. The idea is similar to a tent in that most of the strain in the awning is taken by the ropes that are sewn into the awnings, not by the fabric itself. Figure 14–1 shows how a split rig can use a roped awning entirely over the whole boat. But a sloop often cannot use a roped awning aft, unless it has davits or a gallows frame that the awnings's side lines can tie to. In this case, a battened awning must be used (Figures 14–4 and 14–5).

Characteristics of a Good Awning

1. A good awning gives maximum coverage while requiring minimum storage space.
2. It is strong enough to remain standing in strong winds.
3. Its color deflects glare.
4. It is easy to put up and take down.
5. It exhibits resistance to mildew and sun damage.
6. It pleases the eye and doesn't detract from the lines of the vessel.
7. It is water resistant, if not waterproof.

54

Figure 14–1.
Roped awning
on Ticonderoga.

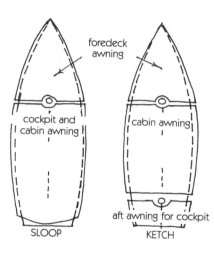
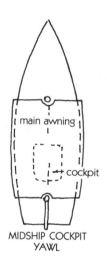

foredeck
awning

cockpit and
cabin awning

cabin awning

main awning

cockpit

aft awning for cockpit

SLOOP

KETCH

MIDSHIP COCKPIT
YAWL

Figure 14–2.
Basic awning layouts.

Figure 14–3.
Awning with bolt rope,
battens, and side
curtains.

*Figure 14–4.
Roped awning for split
rigs.*

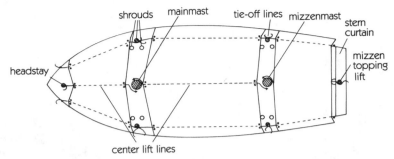

Building a Battened Awning

Materials Needed

- acrylic canvas
- number 1 or number 2 grommets (enough to place on every panel, corner, and slash)
- small rivets or grommets for the roll-up ties to pass through
- number 4 line (1/8-inch Dacron) for rigging
- battens where necessary (wood, plastic, collapsible aluminum, PVC pipe)
- length of 3/8-inch Dacron line the length of the awning, plus 8 to 10 feet, for bolt rope (optional)

Step 1.   First design the awning using Figure 14–2 as a guide.

Decide on the method you will use to cover the area around the mast. Flaps that go from one section to another are suitable (Figure 14–6).

Better than a system of flaps are awn-

ing sections designed to overlap (Figure 14–7) but not attach. Each section is strung independently to rigging, etc.

If your design calls for integral side curtains, measure their dimensions and plan on incorporating a bolt rope or Dacron tape at the corner between the awning top and the curtain. Read ahead in this chapter under "Bolt Rope" and "Building a Roped Awning" for details. Alternatively, you may choose to make side curtains from separate pieces of canvas, snapping or zipping them to the awning. Instructions are given under "Tiedowns and Optional Side Curtains," ahead in this chapter.

Step 2.   Measure the width of the parts of the boat you wish to cover (Figure 14–8). (It's possible to make this awning slightly wider than the boat in order to get a bit more shade from morning and afternoon sun.)

Step 3.   Measure the length of each fore-and-aft section you wish to cover (Figure 14–8).

*Figure 14–5.
Awning for sloops.*

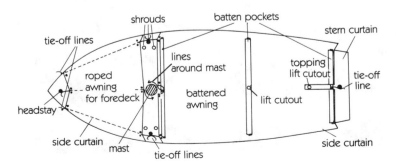

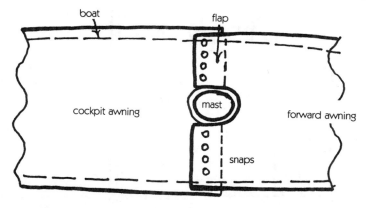

Figure 14–6.
Awning sections designed
to snap together.

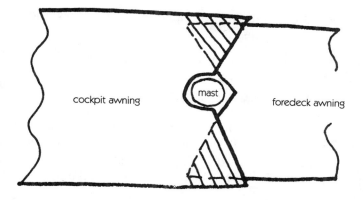

Figure 14–7.
Awning sections designed
to overlap but not attach.
Each section is rigged
independently of the
others.

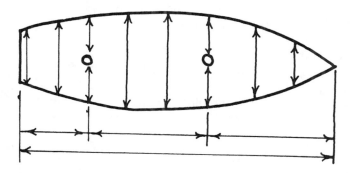

Figure 14–8.
Measure your boat.

Step 4.   Transfer measurements to a diagram.

Step 5.   Take into consideration the width of the cloth you plan to use (refer to Chapter 5), and figure how many panels of what length will be needed to cover each section of the boat. Add enough extra cloth for hems and reinforcing patches and calculate the total yardage required. For large awnings or awnings with considerable curve in the edges, placing the panels athwartships may use less cloth than placing them fore and aft.

Step 6.   Try to determine where battens will have to be placed to extend the awning out to the sides. Also figure as closely as possible where the mast or masts will fit in the canopy, whether slashes will be needed to accommodate backstays, topping lifts, or shrouds, and where reinforc-

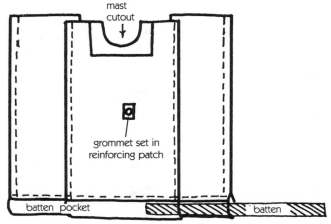

Figure 14–9.
Three-panel awning with
batten.

ing patches will be needed for grommets not placed in hems.

Step 7. Cut the lengths of cloth you will need for each piece. Make sure to allow 2 inches extra for each hem. Where batten pockets are to be used at the extreme ends of the awning, allow an extra 6 or 8 inches on each batten pocket end.

Step 8. Do whatever sewing you can on each panel before sewing the panels together. For instance, the canopy in Figure 14–9 has three panels. The two outer panels can be hemmed along the long sides before they are sewn to the middle panel. The mast cutout can be made and the reinforcing patch for the supporting grommet can be sewn on the middle panel before the three panels are sewn together. The less cloth you have to handle at one time, the easier the job will be. Be particularly careful about matching the right sides of each panel. Refer to Chapter 3 when making the mast cutout, slashes, and reinforcing patches.

Step 9. Sew all the panels together. Begin at an outside panel, and work to the opposite outside panel. Make flat-felled or overlapped seams between panels as you go.

Step 10. Hem the remaining outside edges. In the example in Figure 14–3, a batten pocket is needed at the aft end. For

this type of batten pocket, follow these steps:

a. Fold over ¼ inch and stitch as in hemming.

b. Fold over enough cloth to allow the batten to slip through easily, and stitch the outer edge twice (Figure 14–9). This procedure is identical to making a hem, except that the ends of the hem are not stitched down.

If you should need batten pockets anywhere in the middle of the awning, follow these four steps:

a. Cut a strip of cloth as long as the width of the awning at the point where the batten pocket must be sewn, plus 3 inches, and as wide as the diameter of the batten, plus 2 inches.

b. Make a ¼-inch hem in both long edges of the batten pocket, and make a 1½-inch hem at both ends.

c. Carefully pin the pocket in place, making sure that you are placing the pocket at right angles to the fore-and-aft centerline of the awning.

d. Stitch the pocket to the awning along both long edges. Stitch these edges again for reinforcement.

You may wish to put a curve into the top of the awning by using flexible PVC

Figure 14–10.
PVC pipe provides curved
support for an awning.

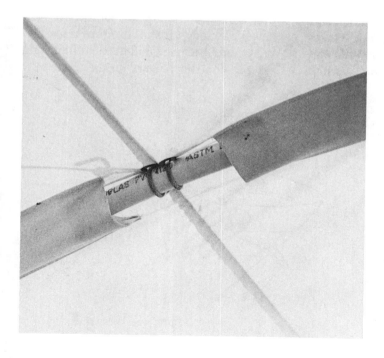

Figure 14–11.
Underside of an awning
showing PVC pipe and
bolt rope.

pipe as in Figures 14–10 and 14–11. In this case, the batten pockets should be sewn on in the same manner, but each batten gets two pockets, one on either side of the centerline, to allow you to slide the pipe through the bridle that lifts the awning. This way, the weight of the awning is carried by the poles rather than by the grommets that the bridle goes through.

Bolt Rope

For extra strength you may choose to sew a bolt rope down the center of the awning to hold up the awning between two masts, or between the mast and backstay. This is highly recommended for large awnings. To sew a bolt rope into an awning, follow these three steps:

Step 1.   Once all the panels have been sewn together and batten pockets have been sewn on, mark the center of the awning on the side that will face the deck. (You must have two batten pockets, one on either side of the bolt rope, as discussed for PVC pipe.)

Step 2.   Fold the awning in half lengthwise on the centerline, and insert into the fold a piece of Dacron rope 8 to 10 feet longer than the awning. Using the zipper foot on your sewing machine, stitch the two sides of the awning together around the rope. Stitch again for reinforcement.

Step 3.   Grommets should then be placed on both sides of the rope so that the bridle can go around the bolt rope. This allows the rope, rather than the grommets, to carry the strain caused by the bridle. (Alternatively, you can place cringles on top of the awning, over the bolt rope, and seize them through the canvas to the rope with waxed sail twine and a large needle. This arrangement does away with grommet holes and their associated leaks in heavy rain.) If battens are needed, place them in line with the bridle grommets, and pass the batten through the bridle as well.

Tiedowns and Optional Side Curtains

After the canopy is all sewn together, tiedowns must be made. This is usually done by spacing grommets around the canopy edges so they will line up with available stanchions, lifelines, shrouds, and deck fittings that can be used to hold the canopy laterally or down. If you haven't already, install grommets for lacing around the mast and in the reinforcing patches for the halyard bridle. You may

Figure 14–12. Grommets in the ends of the batten pockets allow you to tie the battens in and stretch the awning laterally.

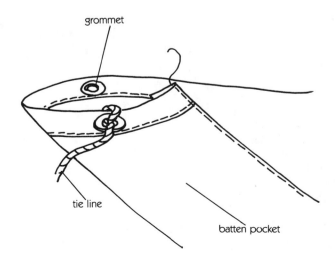

grommet

tie line

batten pocket

want to place grommets in the ends of the batten pockets as well so you can tie the battens in and stretch the awning laterally.

If a removable side curtain is desired to keep out early morning or afternoon sun, or to create privacy in the cockpit, you must first design the curtain to hang from the awning and shade the boat when the sun is low in the sky. One curtain may be sufficient, if it can be moved to follow the sun. This is achieved by setting snaps or grommets at equal distances all around the canopy, and having them line up with the snaps or grommets on the curtain no matter where you put it. Obviously, accurate equidistant spacing is required. Grommets will be required on the bottom of the side curtain to hold it down.

Tie 1/8-inch line to all tiedown and lacing grommets, and rig at least one bridle, to lift the center of the awning. Make a loop of 1/8-inch line through a grommet, around the center batten, and back out

through the top of the awning by way of a paired grommet, then tie off the bridle with a loop to which you can attach the main halyard. When rigging your awning, tighten the halyard so that the center is just above the ends, and be sure to pull the lines tight. A sloppy fit will cause more strain on it than the tension of the lines.

Building a Roped Awning

Materials Needed

- acrylic canvas
- three lengths of 3/8-inch Dacron line the length of the awning, plus 10 feet each
- number 1 or number 2 grommets (enough to place on every panel, corner, and slash)
- small rivets or grommets for the roll-up ties to pass through
- number 4 line for rigging

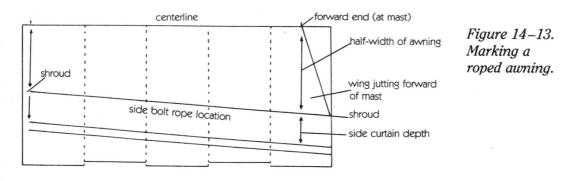

Figure 14–13. Marking a roped awning.

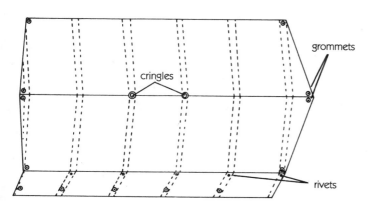

Figure 14–14. Grommet and rivet layout. Cringles might be used in lieu of grommets for the rigging lines, as shown, to avoid leaks through the grommets. See the detail in Figure 14–15.

Step 1. Tie a line from the mainmast to the most forward or aft stay, depending on what you want to cover, at the height at which you want to fly the awning. Next, tie a line from the upper shroud (or most outboard shroud) to the side of the bow or stern pulpit (or to the outermost mizzen shroud) at a height slightly lower than the middle rope. Tie each line very tightly.

Step 2. Measure the length of each line.

Step 3. Take width measurements at the forward and aft ends of the awning. Measure the length of the side curtain at the fore and aft ends. I don't recommend that side curtains be any longer than 3 feet at the aft end. They will almost always have to taper to zero at the forward end. Transfer all the measurements to your drawing, and note if the center of the awning must be slashed for a topping lift for the staysail or baby stay. If so, be sure to take those measurements. Refer to Figures 14–4 or 14–5 for a guide.

Step 4. Add up the width of the awning by combining the width of the top with the width of the side curtain. Cut enough cloth panels to equal these lengths, and stitch them together.

Step 5. Fold this piece of fabric in half, and mark the center of the awning (Figure 14–13). Measure out one-half the width of the aft end, and mark this distance on the awning. Then measure the depth of the side curtain from this mark, and mark again. Measure forward the length of the awning on the center fold, and having marked the center of its forward end, measure out from that point half the width, incorporating the appropriate angle if the awning is to end with wings either side of the mast (Figure 14–13). Make a mark, measure the depth of the side curtain, and mark again. Draw a straight line between the forward and aft half-widths to establish the location of the side bolt rope and to check this distance against the necessary length of the awning

Figure 14–15. Fastening a cringle to the center bolt rope. A rigging line is then rove through the cringle. This alternative to the use of grommets either side of the bolt rope prevents water leaks. Use two cringles for a short awning, three for one 16 feet or longer.

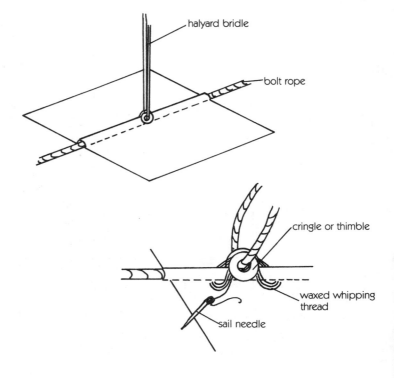

side as measured in Step 1. Adjust as necessary if you find a discrepancy.

Step 6.   Hem the entire edge of the awning with a double-rubbed hem. If you want the awning to be very strong, hide Dacron tape in the hem.

Step 7.   Bind and reinforce all the necessary slashes as described in Chapter 3.

Step 8.   Place the center rope in the middle of the awning as it is folded in half. (See Step 2 under "Bolt Rope," earlier in the chapter.)

Step 9.   Stitch as close to the rope as you can.

Step 10.   In the same manner, place the side ropes in the awning, folding the fabric over the rope. Stitch as close to these ropes as possible. Backstitch several times at the beginning and end of the casing next to the line, since this is the weakest point of the stitching.

Step 11.   Set grommets at every panel seam, corner, and slash. Set grommets on each side of every line. Set small rivets or grommets under the side ropes at each panel seam for the roll-up ties (Figure 14–14).

Rigging the Roped Awning

I cannot stress enough how important it is to fly your awnings as tightly as is physically possible. Just as your sail will wear out more quickly when you allow it to luff in the wind, your awning will wear out if you let it flap in the breeze.

Step 12.   First rig the center line. Tie a bowline in the line about 6 to 12 inches from the awning and then wrap the free end of the line around the mast, shroud, or backstay, taking it next back through the loop in the bowline. Pull hard to get maximum purchase on the line and tie off on the mast, shroud, or backstay side. Use the bowline as a pulley to get more tension on the line. Then tie the side lines between the pulpit and the shrouds as tightly as you can. Use a bowline here as well.

Step 13.   Place a light line in one of the grommets on either side of each bolt rope end. Use this light line to stretch the fabric out on the rope.

Step 14.   Now that the awning is rigged tightly fore and aft, use the tiedown lines attached to each grommet in the side curtains to pull the awning down. If you do this tightly enough, you will be able to pull out any sag in the top of the awning.

Figure 14–16. A roped foredeck awning rigged to headstay, forward lower shrouds, stanchions, and two hoisting bridles. A roped cockpit awning is visible in the background.

15
A Dodger, a Bimini, or Both?

When planning a strategy to keep spray and wind to a minimum in the cockpit or on the bridge, consider using a dodger, a Bimini, or a dodger-Bimini combination. In this chapter we'll look at some of the options, both for sailboats and for power yachts. Since the latter lack the superstructure for a dodger and can only use a Bimini, let's discuss options for sailboats first.

A word of caution: Designing and constructing your own dodger, Bimini, or Bimini-dodger combination will most likely require professional assistance at certain points in the process. The frames, made of tubular stainless steel, will need to be custom bent, and you may want help in detailing their design. As for the full-cockpit enclosures described later in this chapter, you should give serious thought to having a professional build them for you. Working with 30-gauge and 40-gauge vinyl glass on a domestic sewing machine is not easy. You can do it, but it will take a lot of patience and many more hours than it would take a professional with an industrial machine. Even if you decide to have a professional build your cockpit canvas system, however, this chapter will help you to

clarify your options so you can discuss the problems intelligently and get a quality structure that you will be proud of.

The Dodger

A dodger is a self-supporting structure designed primarily to keep spray and wind out of the cockpit. With today's concern about skin cancer, dodgers are also being used for protection from the sun. They provide a warm, dry place for one or two people to sit, and allow the companionway hatch to be kept open when it's raining or wet. They are a particular blessing on a passage, making it possible to sit comfortably in the main hatchway looking about while the boat's steering vane handles the course.

A dodger is supported by a frame that must be bent to the following limitations (Figure 15–2):

1. The position of the close-hauled boom is one factor that limits the height.

2. The position of the traveler may limit spread (fore-and-aft measurement) when the dodger lies in a folded position.

64

*Figure 15–1.
A dodger on a
sailboat, and
a Bimini on a
power yacht.*

Figure 15–2.
Considerations for dodger
size and position.

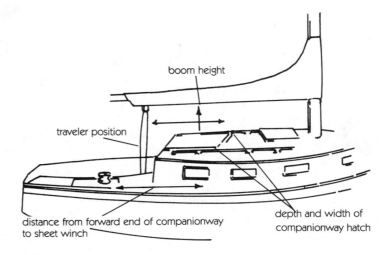

boom height

traveler position

distance from forward end of companionway
to sheet winch

depth and width of
companionway hatch

3. The position of the splash coaming, sea hood, or companionway hatch in an open position may dictate the width of the dodger.

4. The width of the cabin—or companionway—will dictate the width of the dodger.

The optimum dodger gives as much protection as possible, allows for fair visibility for the helmsperson, folds quickly out of the way, is strong enough to keep mist or green seas out of the cockpit, and can withstand frequent grabbing by crewmembers. Technically speaking, if a dodger does all of the above and fits the parameters defined by the boat, it should be wonderful. But it may not be, if you don't take into account what it will do to the total look of the boat. The aesthetics of the dodger—its height and shape—could spoil the fore-and-aft lines of the vessel. If the dodger is boxy on a curved house or curved on a box house, it may look out of place. Likewise, if the dodger comes too far aft, relative to the length of the boat, it could throw the boat's lines out of proportion.

Color will also affect what the dodger does to the total look of the boat (Figure

15–3). My own preference is to make the dodger look like an integral part of the boat by matching its color to the cabintop. Alternatively, though, you may choose to match the color of your hull or of your sailcover.

Helmsman's Awning

Once you have a basic design for your dodger (you might want to seek the advice and help of a professional who has many dodgers under his or her belt), consider the various ways you can use this dodger for a shade system as well (Figure 15–4). You now have a structure at the forward end of the cockpit that can support the forward end of a helmsman's awning. By placing a zipper on the top of the dodger over the aft bow, you can attach the awning at this point. A batten is used to extend the awning athwartships; it ties off to the backstay for the aftermost aftward and upward support. If your dodger is not as tall as you are, you can angle the helmsman's awning up at the aft end so that the person at the wheel can stand under it. The awning can be used for shade when the boat is at rest and often justifies its existence during a downpour at dinner time.

*Figure 15–3A.
Dodger too tall and boxy
(and accentuated by a
contrasting color scheme),
but fits gallows opening.*

*Figure 15–3B.
This dodger lacks fore-
and-aft depth but is
nicely proportioned. It
contrasts sharply with
the deck but matches the
sail cover, the outboard
cover, and the cover on
the horseshoe ring.*

*Figure 15–3C.
Weather cloth, dodger,
and sail cover, nicely
matched to each other
and to the cabintop.*

Figure 15–4. Dodger with helmsman's awning.

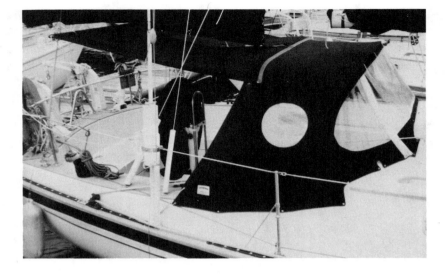

Figure 15–5A. Helmsman's awning with frame support.

Figure 15–5B. Helmsman's awning with aft batten support.

The only situation in which a helmsman's awning cannot be used under sail is when the mainsheet traveler is aft of the dodger. If your mainsheet leads to the bridge deck just aft of the dodger, a cutout must be made to accommodate the sheet where it should pass through the awning. Be sure to decide ahead of time if you want the boom to store to port, starboard, or amidships, because you will make only one cutout in the awning (Figure 15–6). If a traveler is aft of the cockpit, tack the line that ties the batten to the backstay each time the boat tacks. Even on a hot sticky day, this extra work may be well worth it.

For further protection from late afternoon sun and rain, add side curtains and a stern curtain. Because the helmsperson stands so close to the backstay, stern curtains often are necessary on aft cockpit boats in order for him/her to get any shade or rain protection at all. By zipping these curtains to the awning you have a number of options to best protect yourself from the sun and rain.

Zip Window or Not?

Another option in a dodger is a zip-front window, that is, a zipper placed perpendicular to the house top, on either side of the companionway, allowing you to unzip and roll up the center section of the dodger's vinyl glass. If you are using an awning with your dodger, a zip-front window is helpful for air circulation. Even if you're not using an awning, you may still want a zip-front window for improved visibility. If you want the maximum protection from sea and rain however, do not put in a zippered window, because a small amount of water will leak through the zippers. For that same reason, be sure to place any zippers outboard of the companionway hatch so that any leakage will not drip inside the hatch.

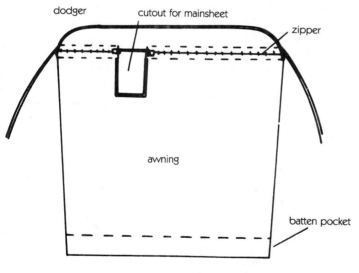

Figure 15–6.
Helmsman's awning with mainsheet cutout.

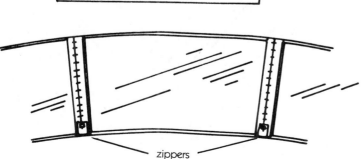

Figure 15–7.
Zippered window.

Materials Needed

- 6 to 8 yards acrylic canvas
- 1 stainless steel frame, 4 eye ends, 2 jaw slides, 2 deck hinges
- 1 sheet vinyl glass
- 1-inch Dacron tape
- 4 grommets
- 2 small padeyes
- number 4 line
- hardware to fasten to deck (snaps, turnbuttons, and/or Lift-the-Dots)
- vinyl binding
- zippers

Frame Construction

I do not recommend the use of aluminum tubing for a dodger frame. It is too soft and flexible to do the job adequately. Imagine the force a 180-pound man on his way overboard in a seaway would exert on the dodger frame. Nor do I recommend the use of brass tubing or rod, which is also too soft and will turn your canvas green. I do recommend using $7/8$- or 1-inch 16-gauge stainless steel. It is flexible yet strong enough, and will not rust and stain your deck or fabric. I also advise using stainless steel or chrome-plated brass fittings to assemble the frame and to mount it on deck. If you should ever try to take a dodger frame apart after it has been used at sea, you will find that the stainless and chrome-plated brass fittings will be the only ones you can disassemble. Aluminum fittings corrode so badly that they freeze on the tubing.

Bending a Frame

Most dodger frames can be made with just two bows. Both bows should be bent exactly the same so that they will fold together perfectly. One bow will mount on the other, thus making the legs of that bow shorter (Figure 15–8).

Instructions for bending your own frame are beyond the scope of this book. The curves involved and the different methods of transferring curves to the various types of tubing benders are too complicated to explain here. However, you can make a paper pattern of the approximate shape you want, take it to your local canvas shop or welder, and have the frame custom bent for you. Or you may find some suitable frames available by mail order.

To make a pattern of the shape you want, use a sheet of cardboard a bit wider than the dodger you have in mind. A splash coaming forward of the companionway is the proper fastening place for the front of the dodger and will dictate its

Figure 15–8. Dodger bows.

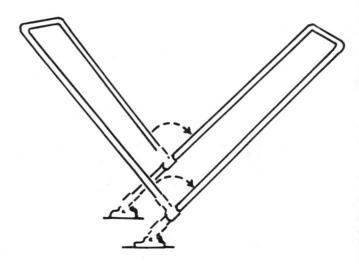

proper folded position. This is probably not a bad curve to follow for the curve of the bow. Or, remembering the parameters listed before, mark the maximum height, see if the cardboard cut to that height can fold down in the proper place when its base is placed on the desired pivot point. Keep the pivot point clear of winches. If all fits, draw in the curve as your eye tells you it should be. Remember to make the center of the bow a bit higher than the sides so the dodger will not collect rainwater. The aft bow will have shorter legs but the same shape.

Mounting the Dodger Frame

Once you have the frame, mount it securely to the deck, coaming, or house top. Be sure you bed the mounting hinge well so the screw holes won't leak. Also be sure

to use at least a number 6 screw so it will hold when weight is thrown against it. If you are mounting on very thin fiberglass, use a backing plate under the glass and through-bolt the hinge in place. Once the frame is mounted you can proceed with your pattern.

Taking a Pattern

There are various methods used by professionals to pattern a dodger, many of which are too difficult for an amateur and would require special tools. If you sew enough fabric together to cover the frame (using flat-felled or zigzagged overlap seams) and use the actual cloth for your pattern, you will be able to build a dodger. This may not be a professional method, but you will end up with a better dodger if you can see what happens to the cloth as it lies on the frame.

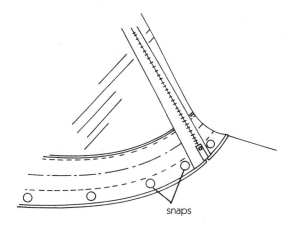

snaps

Figure 15–9A.
Snaps in the hatch coaming.

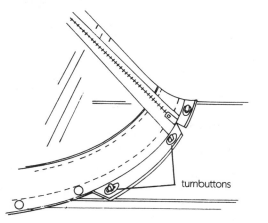

turnbuttons

Figure 15–9B.
Snaps in the hatch coaming and turnbuttons on the cabintop.

Be sure that you hold the fabric tightly. Don't let it slip from side to side, and do not imagine that the boat is symmetrical. Mark the position of the bows on the fabric, the position of the window, and the place at which the deck meets the fabric. Also, if there is too much fabric in a certain area, mark where to take a dart. (See Sewing Techniques in Chapter 3.) If the boat has a coaming, you can run the fabric a few inches over the outside edge of the coaming and fasten it with snaps (Figure 15–9A). If the dodger meets the deck squarely, you will have to add a tab to hold the fasteners (Figure 15–9B). Wherever the fabric lies vertically on the boat, snaps can be used. If you use a tab, you must use turnbuttons or Lift-the-Dots, because snaps will not hold at that angle. For illustration of different types of fasteners, see Chapter 2.

Constructing the Dodger

Step 1. Once your pattern is all marked, true up the lines and cut it out.

Think about where you will need extra reinforcement. The obvious places are wherever there is a fastener. The other major stress point is over the aft bow where the majority of people will grab the dodger. It's a good idea to use Dacron tape for the reinforcement of all fasteners and vinyl or elk hide for the outside of the dodger over the top of the aft bow (Figure 15–10).

Step 2. Cut the reinforcement pieces, and lay them on the inside of the dodger where they belong. Pin them in. Cut the vinyl or elk hide, and pin that to the outside of the dodger over the aft bow.

Step 3. Cut two pockets, one for the top of each bow. The aft pocket should stop about mid-bend of the bow, and the forward pocket should stop before the sharp bend of the bow begins. Cut these pockets 4 inches wide (Figure 15–11).

Step 4. Stitch any darts you have marked with a flat-felled seam (see Chapter 3).

*Figure 15–10.
Reinforcement of the dodger.*

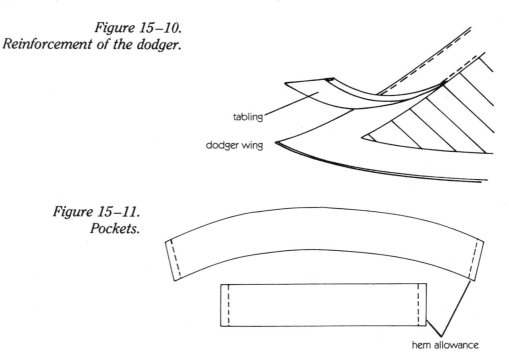

tabling

dodger wing

*Figure 15–11.
Pockets.*

hem allowance

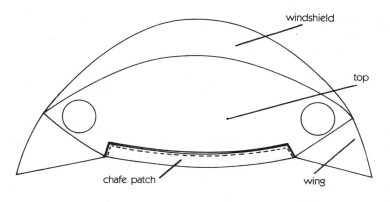

*Figure 15–12.
Stitching a chafe patch
to a dodger.*

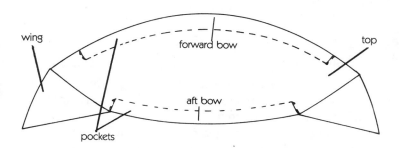

*Figure 15–13.
Pocket layout for
dodger.*

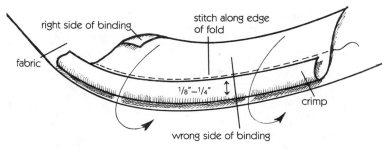

*Figure 15–14A.
Vinyl binding. The vinyl
strip has a 1/8- to 1/4-inch-
wide crimp along one
long edge. Align this fold
with the fabric edge as
shown, and stitch just
inside the raw edge of the
crimp. Then fold the
vinyl over the crimp and
over the raw edge of the
fabric, around to the
fabric's backside. Stitch
again, being sure to
catch the crimp with
your stitches.*

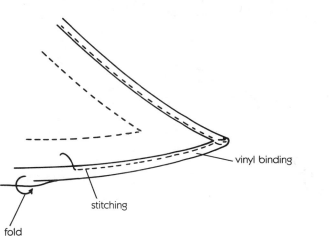

*Figure 15–14B.
Binding the dodger.*

Step 5.   Stitch the reinforcement pieces onto the dodger, folding raw edges under. If you don't want the white Dacron tape to show, cut a piece of matching fabric and cover the Dacron. Stitch this in place. (Refer to Figure 15–10.)

Step 6.   Stitch the vinyl- or elk-hide chafe patch to the top of the dodger (Figure 15–12).

Step 7.   Stitch the pockets to the inside of the dodger so each bow will fit in them (Figure 15–13), being sure to turn the raw edges under.

Step 8.   Bind the entire edge of the dodger with vinyl binding (Figures 15–14A and B).

Step 9.   Cut the glass pieces you need for the front window and side windows. Pin or staple them in place on the wrong side (inside) of the dodger. Stitch the glass close to the edge, and then cut the fabric out from in front of the glass, leaving 1/2-inch seam allowance. Fold this 1/2 inch under once, and stitch it down all the way around each piece of vinyl glass (Figure 15–15).

Step 10.   Use snaps to fasten the fabric where it is in the same plane as the boat. Use Lift-the-Dots or turnbuttons wherever the plane of the fabric is different from that of the boat (refer to Figure 15–9). Set two grommets in each wing, as shown in Figure 15–17.

Installing the Dodger

Step 11.   Place the dodger on the frame, center it, and begin to attach the fasteners to the boat so they correspond to the fasteners in the cloth. Start at the center, being sure to put solid tension on the cloth. Work one fastener on each side of

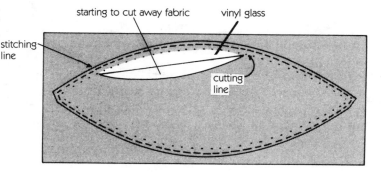

Figure 15–15.
Putting in the vinyl glass.

starting to cut away fabric   vinyl glass

stitching line

cutting line

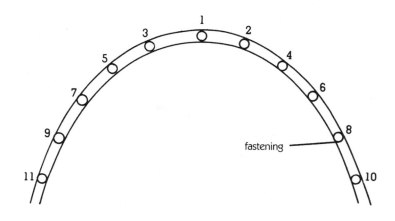

Figure 15–16.
Installing the dodger.

fastening

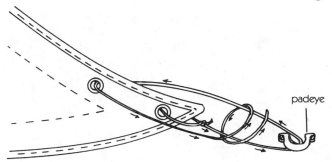

Figure 15–17.
Tying down the wing.

padeye

center, and continue in this fashion, working outward and aft (Figure 15–16). Don't do all of one side at a time or you will disturb the tension and uniformity of the dodger.

Install padeyes to fasten the wings, as shown in Figure 15–17. Tie a line to the grommet in the corner of the wing, run it through the padeye and back to the upper grommet in the wing, and tie it off after tensioning.

The Bimini Top

A Bimini is similar to a dodger in that both are supported by their own metal structures. Because it does not rely on the boat's standing rigging to hold it up and out, the Bimini can be built to fit under the boom and can therefore be used while sailing. If your Bimini will be used in combination with a dodger for a shade system, the two structures should be designed to work well and look good together. Ideally the dodger and Bimini should be the same height, but sometimes this will not work because of the boat's design. Another option is to make the dodger lower than the Bimini and have the Bimini slightly overlap the dodger.

Bimini Top or Helmsman's Awning?

For most aft cockpit sailboats, a dodger-helmsman's awning combination is almost always preferable to a Bimini top. The helmsman's awning is easily zipped on and off when you want to use or stow it, and it will not obstruct the winches and inhibit

your access to the cockpit as a Bimini top could. It will easily support 2½-foot side curtains and a stern curtain (Figure 15–19).

A Bimini is a strong structure capable of supporting a full deck enclosure. If you want to enclose your entire cockpit with vinyl glass curtains, you will need to use a Bimini top rather than a helmsman's awning. But be sure that your Bimini is able to fold down either fore or aft without fouling the winches, and that it is sufficiently portable to be gotten entirely out of the way in bad weather. If this cannot be designed for your boat, you are safer with a dodger-helmsman's awning combination. Full enclosures using the dodger-Bimini combination will be discussed later in this chapter.

Designing a Bimini Top for a Sailboat

The biggest decision you will have to make in designing a Bimini will be where to fold it down. Since it usually mounts on the cockpit coaming in approximately the middle of the cockpit, the Bimini could fold forward or aft, depending on whether the winches are forward or aft of the mounting point (Figure 15–21). Trying to get a Bimini to cover the companionway as well as the helm is usually difficult, because the top will be too large to fold anywhere. Some sailors want shade badly enough to put up with folding the Bimini against the backstay and securing it.

Figure 15–18.
Bimini tops on sailboats.

Figure 15–19.
Helmsman's awning with ties
and stern and side curtains.

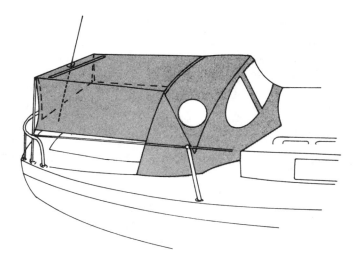

Figure 15–20.
Full enclosure.

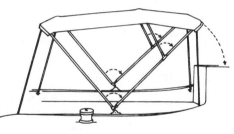

Figure 15–21.
Bimini folding positions on a
sailboat.

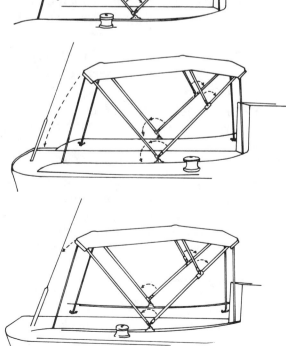

Figure 15–22. Considerations for Bimini size and position on a sailboat.

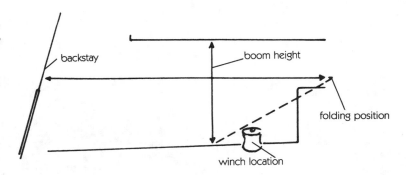

Figure 15–23. Tying the Bimini frame for patterning.

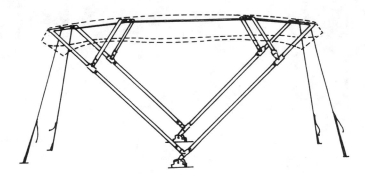

Design Considerations for a Bimini Top on a Sailboat

1. The height of the boom in its lowest close-hauled position will be the maximum height of the Bimini (Figure 15–22).

2. The width of the mounting hinges will be determined in most cases by the distance between the cockpit coamings.

3. The spread (fore-and-aft measurement) is limited by the backstay or mizzenmast and the folding position.

4. If your winches are forward of the mid-cockpit mounting position, the Bimini must fold aft.

5. If your winches are aft of the mid-cockpit mounting position, the Bimini must fold forward.

6. A forward-folding Bimini should not intersect the opening of the companionway hatch in its folded position.

7. A forward-folding Bimini should not hit the house top and therefore stick up higher than the deck.

8. A forward-folding Bimini must not foul a mainsheet traveler on the bridge deck.

9. An aft-folding Bimini must not foul a mainsheet traveler aft of the cockpit.

Constructing the Bimini Top

Again, building a Bimini top is difficult because of the need for a frame. As with the dodger, I would suggest that in designing the Bimini and obtaining the frame, you seek professional help.

Materials Needed

- acrylic or reinforced vinyl
- 3 zippers, one for the pocket for each bow

- vinyl binding to trim each side
- Dacron tape for reinforcing each side
- nylon webbing for 4 tiedown straps
- 4 buckles
- 4 snaphooks
- 4 padeyes

Taking a Pattern

Step 1. Mount the frame on the boat.

Step 2. Using three separate lines, tie the frame securely in position (Figure 15–23).

Step 3. Stitch enough fabric together to cover the top and extend over the edges of the frame by 6 inches.

Step 4. Lay the fabric over the frame, and draw the outline of the bows on the fabric.

Step 5. Mark whatever darts are necessary to make the fabric lie smooth without wrinkling. The fabric should fully cover the bend in the bows.

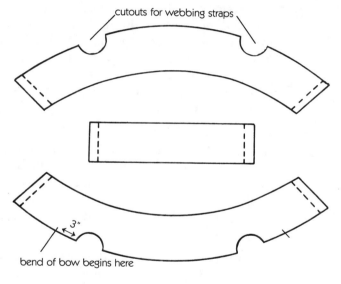

cutouts for webbing straps

3"

bend of bow begins here

Figure 15–24.
Cutting the fabric pockets.

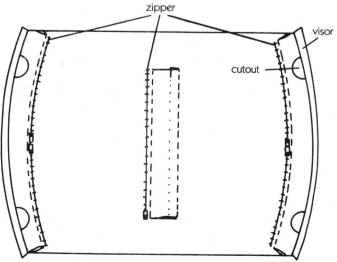

zipper

visor

cutout

Figure 15–25A.
Visors.

Cutting and Stitching the Bimini

Step 6. Cut out the top, leaving a 1/2-inch seam allowance all around.

Step 7. Cut three pockets. The forward and aft pocket should be 4 inches wide (Figure 15–24) and take the exact curve of the top. Proceeding 3 inches in from the beginning of the bends of the bows, make two 2-inch deep half-circle cutouts in the outer edge of each pocket, one on either side of the center. These cutouts will later allow you to fasten the webbing tiedowns to the bows. Bind each cutout with vinyl binding (Figure 15–14). Cut a 4-inch wide middle pocket that stops 6 inches short of the bend in the bow on each side.

Step 8. Cut two strips of fabric the length of the forward and aft edges of the top, making them 3 inches wide with a seam allowance of 1 inch on either end. These will be visors. Fold the inch on each end to the inside, fold each visor in half, and stitch the ends.

Step 9. Stitch a jacket zipper to the inside edge of each pocket. Fold 1/2 inch of the pocket fabric under as you stitch so that the raw edge is finished (Figure 15–25).

Step 10. Stitch any necessary darts in the Bimini, and finish them with a flat-felled seam (see Chapter 3).

Step 11. Staple or pin each visor to the right side or top side of the Bimini, with the raw edges of the visors aligned with the forward and aft edges of the Bimini, respectively. Then stack the forward and aft pockets on top of their respective visors, right sides together. The raw edges of the Bimini, visors, and pockets should now all be aligned. Pin the pockets in place (Figure 15–25B).

Step 12. Stitch 1/2 inch in from the forward and aft edges through the top, visor, and pocket. Turn the pockets to the underside, and stitch the zippers to the Bimini top where the zippered edges of the pockets contact it.

Step 13. Stitch the middle pocket so that the edge without the zipper is stitched on the line marking the position of the middle bow. Fold under 1/2 inch of the edge of the pocket without the zipper, and top-stitch it to the top along that line. Stitch the zipper to the top.

Step 14. Cut a strip of fabric 1 1/2 inches wide and a strip of 1-inch Dacron tape to be used for tabling the side edges. Staple or pin a layer of Dacron and a layer of fabric to the inside of the top. Fold 1/2 inch under to finish the inside raw edge. Topstitch it to the top.

Step 15. Bind the side edges of the Bimini with vinyl binding (refer to Figure 15–14).

Step 16. Put the top on the frame.

Step 17. Make your tiedown straps with one buckle and one snaphook each. Thread one webbing strap through each of the four cutouts in the fore and aft pock-

Figure 15–25B. Schematic layout showing how the visor and batten pocket are stitched to the top.

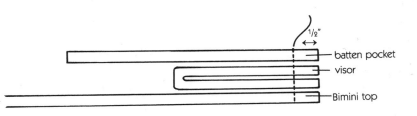

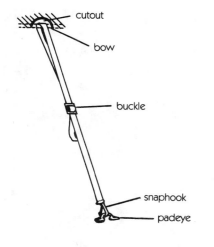

Figure 15–26.
Webbing straps and padeyes.

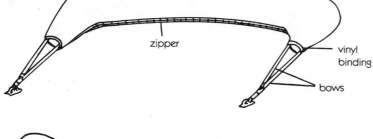

Figure 15–27.
Bimini boot.

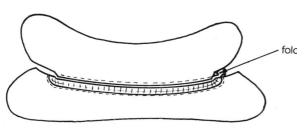

Figure 15–28.
Stitching a zipper in the boot. Although not shown as such here, the two pieces should be sewn together along their top edge before the zipper is installed.

ets, around the bow, out of the cutout, and back to the buckle.

Step 18. Mount the four padeyes on the deck so that the webbing will pull the top out and down when it is fastened to the padeyes. Clip on the snaphooks to the padeyes, and enjoy the shade (Figure 15–26).

A Bimini Boot

If you want to keep the Bimini neat and out of the sun when it isn't needed, make a Bimini boot. This boot holds the bows together in their folded position and contains the fabric as it accordions between the bows.

Materials Needed

- acrylic or reinforced vinyl
- 1 zipper the length of boot (jacket type)
- vinyl binding

Construction

Step 1. On a flat surface, lay a piece of fabric under your folded Bimini with the top on. Fold the Bimini fabric between the bows neatly, but not so neatly that you will never be able to do it again. Trace the outline of the Bimini on your fabric. True up the lines, add a 1/2-inch seam allowance all

*Figure 15–29.
Dodger-Bimini
combination.*

*Figure 15–30.
A Bimini-windshield
combination offers yet another
possibility for sun, wind, and
rain protection in the cockpit.*

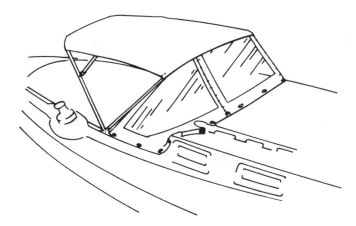

around, and cut two pieces of fabric to the traced shape.

Step 2. Stitch the two pieces with right sides together along the top edge.

Step 3. Stitch a jacket-type zipper in the bottom of the boot (Figure 15–28).

Step 4. Bind the edges of the boot that surround the legs of the bows. (Refer to Figure 15–14).

The Dodger-Bimini Combination

If your boat can handle the dodger-Bimini combination, it is a wonderful rig, giving spray and wind protection when needed and/or sun and rain protection as well. The dodger covers the companionway, and the Bimini covers the rest of the cockpit (Figure 15–29).

In a smaller cockpit, the main consideration is the amount of steel necessary for both frames. It may be that the Bimini frame could make it impossible to get in and out of the cockpit easily. If you are concerned about all those bows blocking you in or out of the cockpit, you might consider borrowing the aft bow of the dodger for the forward support of the Bimini. This will mean that you must always

Figure 15–31.
Full enclosure with zippered
door.

use the dodger whenever you need the Bimini, but it will cut out one bow, which may allow easier access to your cockpit.

Full Enclosures

A fully enclosed cockpit is especially nice for people who spend time in their cockpits in cold weather or on cold nights. Those of you traveling south on the Intracoastal Waterway will appreciate the warmth such an enclosure provides. As I mentioned before, you must use a Bimini or a dodger-Bimini combination if you wish to support the weight of a full enclosure (Figure 15–31). Once the Bimini top or dodger-Bimini combination is in place, you can pattern the boat for the windshield. Decide where you want to enter the cockpit, and whether you will need a doorway or whether you will lift or roll up the entire curtain. Doors are most easily made with zippers.

Materials Needed

- acrylic or reinforced vinyl
- 20-, 30- or 40-gauge vinyl glass
- zippers for the top and sides of each curtain (preferably Number 10 Delrin jacket zippers)
- fastenings (snaps or Lift-the-Dots) to fasten the bottom of the curtains to the deck

Patterning the Enclosure

Step 1. Windshield: Use paper to make your patterns. Be sure that the top and/or dodger is rigged tightly in place. Attach paper to the front of the Bimini if there is no dodger. The windshield should wrap slightly around the side of the Bimini top. There should be a 90-degree angle at the top corner of the Bimini where the windshield and side curtain will meet. Draw the bow and deck line of the Bimini

Figure 15–32.
Windshield pattern.

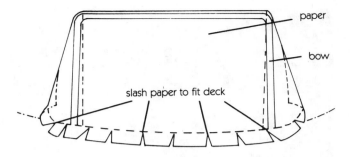

on the paper. Mark each side where you would like the side curtains to meet (Figure 15–32).

Step 2. Side and Stern Curtains: Use the same method to pattern the side and stern. Be sure to mark the edge of the Bimini on the pattern for the sides, and the aft bow on the top of the stern curtain pattern. If necessary, make a cutout for the mainsheet in the stern curtain. Carefully mark each side where it will zip to the next curtain.

Step 3. Preparing the Top for the Enclosure: Stitch zippers to the fore and aft visors. Stitch zippers to the inside of the Bimini. All zippers will be on the inside or underside of the top. Be sure that the zippers start and stop exactly where you patterned the side to start and stop.

Step 4. Constructing the Side Curtains: Cut each curtain out of vinyl glass as you have patterned it.

Step 5. Table each edge with either Dacron or fabric to match your top (Figure 15–33).

Step 6. Stitch the corner zippers to each curtain, making certain that they start and stop at exactly the same place on every curtain. If they don't, your curtains will hang at different lengths.

Step 7. Stitch to the tops of the curtains the zippers from corresponding edges of the Bimini.

Step 8. Hang all the curtains in place. Make whatever minor adjustments are necessary, and install the fasteners in the bottom so the curtains are tight against the boat. Snap fasteners usually work well for this application.

Navy Tops for Small Power Yachts

Staying protected from wind and heavy spray on a power yacht is a bit easier than

Figure 15–33.
Tabling the Bimini
curtains.

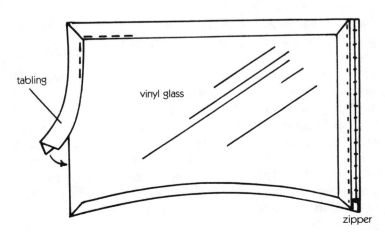

Figure 15–34.
Navy tops for small
boats.

Figure 15–35.
A Navy top that's too tall.

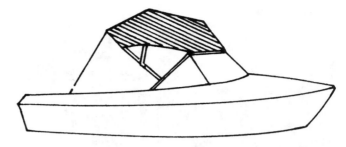

on a sailboat. Spray rarely reaches a flying bridge. If you're out in very windy weather, most large yachts have interior steering stations where you can comfortably take refuge. On board a small runabout—without the luxury of a bridge or an interior steering station—you can make life vastly more comfortable by constructing a navy top. A navy top is a fabric awning that is supported by the boat's windshield and a steel frame. It usually covers the steering station and provides shade and weather protection for the boat's occupants. Side curtains made of vinyl glass provide further protection without limiting visibility. If you want to sleep aboard or protect the boat from rain and dirt when she's not in use, you can build a backdrop that attaches to the aft edge of the navy top and extends to the stern, thereby enclosing the entire boat.

Design Considerations for a Navy Top

1. The windshield is the first point of attachment and therefore dictates the top's height and where it will fold when not in use.

2. The metal frame can be taller than the windshield. However, it usually isn't advisable for the frame to be more than 6 to 8 inches taller, since you could destroy the lines of the boat. On a small 16-foot power yacht, don't try to create a covered space with standing headroom unless you

don't care what it looks like (Figure 15–35).

3. The width of the navy top is dictated by the width of the side deck or the coaming on which the top will mount.

4. The height is also dictated by where the top will fold (on the windshield or the foredeck).

Construction

Construction of a navy top is the same as for the Bimini top described for sailboats. You must get a frame, install it, pattern the fabric, and stitch it in the same manner. The side curtains will be made just as the enclosure curtains were, and the backdrop should be patterned in the same way. The backdrop is usually not made of vinyl glass because of the expense and lack of flexibility. Make the backdrop out of fabric to match your top, with a zipper to connect it to the navy top. Use zippers to attach the backdrop to the side curtains. It is probably advisable to put a vinyl glass window in the middle of the backdrop so that you can see out of it when sleeping aboard or when taking refuge from the rain. This glass will also allow more light in.

Bimini Tops for Flying Bridges

On a larger power yacht with a bridge deck and/or flying bridge, you can create shade and spray protection with a Bimini top. As with sailboats, a Bimini top is an awning supported by a steel frame.

Figure 15–36.
Bimini top for a flying bridge.

Design Considerations for a Bimini Top on a Large Power Yacht

1. Height is dictated by where you want the top to fold down. Possibilities include on the windshield, on the chocks forward of the windshields or on struts that help support the top (Figures 15–37A and B). If the top can fold on the windshield without harming it, that is the easiest solution. In many cases, the design of the windshield, or antennas, searchlights, or fishing gear, may prohibit the Bimini from folding there. You can, however, build wood or metal chocks to hold the Bimini when it folds just in front of the windshield. It is usually necessary to place a chock on either side of the bridge, as well as in the center of the bridge, so the top will be well supported when the boat is running fast.

2. Spread (distance the Bimini covers fore and aft) may also be determined by where you want the Bimini to fold. If you want the Bimini to have a large spread and more height than the windshield or chock folding position will allow, fold the Bimini on struts that will stay permanently in position. These struts are highly recommended for large tops because they are made of stainless steel tubing and prevent shifting as the boat pounds on the waves.

A Bimini protects you from the sun primarily and from the rain to a lesser extent. For more rain and spray protection, add a windshield. For total protection, add sides and a stern curtain and completely enclose the bridge (Fig 15–38).

Figure 15–37A & B.
Folding positions for a
Bimini top on a flying
bridge.

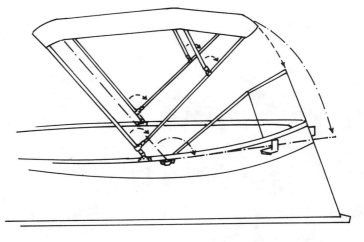

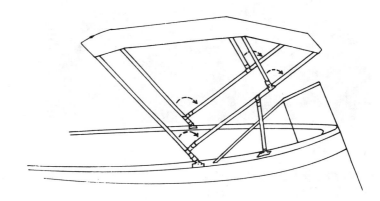

Figure 15–38.
Bimini with full enclosure.

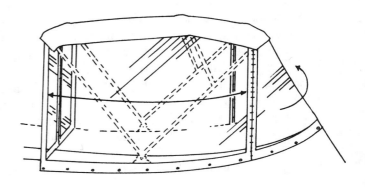

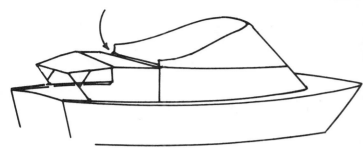

Figure 15–39.
Navy top on the aft deck of a
power yacht.

Navy Tops for Aft Cockpits on Larger Power Yachts

A navy top can be built for your aft deck to give it some shade (Figure 15–39). It usually attaches to the underside of the overhead with a rope track, extends aft to a two- or three-bow frame (depending on the spread of the top), and is tensioned aft with nylon webbing straps. The limitations that the boat places on the navy top are as follows:

1. The top should slope slightly toward the stern to permit water to run off. Thus, the frame should be slightly lower than the overhead.

2. The width will be dictated by the distance between the side decks and where you mount the frame. Be sure to mount the frame so the angle of the aft bow is great enough to create some tension when the webbing straps are fastened to the transom.

Maintaining Dodgers, Biminis, and Navy Tops

In Appendix A you will find cleaning instructions for acrylic and vinyl glass. Note that scrubbing acrylic canvas with a stiff brush will cause it to lose its water resistance. If you choose to leave this gear on board in the winter, you will shorten its life expectancy. Vinyl glass gets very brittle in cold weather. If you must move it when it is cold, do not bend it or it will shatter. When vinyl glass gets yellow or orange, it has deteriorated to such a point that it could rip at any moment. Replace it before it rips or you will lose the shape of the dodger or curtain. Put the new glass in before you remove the old; this is accomplished most easily by making the new glass slightly larger and stitching it just outside the perimeter of the old. This method helps you retain the shape of the original piece.

16
Rigging a Rain Catcher

When cruising to places where drinking water is expensive, brackish, or nonexistent, it's practical to have a simple means of collecting rainwater, which is delicious to drink and great for bathing. The heavily chlorinated water that most of us drink is awful compared with pure rainwater.

The following instructions are for a 6-by-8-foot rectangular rain catcher, a size I find practical. It consists of a canvas tarp with a funnel in the middle. It has grommets all around the edge for convenient rigging anywhere on the boat. A garden hose is attached to the funnel and then led to the filler pipe on deck (or through a hatch or port, directly to a water tank). This rain catcher is easy to keep clean and free of salt spray (unlike a Bimini top, dodger, or awning) and folds up to stow nicely in any small place. I find that I can set it up permanently when I am moored at one place for a while, or, when I am sailing, I can rig it under the main boom to catch the rain as it runs off the sail and funnel it into the tanks. (It is important to let sufficient rain wash all salt out of the sail before beginning to catch water.)

Materials Needed

- 6 yards treated canvas 36 inches wide
- 1 PVC pipe fitting (1/2- by-1/4-inch insert coupling)
- 1 small stainless steel clamp to fit over pipe fitting
- 1 length of garden hose
- 1 light line, number 4, 1/8 inch
- 8 grommets

Construction

Step 1.   Cut 18 inches off the length of the material to use for the funnel.

Step 2.   Cut the remaining cloth in half lengthwise.

Step 3.   Hem the long outside edges of both pieces.

Step 4.   Place the two remaining long edges, right sides together, and join with a flat-felled seam.

Step 5.   Make a funnel out of the extra 18 inches. Roll this piece into a funnel

90

Figure 16–1.
Rain catcher.

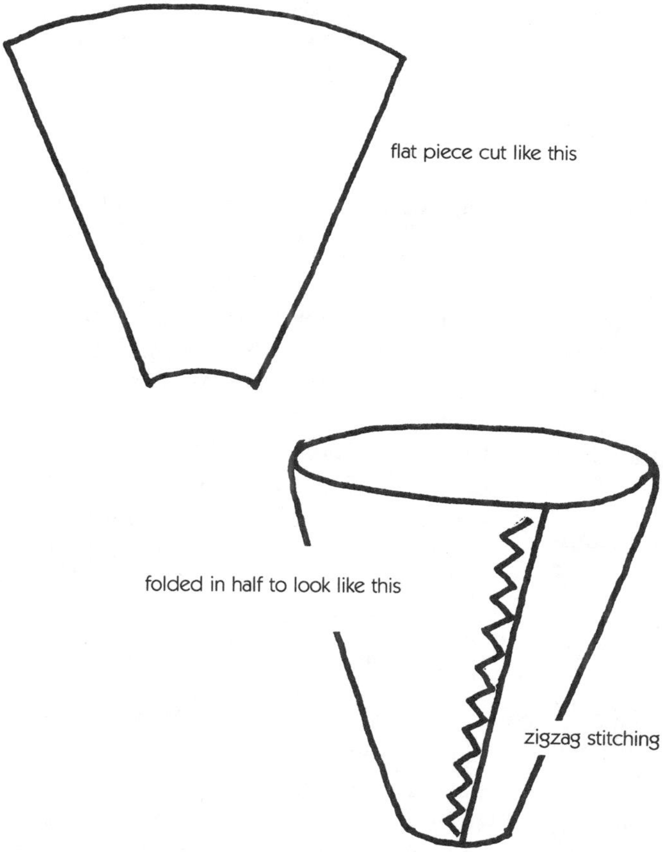

Figure 16–2.
Funnel layout.

flat piece cut like this

folded in half to look like this

zigzag stitching

shape, and cut the excess material away. Sew the side seam, and zigzag the raw edge. The top diameter should be at least 6 inches, and the bottom diameter should be slightly larger than the PVC hose fitting (Figure 16–2).

Step 6. Place the funnel on the very center of the main piece, and trace lightly around it. Or, measure a circle of the same circumference as the funnel in that exact spot. Cut 1/2 inch in from the circle just drawn. This will provide a hole in the main

Figure 16–3.
Funnel arrangement.

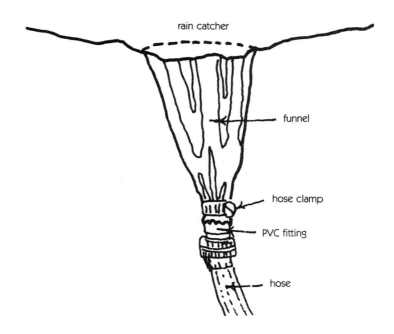

piece 1 inch smaller in diameter than the funnel.

Step 7. Pin the funnel edge to the edge of the hole, with the wrong side of the funnel facing the top of the rain catcher. Straight stitch around the edge three times, or zigzag around once, then invert the funnel through the opening and stitch again.

Step 8. Hem the ends of the rectangle.

Step 9. Place eight grommets at the edges and corners of the panel.

Step 10. Insert the PVC fitting in the funnel, and snug the cloth down tight on it with the hose clamp.

Step 11. Attach light line to the grommets where necessary, to rig it low on the boat.

Step 12. Screw the garden hose to

the PVC fitting, lead the other end of your hose to the tank filler, and wait for rain.

If you have a Bimini top or dodger that is normally kept rigged, it's a simple matter to install rain-draining funnels in the top of it, using the above instructions to construct and install the funnels. Locate the lowest point on the Bimini top or dodger, and position one or two funnels there. Experiment with slacking off the tension on the top's supports to create better drainage.

A rain catching system must be capable of being operated in strong winds, so it's not advisable to rig a rain-catching funnel in a large awning that could be damaged in bad weather. If, however, you have a small cockpit awning that is likely to be rigged when it rains or storms, placing a rain-catching funnel in it will relieve you of carrying a separate rain catcher.

17
Secure Your Ship with Weather Cloths

Weather cloths, or splash curtains, are designed to make the cockpit or bridge area of a boat more comfortable and less vulnerable to spray. They also add to the psychological security of the crew and increase the privacy of the cockpit. Weather cloths are usually laced to the lifelines with light line through grommets or, in the case of some power yachts, snapped or screwed onto permanent structures and railings. Weather cloths not only increase the comfort and security of a vessel, but also can add to the beauty of the boat.

Materials Needed

Weblon can be used for weather cloths because they are freestanding and don't seal off wood or metal. Weblon also cleans easily. Power yachts traditionally use Weblon, but auxiliary yachts often shy away from the shiny plastic and choose acrylic or treated canvas. All three of these fabrics are excellent for weather cloths.

If you plan to lace the curtains between lifelines and railcap, you will need enough grommets to put one every 6 to 8 inches along the top and sides of the curtains. You will also need some tiedowns along the bottom, but be careful to place them only where you have something to tie to. One continuous length of light line will be necessary to tie the sides and top of the curtain. Small pieces can be used to tie the bottom edge. Have enough thread to do the whole job. Three large spools of polyester thread should be enough to sew two 8-foot by 30-inch curtains.

If you plan to fasten the weather cloths to permanent wooden or metal structures, choose the proper Lift-the-Dot snap tops and wood or metal screw-type snap bottoms. Be prepared to replace these fastenings occasionally.

Measuring

An effective weather cloth on a sailing vessel should run from about amidships all the way aft. If you have a gate aft of amidships in your lifeline or railing, a separate weather cloth should be made for the gate area. Otherwise, a weather cloth should be one continuous piece of cloth. Sailboats rarely need a weather cloth across the stern, but the design of your stern pulpit

Figure 17–1.
Weather cloths for a
power yacht.

may make it advisable to continue the cloth right around to the other side. On power yachts, weather cloths usually enclose the bridge area entirely, ending and restarting at appropriate corners or gates.

When lacing the weather cloths between lifelines and stanchions, it is advisable to sew the cloths slightly smaller than the space to be filled so that the cloth can be stretched tightly. When fastening the cloths with snaps, it is essential that the cloths be sewn exactly to size.

Step 1. Measure the length at both top and bottom.

Step 2. Measure the width at several intervals and at both ends. Note these measurements on a sketch diagram.

Step 3. Make note of any slashes or cutouts that are necessary for gear attached to stanchions, winch leads, or mooring chocks. The weather cloth should be rigged outboard of your stanchions, but inboard of liferings, if you carry them.

Step 4. Add extra cloth for a 2-inch hem all the way around the outside.

Construction

Step 1. Cut out the weather cloths.

Step 2. Hem all edges. Stitch once on the outside and once on the inside edge of the hem.

Step 3. Make any necessary slashes or cutouts. You may want to remeasure at this point by holding the weather cloth in place to make sure the cutouts are located accurately.

Step 4. Measure and mark for grommets, snaps, or screws by placing four grommets in the corners of the cloth and rigging them tightly in place. With a marking pen, mark where the additional grommets should go. On the top lacing, the grommets should be 6 to 8 inches apart. On the bottom and sides, place grommets where they will reach something you can tie to on the rail or deck. For instance, padeyes, stanchions, or cheek blocks make excellent tiedowns for weather cloths. Or you can install special eyes to use as tiedowns. The heavy stress is on the top and ends of the cloths, so not as many tiedowns are needed on the bottom.

Step 5. Install the grommets or snaps in the cloths.

Step 6. Rig the weather cloths. If you are using the grommet system, with a continuous length of light line, lace the

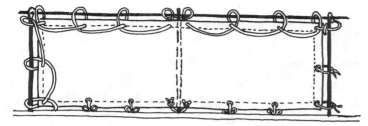

Figure 17–2.
Lacing the weather cloth.

top with half hitches all along the lifeline. Then attach the sides and bottom with appropriate lengths of line (Figure 17–2).

If you are using snaps, fasten to a railing or deck. Install the snaps in the appropriate place, beginning at one end, then working along the top and bottom equally, stretching the cloth tightly as you go until you reach the other end. Install the final end snaps.

To cover the windows of a power yacht, follow the instructions for making weather cloths. Be sure to make the cover wide enough to be fastened securely to the frame of the window with snaps.

Lettering for Weather Cloths

For those of you who are making ocean passages or racing, here's how to add letters or numbers to your weather cloths.

Step 1.   Measure the length of the weather cloth that will receive the name.

Step 2.   Count the number of letters in the name or number.

Step 3.   Divide the length of the cloth by the number of letters plus two for the spaces at the beginning and end of the name. If there are two or more words, add one space between words.

Step 4.   Once you have decided on the lettering, buy stencils of the appropriate size, trace them to "sticky-back" nylon ripstop of the color of your choice, and cut out the letters. (If you want the letters to last as long as the weather cloth, cut them out of a contrasting color of acrylic. Light a candle, and very carefully pass the edge of each letter through the flame. When you get the hang of it, you will be able to

Figure 17–3.
Weather cloths for windows. See also pages 125–126.

Figure 17–4.
Ship name appliqued to
weather cloth.

sear the edge without burning small bits in the fabric. This will keep the fabric from unraveling.)

Step 5. Draw one line on the weather cloth to mark the bottom of each letter.

Step 6. Mark off where each letter will go. Peel the paper off the "sticky back," and place the letter on the weather cloth. If your letters are 6 inches or more in height, peel back only the bottom third of the paper and stick that much of the letter in place before removing the rest of the paper. Peel the paper and stick down the letter as you go. If you are using acrylic letters, use double-sided sticky tape to hold the letters in place while you stitch.

Step 7. Set the zigzag stitch setting at 4 on a 1-to-6 scale and the stitch length at 3 on a 1-to-5 scale.

Step 8. With thread that matches the letters or number, zigzag all the way around each figure. Make sure, when you turn a corner, that the needle is down and that the next stitch lands in the letter and not on the weather cloth.

18
Hatch Dodgers

A hatch dodger is a canvas cover for a forward or main deck hinged hatch that uses the hatch cover as a supporting frame. The dodger can be used whether the hatch is all the way open or nearly shut. Its purpose is to keep rain out of the hatch when the boat is at anchor, docked or underway. In fact, it should work in most sea conditions, allowing for ventilation even though spray is washing over the deck. The dodger can be used on sailboats or powerboats. It is especially useful if you are away from the boat and don't want to close it up tight while you're gone.

A proper hatch dodger should be watertight on the forward and side edges. It should be large enough to allow the hatch to be open all the way (80 degrees maximum) and should have sides that completely enclose the area between the hatch lid and the deck. The dodger should also extend far enough aft so that rain coming from aft doesn't reach the hatch opening. If you have Plexiglas in your hatch cover, vinyl glass can be used in the top of the dodger to continue to let light shine through. You should realize, however, that the vinyl glass will need replacing before the canvas.

Materials Needed

- acrylic canvas
- vinyl glass (optional)
- 3/8-inch Dacron line to be sewn around three sides of the hatch
- rope track to hold the line
- number 1 grommets
- Dacron tape to go around three sides of the dodger
- vinyl binding

Construction

Step 1. Mount the rope track around the port, starboard, and forward sides of the hatch.

Step 2. Fill in the measurements on the drawing in Figure 18–2. Be sure to measure all sides of the hatch, because it may not be symmetrical. I suggest that you construct the dodger to function while the hatch cover is open to no more than 80 degrees, because you will lose your protection from the water otherwise.

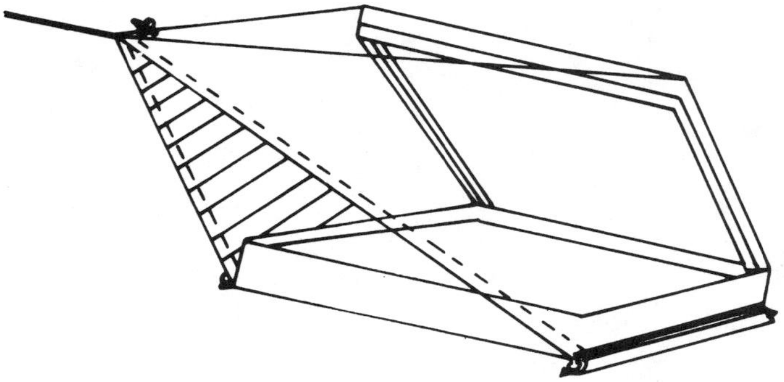

Figure 18–1.
Hatch dodger.

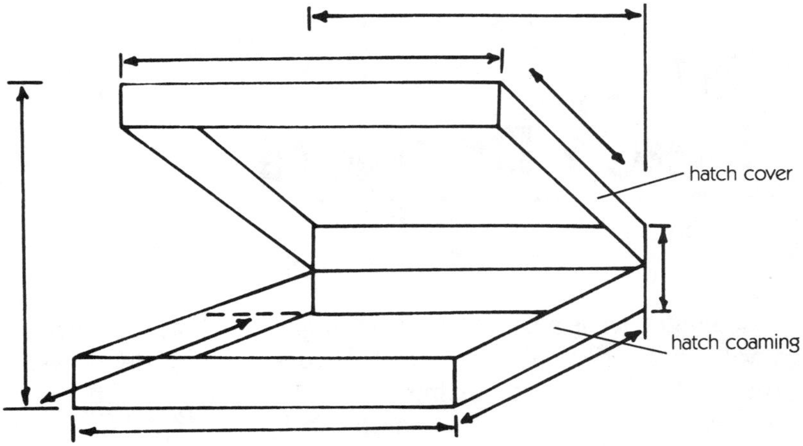

Figure 18–2.
Measuring for a
hatch dodger.

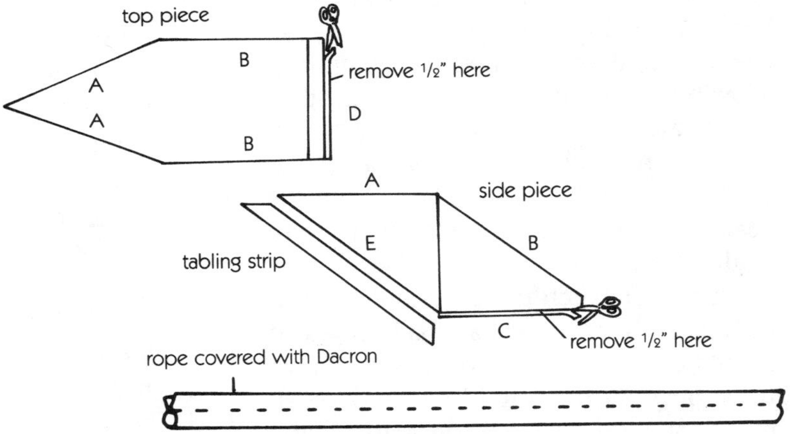

hatch cover

hatch coaming

Figure 18–3.
Pieces of a hatch
dodger.

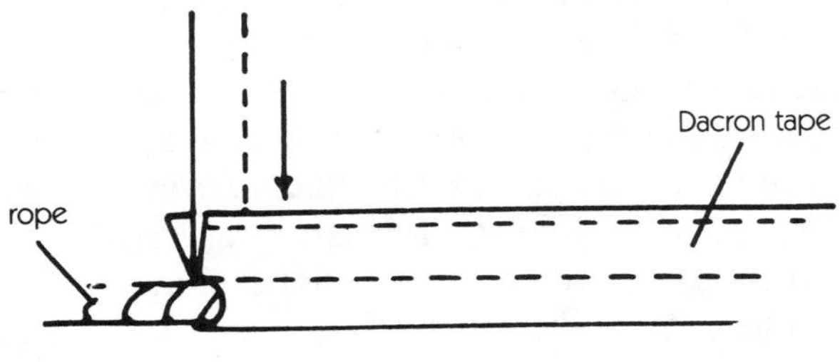

top piece

A
A

B

B

D

remove ½" here

side piece

A

E

B

tabling strip

C

remove ½" here

rope covered with Dacron

Figure 18–4.
Stitching the Dacron-bound
line to the dodger.

Dacron tape

rope

Step 3.   Transfer all your measurements to the cloth. You will probably have three pieces of fabric to sew together.

Step 4. Top piece: The top piece will cover the top of the hatch and the forward edge of the hatch frame, and includes the aft overhang (Figure 18–3).

Step 5. Side pieces: The side pieces will attach to the top and forward edge of the dodger.

Step 6.   Add a ½-inch seam allowance to edges A, B, and C.

Step 7.   Cut the bottom of the hatch cover (edges D and C) ½ inch shorter than the deck measurement dictates (Figure 18–3) so you have room to sew the rope onto the dodger.

Step 8.   Cut to the exact measurement the overhang part of the top. Cut strips of tabling 2½ inches wide to be sewn to the E edges for reinforcement and appearance.

Step 9.   Sew the Dacron line into the 3-inch wide Dacron tape by folding the tape in half and placing the line in the center. Using a zipper foot, sew as close to the line as possible.

Step 10.   Stitch the top to the sides at edges A and B, with right sides together.

Step 11.   Staple the tabling strips to the E edges. Stitch the raw edges together. Fold under ½ inch of the free edge of the tabling and stitch it down.

Step 12.   Stitch the Dacron-bound line to the bottom edge where the dodger meets the deck (edges D and C). Sandwich the acrylic between the two layers of Dacron and stitch close to the edge of the Dacron and again close to the edge of the acrylic (Figure 18–4).

Step 13.   Stitch vinyl binding to edges E. (Refer to Figure 15–14).

Step 14.   Set a grommet in the point of the overhang.

Step 15.   Slide the hatch cover in place. Tie off the overhang with a piece of line that ties to the grommet and the mast or any other suitable item on deck.

19
A Simple Wind Chute

A wind chute is a device that funnels breezes below decks to cool the interior and ventilate stuffy places. It is a necessity and a blessing when cruising the tropics, and a welcome addition in most climates where little breeze flows in the evening. In poorly ventilated boats that lack opening ports or Dorade ventilators, a wind chute will do wonders in helping keep the boat's interior fresh and dry.

This particular wind chute has four wind catchers that will catch air from any direction and divert it below. Whether you are sitting at dockside or lying at anchor into the wind or current, this wind chute will funnel air below without having to be repositioned as the wind changes direction. The chute is placed in a forward hatch and is secured by two wood dowels that are placed in the chute from below decks. A jib or genoa halyard is then used to lift the chute and hold it taut, and this lift causes the dowels to pull up tightly against the underside of the hatch frame.

The chute described here is designed to fit any forward hatch up to 30 inches square. You can, however, customize the chute so that the bottom of it fits tightly around the outside of your forward hatch frame and fastens with snaps rather than dowels. This can be done by making the bottom measurements of the wind tunnel the same as the size of your hatch. For instance, the wind chute here is 30 inches square. If your forward hatch frame is 24 by 30 inches, cut two of the side panels of the wind tunnel 25 inches wide at the bottom, and cut the other two panels 31 inches wide. Allowing for half-inch seams, this will give you finished dimensions of 24 by 30 inches. If you choose to fit your wind chute around the hatch frame, the screen will have to be sewn higher in the wind chute to accommodate the hatch frame.

Materials Needed

- 6 yards nylon spinnaker cloth, preferably 1.5-ounce
- 248 inches of nylon webbing, 1 to 2 inches wide
- 9 grommets

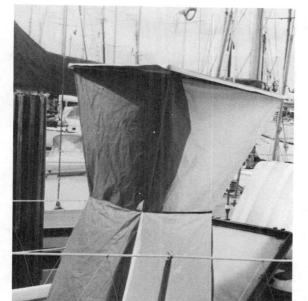

Figure 19–1.
Wind chute.

- 12 inches of light line
- 4 ½-inch wood dowels, 42 inches long
- 1 piece of fiberglass screen 31 inches square

Construction

Step 1.   Cut the following pieces:

4 panels for wind tunnel (A), 30 by 36 by 18 inches

2 panels for wind catcher (B) 40 by 36 inches

1 top (C), 30 inches by 30 inches square

Step 2. Wind Tunnel: Place two of the "A" pieces right sides together so that the edges match. Stitch along one long edge ½ inch from the edge of the cloth. Open the two pieces so that they lie flat. Sew a flat-felled seam, folding the seam allowance under. Repeat this procedure with the remaining two "A" pieces, then sew the third and fourth seams to complete the tunnel (Figure 19–3).

Step 3.   Fold ¼ inch of the bottom edge of the wind tunnel to the outside. Stitch. Stitch the nylon webbing around the bottom of the wind tunnel so that it covers the raw folded edge yet extends a bit

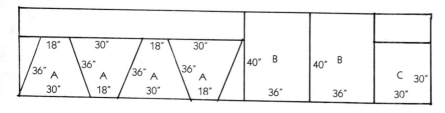

Figure 19–2.
Layout for a
wind chute.

Figure 19–3.
Stitching the wind tunnel.

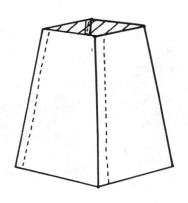

Figure 19–4.
Placing webbing and hem in the
wind tunnel.

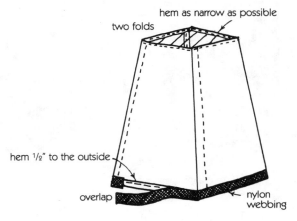

hem as narrow as possible

two folds

hem ½" to the outside

overlap

nylon webbing

Figure 19–5.
Pinning the screen in position.

bottom edge of wind chute

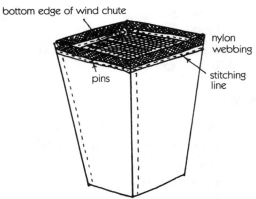

nylon webbing

stitching line

pins

Figure 19–6.
Wind catcher.

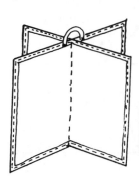

below the bottom of the spinnaker cloth. Overlap the beginning and end of the tape and stitch securely.

Step 4.   Hem the top edge of the wind tunnel by folding the material over twice. This hem should be as narrow as possible (Figure 19–4).

Step 5. Screen: Pin the screen level with the top edge of the nylon webbing and inside the bottom of the wind tunnel. Place pins perpendicular to the stitching line. Pinch the fabric in the corners of the screen to take up the excess. Stitch all the way around the screen (Figure 19–5).

Step 6. Wind Catcher: Hem all four outside edges of both B pieces by folding over 1/4 inch twice, and then stitching all around. Place one "B" piece over the other, matching all edges. With the longest edges as top and bottom, find the center line by folding the two pieces in half and matching the 36-inch edges. Pin the center line, and stitch the two pieces together along this line. Sew a small loop of nylon webbing to the top of the wind catcher over the center seam to use as a lifting ring (Figure 19–6).

Step 7. Sewing the Wind Catcher to the Wind Tunnel: The wind catcher should fit inside the wind tunnel as if it were an X. To accomplish this, sew the bottom corners along the vertical edges of the wind catcher to the corner seams of the wind tunnel, so that 6 inches of the wind catcher is inside the tunnel (Figure 19–7).

Now you will find that the diagonal of the wind catcher (36 inches) is longer than the diagonal of the top of the wind tunnel (25 1/2 inches), thus creating a bagginess in the catcher. This extra material balloons inward as the wind is caught, directing a maximum flow of air below decks.

Step 8. Top: Hem all edges of the top piece "C" as you did the wind catcher pieces. Sew the nylon webbing to the outside edge of the top so that it makes a curtain that hangs down below the top 3/4 inch. The grommets that hold the dowels in place will be set in this webbing, so there must be enough room for them. To do this, begin sewing the webbing onto the top in the middle of one edge. When you get to the corner, put the needle of the machine down through the webbing and

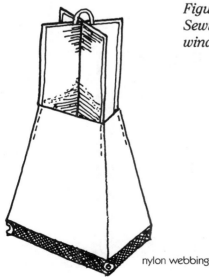

Figure 19–7.
Sewing the wind catcher to the wind tunnel.

nylon webbing

Figure 19–8.
Sewing the top to the
wind catcher.

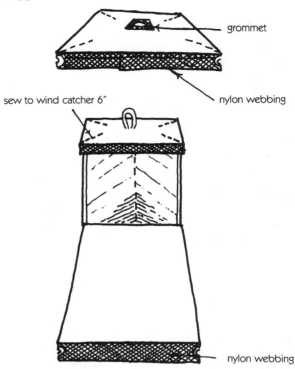

cloth exactly at the corner. Then turn the top 90 degrees and bend the webbing around so that it matches the edge of the top again. Stitch the webbing flat until you reach the next corner and repeat the corner procedure. Continue in this manner until the webbing has been sewn all around the top. Overlap the ends of the webbing and stitch securely. Turn the corners right side out so that the tape extends

down from the top like a short curtain all the way around. Find the middle of the top and sew a small patch of nylon webbing to the very center on the wrong side of the top. This patch will reinforce the grommet that will eventually be placed there (Figure 19–8).

Step 9. Now you will find that the diagonal of the wind catcher (40 inches) is

Figure 19–9.
Setting the dowels.

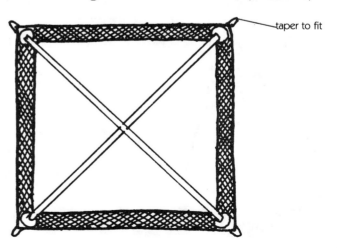

shorter than the diagonal of the top (42½ inches). The fact that the sewn flaps do not extend all the way to the corners of the top leaves room for the installation of dowels. Secure the top to the wind catcher by sewing 6 inches of the top edge of each wind-catcher flap to the top piece, placing each flap as close to the corners as possible.

Step 10. Finishing: Set grommets in all four corners of the top and bottom nylon webbing. Set one grommet in the center patch of the top. Tie the small piece of line to the nylon loop at the top of the wind catcher. Thread the other end of this line through the grommet in the middle of the top. Place two dowels corner to corner in the bottom and the top of the wind chute. Center them and mark them so that they will extend slightly beyond the edges of the wind chute. Cut the dowels to size and taper the ends to points so that they will fit tightly into corner grommets (Figure 19–9).

Rig the chute aboard and enjoy wonderful fresh air below.

20
Deck Cushions

Interior and exterior cushions add much to the beauty and comfort of a vessel. Their placement, size, and fabric will directly affect their usefulness and durability. They are well worth careful planning.

The steps for designing and constructing cushions are laid out in detail in Chapter 29. No matter where you want cushions on deck—cockpit, deck, foredeck, flying bridge, or fishbox—you can make them according to those instructions. In this chapter I will limit myself to a few comments specifically related to appropriate materials and design.

Suggested Materials

Airex is a closed-cell foam that is softer than the first closed-cell foams and doesn't shrink with age as much as the original unicellular foams. Airex foam is twice as expensive as polyurethane foam, which I use for interior cushions, but it lasts four times as long and is much easier to care for. Because it will not absorb water, you won't have to store soggy cushions or sit on wet ones. Closed-cell foam also floats and, if used in cockpit cushions, will al-

ways be handy to throw to anyone who has fallen overboard.

For covers, I suggest one of the darker shades of acrylic canvas. It wears as well as vinyl and is almost as easy to clean when covering Airex foam. Squirting a bit of dishwashing liquid and seawater on the cushions, and then rubbing them with a soft brush, easily cleans the covers while they are still on the foam. And unlike vinyl covers, which get hot and sticky in the sun, acrylic canvas breathes.

Another cover fabric that has gained popularity in recent years is Textilene (see Chapter 4). If you are using polyurethane foam, Textilene will allow the water that gets into the spongelike foam to escape. If you are using Airex, this additional precaution (with its additional expense) is not necessary.

Fastenings

The perennial problem on a rolling or heeling boat is how to keep the cockpit and/or deck cushions in place. A standard procedure is to use snap-on fabric tabs to

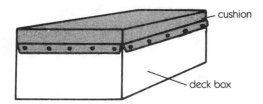

Figure 20–1.
Deck box cushion fastened
with tabs.

cushion

deck box

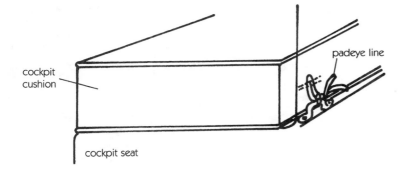

Figure 20–2.
Cockpit
cushion
fastened to
padeyes.

padeye line

cockpit
cushion

cockpit seat

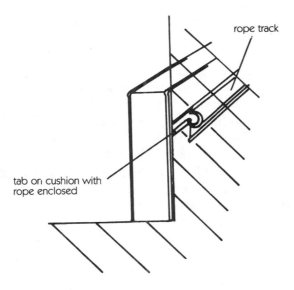

Figure 20–3.
Cockpit cushion backrest
fastened with rope track.

rope track

tab on cushion with
rope enclosed

fasten the cushion to available lips or fiddles (Figure 20–1). The major strength of the system comes from using enough snaps so that weight is evenly distributed. One or two snaps will not be sufficient in most cases.

As an alternative to snaps, tie a line stitched into the cushion seam to a padeye mounted directly behind or below the cushion (Figure 20–2). This system gives

you positive tension anytime there is force on the cushion—either from someone sitting on the cushion or from gravity pulling the cushion down to leeward as the boat heels. This system will not cause the fabric to tear as easily as the snap tab system will.

If you have a backrest on your boat, a very strong way to secure it is with a rope track. Mount the track just below where you want the top of the cushion to stop; it

*Figure 20–4.
Layout of cockpit
cushions.*

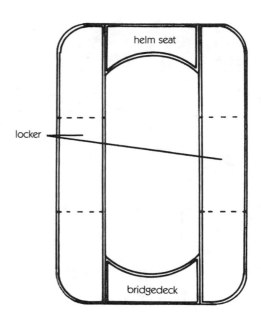

will hold the backrest in a straight line and provide even tension (Figure 20–3). It is necessary to stitch a piece of ¼-inch Dacron line into a piece of Dacron tape 4 inches wide. Fold the tape around the line and stitch it in place. Then sew both tabs of the tape to the cushion. Be sure to stitch the tape to the cushion so it will hold the cushion at the proper height when the rope is in the rope track. It's nice if you can hide the track behind the cushion.

Dividing Cushions

In a U-shaped cockpit with lockers under the cushions, how do you split the cushions so they will stay in place, be comfort-able, and yet allow access to the lockers underneath? Figure 20–4 shows one possible solution. Remember that the smaller the cushions are, the easier they are to store.

Whether or not to put a cushion in front of the companionway is another consideration. My suggestion is not to, unless you have a very comfortable seat athwartships on the bridge deck that would be less comfortable if only part of it were cushioned. When possible, split the cushions in such a manner that the cushion in front of the companionway may be removed when traffic is expected.

21
Sail Covers

Since most sails today are made of fabric that is very susceptible to the ultraviolet rays of the sun, it is important to cover them. Cotton sails also require a good cover of water-resistant material to keep out rain and thereby resist mildew and subsequent deterioration. A well-fitted sail cover will also add to the trim appearance of the vessel. This chapter will discuss how to make a simple sail cover that can be modified to fit any boat's boom. As you design your own sail cover, take into account any fittings, lines, winches, or special requirements that your particular cover should have to do the job attractively and adequately.

Suggested Materials

There are a number of materials to choose from for sail covers. Eight or 10-ounce canvas is adequate when you treat it with waterproofing. However, since the waterproofing will not last long and since untreated canvas is susceptible to mildew, I suggest a synthetic such as acrylic or a factory-treated canvas such as Vivatex. The treatment given to Vivatex is far superior to a "home" treatment of plain canvas.

Plastic- or rubber-coated materials are not suitable for sail covers. It is important that the cover breathe so that the sail will not mildew. Coated materials are also poor choices because they eventually lose their coating from the repeated rolling or wadding a sail cover undergoes when not stretched on the boom. Nylon is a suitable choice because it is lightweight and will stow in a small space when not in use. However, nylon will crinkle noisily in the wind and may stretch after it has been pulled tight for a while. It also allows considerable sunlight to reach the sails and will not last as long as Vivatex or acrylic.

Fastenings

Of all the fastenings discussed in Chapter 2, I recommend using a grommet-and-sailhook combination to fasten most sail covers. This system is simple and easy to install and will not fail from repeated use or water corrosion. It consists of a pair of grommets placed on one side of the cover to oppose each sail hook. Shock cord is then knotted through the grommets and hooked over the sailhook.

If you have a zigzag sewing machine

*Figure 21–1.
Sail cover customized for
climbing brackets.*

with an adjustable feeder, you can sew the hooks on easily by putting the feeder in its lowest position, as if sewing on a button, and setting the zigzag scale to just miss the metal. Otherwise, the hooks can be sewn on by hand. I don't recommend that you use one continuous length of shock cord, threaded through all the grommets the length of the sail cover, for two reasons. The first involves cost. Shock cord is expensive, and if the shock cord breaks in one place, the entire length will need replacing rather than, say, a 6-inch piece. The second reason has to do with safety. If a 12- or 16-foot shock cord should snap loose in a storm and snag on gear or people, it could cause an injury.

Lightweight line can be used to tie the sail cover snugly around the top of the sail and mast to make fastening the shock cord easier. Such line can also be used to tie the after end of the cover around the boom. If cutouts are necessary for lines, etc., light line can also be threaded through grommets to lace the cutout together after the cover is in place.

You will see some beautiful sail covers that are fastened at the front of the mast with a zipper. This is very attractive and impressive, but I don't think the amateur should attempt this type of closure on a sail cover. The fit of the cover must be exactly right or the zipper will be nearly impossible to close or, in the case of an oversize cover, will bump and hang terribly. The grommet-and-sailhook system allows you to take up the slack in the cover in case it doesn't fit exactly the way you had planned.

Making a Pattern

If you have old sail covers that fit to your satisfaction, you will have no problem using them as patterns for your new covers.

*Figure 21–2.
Grommet and sail hook
system.*

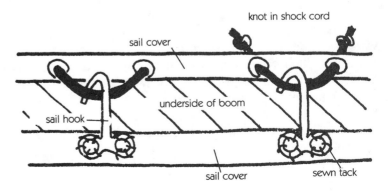

Simply rip the old cover apart carefully, add seam allowances and cut the new pieces around the old ones. Be careful to note right side and wrong side in pieces that are not reversible. If you don't have a cover to use as a pattern, a few measurements will give you the basic shape needed, and careful fitting as you sew will enable you to achieve a good fit. The measurements should be taken with the sail on the boom, furled no better or worse than usual.

Figure 21–3 gives the basic shape of most sail covers for sails on booms connected to masts. Covers for sails on booms connected to stays or for gaff-headed sails will have a flatter and smaller inset but will be basically the same shape. This figure is also optimum because there is no seam down the middle of the cover. This portion of any sail cover receives the most direct sunlight and the most wear. If your sail cover must be considerably wider than the width of the cloth you are using, you will have to put a seam down the middle of the cover. If it needs to be only slightly wider, however, it is advisable to make the cover as it is described here and add the extra width to the bottom edges of the cover.

One more tip before measuring: The sail cover should have at least a 2-inch gap at the underside of the boom to allow the shock cord to stretch and create tension on the cover. Be sure to remember this when adding hem allowances.

Figure 21–4 gives all the measurements needed for most basic sail covers. After you have these measurements, you can measure for cutouts, winch covers, or other adaptations for your particular rig. It is usually not advisable, though, to cut any holes or slashes until most of the basic cover is put together. Measuring for these custom changes on the sail cover itself, rather than the boom, ensures a more exact fit.

Cutting and Construction

Step 1. Main Piece: Take measurements A, L, H, G, F, and E, as shown in Figure 21–4. These measurements will give you the shape of the main piece of the cover. Allow for a 2-inch hem and a 2-inch gap under the boom. Allowing for a 1-inch hem, but actually sewing a 2-inch hem, will provide the space required under the boom.

Step 2. Mark these measurements on the cloth, being sure to center the measurements on the material. At this point you can tell if you will need to add cloth to the bottom edges of the cover, or if you will have to cut two main pieces and sew them together. H, G, F, and E measurements are circumferences. Use them as flat measurements when making the main piece in one piece; divide them in half when cutting the main piece in two pieces.

Step 3. Being careful to add hem and seam allowances where you need them, and remembering the fore and aft ends as well, cut out the main piece and hem the side or bottom edges. Fold over the aft end of the main piece to make a casing for the drawstring that will tie around the end of the boom, and stitch. Light line can be threaded through this

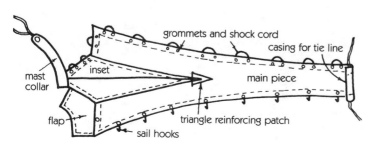

Figure 21–3. Basic shape of sail cover as seen from below.

Figure 21–4.
Measurements for a
sail cover.

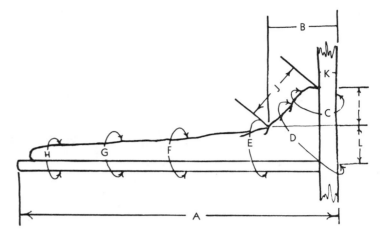

casing by stabbing a large safety pin into the line and using it to thread the line through.

Step 4. Mast Inset: Measurements J and B will help you determine how far to cut the main piece for the mast inset, but do not cut this until the mast inset has been cut. Use measurements J, B, I, and K to get the angles for the mast inset (Figure 21–6). First take measurement B and mark it on a straight edge of cloth. Then take measurement I and mark it on your cloth, using one end of your B measurement as the bottom starting point. Then place the K measurement, which is the diameter of the mast, parallel to the B measurement, using the top of the I measurement as a starting place. The J measurement should be the same as the distance between the open ends of K and B. If it is not, juggle the I measurement until it fits or make J a curved line to accommodate the sail. Allow 2 inches for hemming the I edge, 1 inch for hemming the K edge and 1/2-inch seam allowances on the J and B edges. Cut this out to get one-half of the inset, and repeat the process to get the matching half, then stitch the halves together along edges J with a flat-felled seam.

Step 5.   Cut a slash of length B in the main piece, along the centerline, starting from the forward end. Place the right sides of the main piece and the mast inset together, lining up the middle of each piece. Stitch the B seam on the left side, lift the

Figure 21–5.
Staysail sail cover with
flat inset.

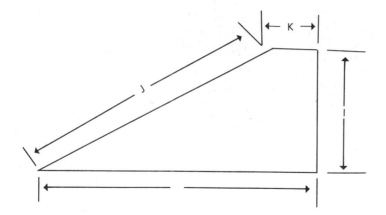

Figure 21–6.
Mast inset.

presser foot, and rotate the pieces so you can stitch the right side. Pinning these parts together will undoubtedly make your sewing more accurate. Flat-fell this seam as in Figure 3–2 if there is enough cloth to turn under. If not, zigzag the seam allowance to the cover as in Figure 3–1. Sew a reinforcement patch over the point at which the apex of the inset meets the main piece. This will strengthen this area and camouflage any trouble you had in making this corner. Hem the right and left forward, or I and L, edges of the sail cover. Make a 1-inch hem at the K edge.

Step 8. Flap: The flap is used to cover the front of the mast and any winches that may be mounted there. It should be as tall as the sail cover and as wide as needed to do the job. Hem the flap on all edges with a 1/2-inch seam. Sew the right side of the flap to the wrong side of the starboard side of the sail cover.

Step 9. Mast Collar: The mast collar is used to secure the forward end of the cover around the mast and external halyards to make fastening the shock cord easier. This piece of cloth should be approximately 2 inches wide and long enough to go around the mast at least 1½ times. Hem this piece all the way around and sew it to the top of the mast inset at K. The collar is usually most effective if it is sewn to the outside edge of the mast inset. A grommet should be placed in the very end of the tail, and a line that will go around the mast fastened to it.

Figure 21–7.
A handsome cover on a gaff-rigged mainsail.

Step 10. Finishing: Place grommets on the port side of the bottom and forward edges, and position the hooks opposite them on the starboard side of the cover. Place these pairs about 15 to 18 inches apart. The hooks should be tacked in each loop. Put the cover in place and thread shock cord through the grommets, adjusting the length of the cord so that the cover fits snugly. An overhand or figure-eight knot works very well for securing the shock cord. If you have mast-mounted winches and wish to make built-in covers for them in the sail cover, refer to Chapter 28 and modify the design to fit into your sail cover. Usually these covers wear out quickly; it is just as attractive to allow enough length in the main piece of your sail cover simply to go around the winches as it circles sail and mast. A sacrificial piece of cloth can be sewn to the inside of the sail cover where winches may rub, to save wear on the cover itself.

22
A Cover for the Yacht Tender

Whether you're carrying a 25-foot runabout on the upper deck of a motor yacht or a 7-foot pram in davits, you will find that a cover will reduce your maintenance time, protecting varnish, gelcoat, and upholstery from the damaging effects of sun, water, and dirt. A cover can also convert a dinghy into extra storage space. Gear usually associated with the tender, such as life jackets, diving gear, water skis and gas tanks, can be stowed inside the tender when not in use. The cover keeps everything shipshape and dry. The size of the tender has less effect on the difficulty of the project than does the number of projections above its deck level, such as windshields or outboard motors.

Suggested Materials

Treated canvas is the best cover material for tenders because it is waterproof. Acrylic canvas is not especially good for tender covers because it will allow water to leak through if puddles form. If a ridge pole, arched bows, or something similar can be rigged to keep water from collecting, acrylic canvas can be used, and it will outlast treated canvas.

Weblon is also a good material for tender covers. It is waterproof and easy to clean. However, a Weblon cover left on a tender for long periods of time will cause condensation underneath, which will eventually cause mildew unless some means of ventilation is designed into the cover.

Nylon sailcloth has been successfully used for tender covers but should not be expected to last very long as the sun will devour it.

Fastenings should be chosen before the cloth portion of the cover is designed. Small dinghies with overhanging gunwales may require only a cover held by a drawstring or shock cord threaded through a casing that runs all around the dinghy and snugs up under the gunwales. A larger tender with a windshield, motor, or tow bar might need to have its cover snapped directly to the hull.

A cover will work more efficiently if an oar, boathook, mop, or a specially designed dowel or batten can be used for a ridge pole. This will reduce leakage in the cover and provide better ventilation. Such a pole can run from bow to stern or from gunwale to gunwale, or stand vertically

Figure 22–1.
Boston Whaler under
cover.

Figure 22–2.
Davits used for ridge
pole.

Figure 22–3.
Rigging a
ridge pole.

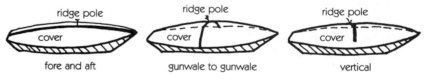

and poke through a grommeted hole in the cover. The position of the ridge pole or flexible batten should be designed into the cover at the time measurements are made.

Measuring

Step 1. Measure the beam of the tender at key points to establish the shape of the cover, incorporating any extra length necessary to arch over a ridge pole, windshield, or other superstructure. It is usually helpful also to measure the distance between these measurements. Transfer all measurements to a clear diagram.

Step 2. Measure the overall length of the tender, and transfer this measurement to the diagram.

Step 3. Measure for windshields, etc. A paper pattern of the windshield and the area of the bow in front of the windshield is usually necessary for proper fit, and is definitely worth the extra work involved. Lay a piece of pattern paper over the windshield and mark its outline on the paper. Similarly, lay pattern paper on the foredeck and draw the curve where the base of the windshield meets the deck. Mark both patterns at the fore-and-aft centerline, and

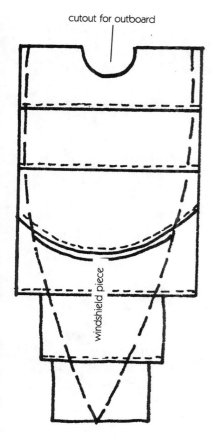

cutout for outboard

windshield piece

Figure 22–4.
Panels of tender cover with
windshield and outboard
pieces.

transfer these marks to the fabric when you trace the patterns, so that when you sew these shapes together you'll align them properly. Alternatively, let the windshield support a fore-and-aft ridge pole anchored at bow and stern, and bypass the minor complication of having to fit the windshield.

Step 4. Measure the extra length of material necessary to overlap the gunwale. Remember to add seam allowance and hem and/or casing allowance to each width measurement.

Construction

Step 5. Based on your measurements, decide whether it is better to run the cloth panels fore and aft or athwartships on the tender. Most covers are made with the panels sewn in strips from gun-wale to gunwale. Decide how many panels it will take to cover the boat, and how long each one should be. For instance, if panels will run athwartships and your cloth is 36 inches wide, measure 35 inches forward from the stern, less hem allowance, and see what the width should be. Cut the first panel, remembering to allow for seams and hems. Then measure 35 inches forward from the last "station" (seam between panels), and check for the greatest width necessary within that 35 inches. Continue to measure and cut these panels until you have enough of them to cover the tender, or at least the area aft of a fitted windshield panel.

Step 6. Sew these panels together with overlap seams.

Step 7. Using the paper patterns you have made of the windshield (if any) and

*Figure 22–5.
Beautifully made cover with
cutouts for cleats.*

*Figure 22–6.
Tabling the edge of
the cover.*

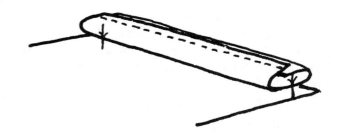

*Figure 22–7.
Ridge pole pockets.*

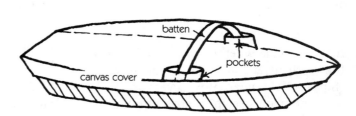

Figure 22–8.
Dinghy cover fastened with
tiedowns and shock cord.

the curve of the windshield where it attaches to the foredeck, cut the piece of cloth that will cover the windshield. Then, with the foredeck pattern, cut the curve into the aftermost edge of the foredeck section of the cover. Sew the windshield piece to the foredeck section. Then sew the rest of the panels to the top of the windshield piece.

If an outboard motor cover is part of the tender cover, it is usually made with two side pieces and a strip that covers the front, top, and back of the motor. It should be sewn together first and then sewn into the tender cover. Usually a drawstring that goes around the stern half of the motor is required to keep this portion of the cover securely on the motor.

Step 8.   Place the cover over the tender, and mark the outside edge all around the boat so that it will fasten where you want it to. Then, allowing a 2-inch hem (or a 3-inch casing if you are using a drawstring), cut the shape of the cover. If there is considerable curvature, allow 4 inches of hem. Then cut 3½ inches of that hem off, and use it as a tabling to be sewn to the cover in place of a hem (Step 9). This will keep puckers and darts to a minimum. Mark cutouts for cleats or chocks that might be used with the cover in place.

Step 9.   Hem the outside, being care-

ful to match the measurements exactly, or sew a casing around the outside. If using a tabling, first sew the raw edges of the tabling strip by folding over ¼ inch and stitching. Then fold the tabling strip in half, and place it over the outside edge of the cover (Figure 22–6). Stitch through all three thicknesses at once. Be sure to match the tabling to the place it was cut from on the cover and stitch around the edge twice. Stitch, cut, and finish the necessary cutouts (Chapter 3).

Step 10.   Make pockets for the ridge pole, if necessary. For instance, a horizontal ridge pole could have pockets at either side of the cover to hold the pole and force it to bend (Figure 22–7).

Step 11.   Attach fastenings. If you are using snaps, first attach them to the boat and then to the cover. They will need to be placed every 8 to 10 inches. A drawstring can be inserted with a safety pin and worked through the casing.

Optional. Buy plastic scoop ventilators from a canvas shop and stitch them fairly high on the cover to catch maximum air. Cut away the fabric from within the perimeter of the scoop's base.

Step 12.   Fit the cover to the tender and test it on the first really windy day to make sure it cannot be blown off.

23
Building a Winter Cover

A winter cover is expensive. Many boaters think about buying one but never do because of the cost. If you make one yourself, you will at least save on labor costs. Expensive as it is, a winter cover will save you time and money in the long run, because it protects your boat from the damage that sun, snow, and dirt can cause. More important, it will keep water out of those little cracks in the deck or the house top that freezing and thawing water will enlarge.

Those of you who live aboard in cold climates will certainly appreciate the added protection that a winter cover offers. It will turn your cockpit into a cold room suitable for extra storage or for working space on relatively nice days.

Design

A winter cover consists of two parts: a frame and the canvas covering. Powerboats will almost always need a frame of some type. Sailboats can also use a frame, such as the one shown in Figure 23–1, but if the mast is left in place during the winter, they can get by with a line sewn

into the fabric as a ridge pole, using the boat's standing rigging to support the cover—essentially, the same principle as an awning. Kover Klamp manufactures a beautiful frame system designed for the do-it-yourselfer. Figure 23–1 shows Kover Klamp's suggested method for building a frame for either type of boat. Whether you use Kover Klamp's pipe frame or devise your own out of wood, the designs shown here will enable the cover to remain taut even while heavily laden with snow.

Covers for boats less than 25 feet long may be sewn as one piece, but for larger boats it is best to construct the winter cover in two parts, so that you can more easily handle the considerable fabric involved. Covers for sailboats should be split at the mast or masts; powerboat covers should be divided either at the windshield or halfway aft on the flying bridge.

Wherever there is a split in the cover, design the fabric so you have an overlap of at least 12 inches. The forward piece then overlaps the aft piece or vice versa. Do not lace these two pieces together as that will cause stress where the cover is not built to

120

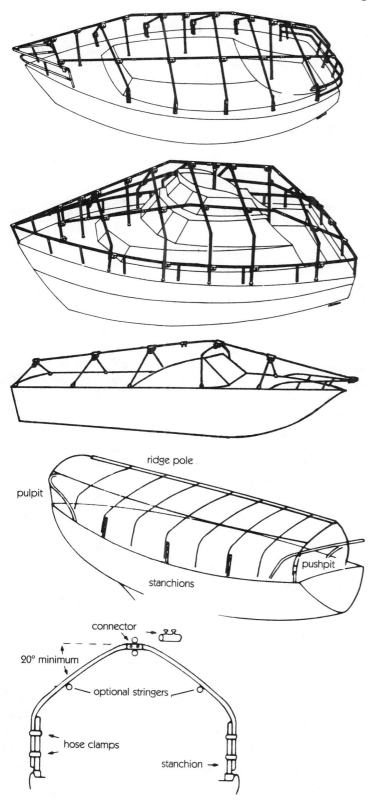

Figure 23–1.
Designs for winter covers
with Kover Klamp frames.
(Note: The Kover Klamp
company could not be
reached at their old
location as this book
went to press, and the
editors are unable to
verify if and where the
company is currently
operating.)

Figure 23–2. Measuring a winter cover for a sailboat with rig in place.

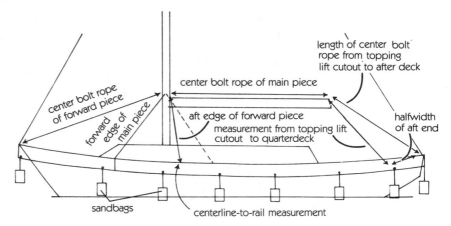

take it. When the covers overlap, the slight movement in the cover will merely act as a means of ventilating the boat. If you lace the covers together, you must create an elaborate flap system to keep the water out of the grommets used for lacing. Overlapping eliminates that problem.

It is imperative that the cover be tied tightly so that it will not flog in the wind. The two most effective systems for anchoring a winter cover to the boat are tying lines under the boat, or else attaching sandbags to the cover so they extend below the deck coaming. The latter is the obvious choice if the boat will be stored in the water, and it has the added advantage of being easier to install. Grommets are placed in each seam overlap (as discussed in the chapter on awnings) to be used for tying on the cover.

Materials Needed

- Vivatex or acrylic canvas
- grommets
- 3/8-inch Dacron line for center bolt rope (sailboats)
- line for tiedowns
- Dacron tape
- webbing for each sandbag

Measuring

For powerboats and sailboats being dismasted and stored out of the water, start by installing your frame system. Then measure and pattern the frame, using steps 1 through 5 in Chapter 22 as a guide. If your cover will be split, be sure to allow for the 12-inch overlap. Note all cutouts necessary and their position relative to the centerline of the boat. Mark cutouts for docklines if necessary.

Figures 23–2 and 23–3 show you how to measure a winter cover for a sailboat whose mast will remain in place during storage. Figure 23–3 is a detail of the forward cover. Notice that whatever cutouts needed for stays are measured and marked on the drawing. Measurements for a winter cover should be taken at 1-foot stations all along the boat. To measure for the top of a sailboat, tie a rope along the centerline at the projected cover height and angle, and measure from the rope to the lifeline at 1-foot stations. At these same stations, measure from the lifeline to 6 inches below the caprail to find the length of the side of the cover.

Cutting and Stitching

The process of cutting and stitching a winter cover is exactly the same as for making an awning. Refer to Chapter 14 for those instructions. Keep in mind that a winter cover will need to be stronger and more carefully reinforced than an awning. I suggest that you put Dacron tape in all of the hems, reinforce the area where any cut-

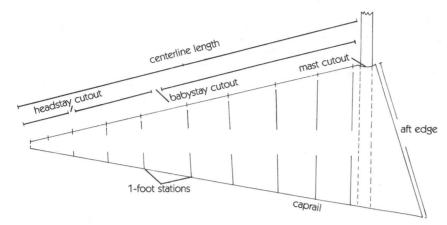

*Figure 23–3.
Detail of
measuring the
forward piece
in Figure 23–2.*

outs are made with Dacron and extra fabric, and doublestitch areas that will take extra strain.

Making a Sandbag

Make a 10-by-5-inch bag out of heavy canvas, with a loop of heavy webbing at the top edge. Fill the bag three-quarters full, and stitch the top edge closed. Each hem grommet in the awning will require its own sandbag.

Installation

Try to put the cover on before it gets too cold to tie knots with bare hands. Align each piece fore and aft before you begin to tie the sides down. Overlap the fore and aft covers so that the split does not face the prevailing wind. Tie the cover on by starting from the middle of the boat and working fore and aft. Tie it tightly. If you use sandbags, attach them with line and drop them over the side of the boat.

*Figure 23–4.
Winter cover with door.*

Storing the Cover for the Summer

The most dangerous time for the winter cover is the time it spends folded up in a corner of the basement. It is likely to mildew and rot if it is not properly stored. Be especially careful of cotton canvas, which mildews very quickly. Hose off all dirt and salt water before removing the cover from the boat. Allow it to dry completely. Remove the cover and fold it up neatly without enclosing any leaves, grass, bugs, etc. Store it in a cool, dry place. Also, repair any rips and/or chafed areas before you put the cover on in the fall. A good winter cover, properly cared for, should last 10 to 15 years.

24
Windshield Cover

Power yachts and/or motorsailers with large windows often require the privacy and sun protection that a curtain or windshield cover provides. It's a fairly simple project to construct these out of acrylic canvas and fasten them with snaps. If you install enough snaps, the covers will hold even if you are running the boat fast.

Materials Needed

- acrylic canvas
- snaps
- Dacron tape
- vinyl binding

Figure 24–1. Windshield covers.

Patterning and Cutting

Step 1. To create a pattern, place a piece of brown wrapping paper on top of the windshield or window. Using a pencil on its side, trace the edge of the window on the paper. Notice whether the fastenings can be inside or outside of the edge. If they can be inside, you need not add anything to the pattern when you cut out the fabric. If you need to fasten the cloth outside of the line, add 2 inches to your pattern.

Step 2. Lay out the patterns and carefully cut them out. Position them on the fabric, and cut out the cloth.

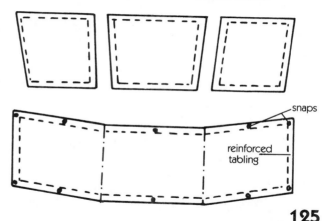

snaps

reinforced tabling

Figure 24–2.
Windshield covers in
operation.

Step 3. Cut tabling strips 2 inches wide to go around the curtain. Cut Dacron tape to be placed in the hems as reinforcement for the fastenings.

Step 4. Staple or pin the Dacron and the tabling on the edge of the curtain's inside face (refer to Figure 15–10). Stitch once next to the raw edge and then again when you fold the raw edge under.

Step 5. With vinyl binding, bind the edge of the curtain (Figure 15–14).

Step 6. Install the male halves of the snaps in the boat. (For instructions on how to drill into wood or fiberglass, refer to Figure 31–26.) Then position the female halves along the reinforced edges of the cover to match. The covers should fit tightly, so don't be afraid to put a bit of tension on them.

25
Hatch Covers

Hatch covers are nice for two reasons: They keep the sunlight off the varnish and Plexiglas and they also provide privacy and shade below decks. If your hatch presently has a Plexiglas center and you like the light below, you can put a matching vinyl glass center in your hatch cover. If you'd rather have shade, make the cover out of solid fabric. (Note that the vinyl glass will rot out in the sun very quickly and will have to be replaced more often than the fabric.)

Materials Needed

- acrylic canvas
- vinyl glass (optional)
- a snap for each corner or cutout
- vinyl binding (for hatches with deeply inset hinges)

Measuring and Patterning

To measure a square or rectangular frame with 90-degree corners, simply take the length and width of the hatch. Measure the depth of the hatch (or height off the deck), and transfer all measurements to the drawing. Be aware that the height may vary fore and aft or port to starboard.

To measure a hatch with beveled or rounded corners or corners with an angle, take a paper pattern. Lay a piece of paper over the hatch and mark darts in each corner as the paper goes over the top of the hatch and down the side (Figure 25–1).

A butterfly hatch must be thought of as having two tops. Measure each side carefully. If the ridge is rounded, be sure to mark the middle so that you will correctly measure the width of the hatch. If the hatch top overhangs the hatch frame, use the measurement for the top, not the frame. If you dart out the corners to fit the frame, you will not be able to get the hatch cover on (Figure 25–2).

Cutting and Stitching

Step 1. Look at the hatch, and see how many pieces of fabric are required. Most hatch covers can be made with a top and a band for all the sides. Some can be made with one piece of fabric that covers the top and sides by using darts in the corners.

Step 2. Cut each piece of fabric. Be sure to add a ½-inch seam allowance

127

*Figure 25–1.
Patterning beveled,
round, or mitered
corners.*

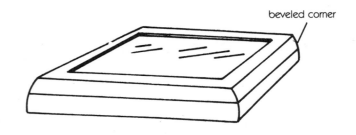

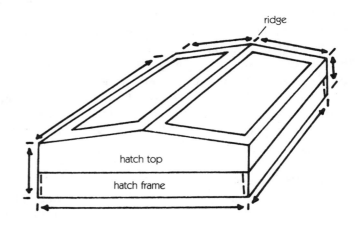

*Figure 25–2.
Butterfly hatches. If the
frame is recessed (dashed
lines) and you dart the
cover corners to fit the
frame, the cover won't fit
the hatch top.*

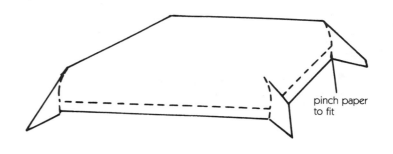

*Figure 25–3.
Hinge cutouts and vinyl
binding (dashed lines).*

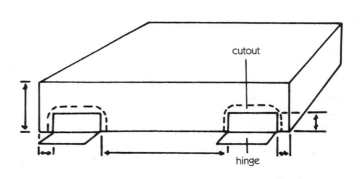

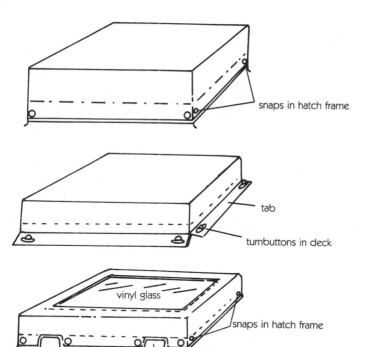

Figure 25–4.
Fastening hatch
covers.

snaps in hatch frame

tab

turnbuttons in deck

vinyl glass

snaps in hatch frame

hinge cutouts

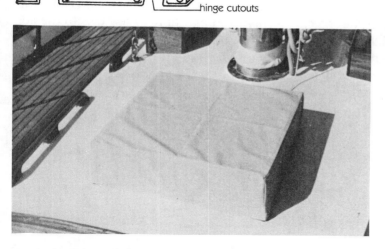

Figure 25–5.
Square hatch cover.

Figure 25–6.
Custom hatch cover.

wherever two pieces of fabric join together, and 1½ inches wherever there will be a hem.

Step 3. If there will be a curve to the bottom edge of the side piece, stitch tabling to that edge and bind it.

Step 4. Stitch the top to the sides with right sides together.

Step 5. Hem the bottom.

Step 6. If you are using vinyl glass in the center of the cover, staple or pin it to the inside face of the cover, and stitch close around the perimeter. Cut the fabric away where the vinyl glass has been stitched, leaving a ½-inch seam allowance next to the glass. Fold over the raw edge, and stitch it down all the way around.

Step 7. Hinge Cutouts: If your hatch hinges come up into the hatch frame by a considerable degree, it will be necessary to make cutouts so that the cover will not foul the hinges. Measure the position and depth of the hinge, and mark it on the cover after it is hemmed. Cut this fabric out and bind the raw edge with vinyl binding (Figure 25–3). Refer to figure 15–14 for instructions on using vinyl binding.

Step 8. Fastenings: If you want to leave your covers on when the hatch is open, you must fasten the cover to the hatch rather than to the deck. Wooden hatches will hold a snap easily, but hatches with aluminum frames will not. If you must fasten the cover to the deck, this is usually done by putting snaps in the deck or in the lower hatch frame (Figure 25–4).

Install the fastenings in the cover at the same time that you install them on the boat. This way you'll avoid putting a snap where there is a hinge or other obstruction. You may have to sew tabs to the bottom edge of the cover as shown in Figure 25–4.

26
Custom Covers for On-Deck Equipment

Because of the damaging effects of the elements to almost anything on a boat, it is often desirable to cover items such as brightwork, brass, and machinery as much as possible whenever they are not in use. A binnacle is a good example, as are winches, windlasses, deck boxes, air conditioners, hatch covers, depth sounders, and steering wheels. Covers for these items are usually customized. With a few instructions you will be able to design and construct your own custom covers. Note, for example, the resemblance between a ditty bag and many other covers. The methods of design, measurement, and construction you have learned from other projects in this book will help in making a customized cover.

Materials

The cloth to use is canvas, preferably treated, or acrylic. When you cover something to protect it from sun, wind, and water, don't create a new problem by covering it with a material that doesn't breathe. Moisture will eventually get under any cover, and it must be allowed to get back out. Choose fastenings that close

simply. Often a drawstring around the bottom is the best (and easiest) method of fastening a cover.

Designing a Pattern

Step 1. Look at the object and analyze the angles and surface areas to be covered. For instance, a winch has a top, continuous sides, and a 90-degree angle between them. A hatch has a top and three or four sides, three of which could be of different shapes, and the angle between a side and the top may be greater than 90 degrees. The top of a hatch may be curved, and the two pairs of sides may be of different heights. An air conditioner will probably have a top, three sides, and an exposed bottom and back. The angles will probably be 90 degrees. Draw a sketch of the object that you want to cover, and label each surface area to be covered.

Step 2. Decide which sides you can make with one continuous piece of cloth and which sides must be cut exactly to shape. For instance, a winch cover needs one circular piece of cloth for the top and

131

Figure 26–1.
Winch cover.

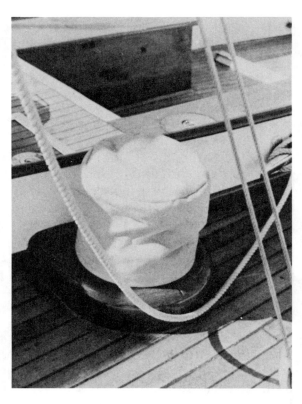

one continuous length of cloth for the sides that will go all the way around, much like a ditty bag. A hatch cover can probably be made with one piece for the top and one strip for the sides. However, depending on the type of hatch, it may be better to make separate pieces for each side, which will eventually be sewn together to make one strip.

Step 3. Take accurate measurements for the pieces you have decided to use. Remember to allow 1/2 inch for seams and 1 1/2 to 2 inches for hems. Transfer these measurements to your drawing.

Step 4. Calculate the amount of cloth required to complete the job. Refer to Chapter 5 for the widths of cloth that are available.

Step 5. Decide how you will fasten the cover: snaps, grommets, Velcro, drawstring, etc.

Step 6. Measure and draw the pieces on the cloth. If the cover you are making has many angles or curves that are important to fit, making a paper pattern first may simplify the job considerably.

Step 7. Stitch the pieces together, remembering to do all the sewing you can on the small pieces, and planning ahead so that you do not forget anything.

Step 8. Attach the fastenings and fit.

Winch Covers

A beautiful winch cover can be made with a yard of treated or acrylic canvas, some 1/2-inch elastic, and thread. All it really involves is making a ditty bag within a ditty bag and placing it upside down on the winch.

Step 1. Refer to Figure 26–2 and fill in the required measurements.

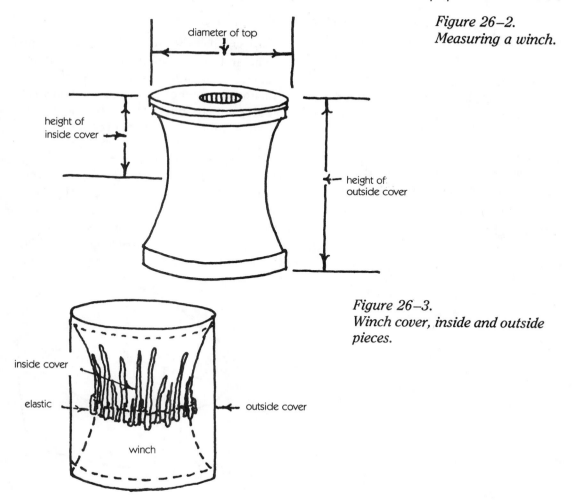

Figure 26–2.
Measuring a winch.

Figure 26–3.
Winch cover, inside and outside pieces.

Step 2. Top: Cut one circle of cloth the exact circumference (diameter times 3.14) of the top of the winch, plus a 1/2-inch seam allowance (refer to Chapter 6 on how to draw a circle).

Step 3. Outside Piece: Cut one piece of cloth the width of the circumference of the circle and the height of the winch, plus 1/2 inch for seam allowance and 1 1/2 inches for the hem. This will be the outside layer of cloth.

Step 4. Inside Piece: Cut one piece of cloth the same width as the outside piece, but make it the height of the winch from the top to its narrowest circumfer-ence (C), plus 1 inch for the casing and 1/2 inch for seam allowance. This piece will fit inside the outside cover and will grip the winch with elastic.

Step 5. Stitch the side seam of the inside piece. Make a 3/4-inch casing at the bottom edge. Stitch close to the edge. When stitching, leave an opening 1/2 inch wide through which to thread the elastic.

Step 6. Cut a piece of elastic that will fit snugly around the smallest part of the winch, and add 1/2 inch for sewing. Put a safety pin through one end of the elastic, and thread it through the casing. Holding both ends of the elastic, overlap them and stitch them together. Allow the elastic to slip into the casing, and stitch the opening in the casing closed.

Step 7. Stitch the side seam of the outside piece. Hem this piece so that it will just cover the winch, allowing 1/2 inch for the top seam allowance.

Step 8. Place the outside piece inside the inside piece so that the wrong sides of both pieces are facing you.

Step 9. Pin the top piece to both side pieces, right sides together. Stitch twice around. Turn right side out and cover your winch.

Windlass Cover

Your windlass, whether it is electrical or manual, is a piece of machinery that must function smoothly when lowering and raising the anchor. If it doesn't, you may find yourself much closer to the beach than you intended. To protect your windlass from saltwater corrosion, keep it covered while you are underway. To protect it from fresh water, keep it covered when you are at rest. Obviously, the only time the windlass should be uncovered is when you're actually lowering or raising the anchor. If the cover is designed properly, both chain and rope rodes can easily be led

*Figure 26–4.
Windlass cover.*

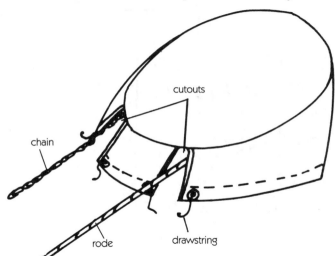

*Figure 26–5.
Pieces of canvas for the
Simpson Lawrence 555
windlass.*

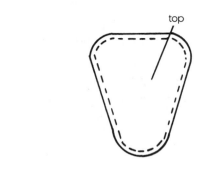

over the windlass gypsies when the cover is on. The cover needs to be fastened securely enough to keep a breaking wave over the bow from tearing it loose. But it must be easy to remove in case you need to anchor quickly. And it needs to breathe so any water or condensation that does get inside can get out. I suggest using a dark color so that windlass grease and anchor rode mud won't show so easily on the cover. A bottom drawstring that can be snugged up and tied to the windlass will provide both security and easy removal.

Materials Needed

- acrylic canvas
- number 4 line for drawstring
- vinyl binding

Design

Normally, a windlass cover can be made with two pieces of fabric, a top and a band for all the sides. You will need a slot for each anchor rode to exit from the cover. The windlass used as a model in this chapter is the very popular Simpson Lawrence

Mechanical 555. Pieces for the 555 cover appear in Figure 26–5.

If the sides of your windlass change shape, you will have to cut out individual side pieces rather than using a single band. Picture the windlass as having a top and four sides. It may be more complex than that, but usually you can visualize the necessary pieces of fabric (Figure 26–6).

Measuring

Step 1. Take measurements of each angle of the top, or make a pattern with paper.

Step 2. Measure the length and height of each side.

Step 3. Measure the width of each rode slot.

Step 4. Transfer all measurements to a drawing.

Step 5. Add ½ inch all the way around the top for seam allowance.

Step 6. Add 1½ inches to the bottom of the side band to make a casing for the

Figure 26–6.
Windlass cover with
irregularly shaped sides.

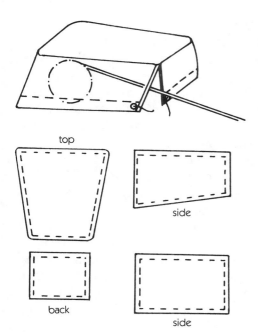

Figure 26–7.
Line and cutout in the 555
windlass cover.

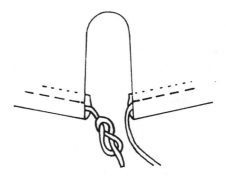

Figure 26–8.
Binnacle bag with zipper.

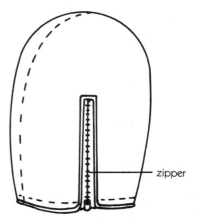

zipper

drawstring. Add 1/2 inch to the top of the band for seam allowance.

Construction

Step 7.   Cut all the pieces necessary for your cover, being sure to add and mark all seam allowances and hems.

Step 8.   If the sides require more than one piece of fabric because they change shape, stitch these sides together.

Step 9.   Bind the cutouts with vinyl (Refer to Figure 15–14).

Step 10.   Stitch the top to the side piece with right sides together.

Step 11.   Hem the entire cover. If you are using a drawstring, place the line in the casing before you stitch the casing down. If you want to be sure the line does not slip inside the casing, stitch very close to the line where it enters and exits from the cover. Knot the ends of the line with a figure-eight or overhand knot (Figure 26–7).

Binnacle Bag

On production sailboats, as well as on semi-custom designs, the Edson-type steering column, with a wheel, compass, engine controls, and sometimes a table and extra instruments all mounted on one base, has become very popular. It is probably simpler and more effective to cover this entire binnacle arrangement than to make separate covers for each item. A binnacle bag slightly resembles a canvas bag, but in fact it is quite fitted. It should be made with a breathable fabric so any moisture that collects under the cover can escape.

This particular bag has been designed with a zipper, allowing the bag to taper, which helps to hold it in place. A simpler bag can be made by taking the maximum circumference of the binnacle—which is usually at the point where the wheel extends beyond the binnacle—and carrying that width all the way down to the cockpit sole. To keep the bag from blowing away, use a drawstring in the bottom to cinch it up.

Materials Needed

- acrylic canvas
- zipper (or number 4 line for drawstring)

Measuring and Cutting

Step 1. Refer to Figure 26–10 and fill in the required measurements.

Step 2. Transfer all the measurements to the cloth. You will be using three pieces of fabric: a front, a back (wider than the front to match the wheel diameter), and a middle band for the sides (Figure 26–11). In order to obtain front and back pieces that are symmetrical, mark a centerline on the fabric, then transfer half-width measurements for the front or back

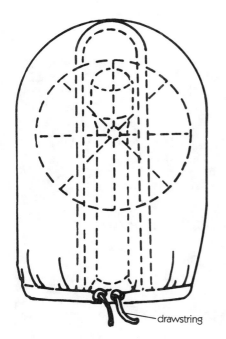

Figure 26–9.
Binnacle bag with drawstring.

— drawstring

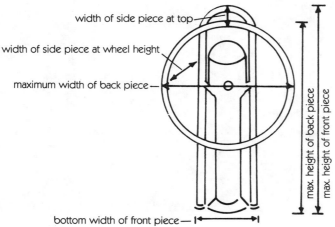

Figure 26–10.
Binnacle bag measurements.

width of side piece at top

width of side piece at wheel height

maximum width of back piece

max. height of back piece

max. height of front piece

bottom width of front piece

Figure 26–11.
Pieces of binnacle bag.

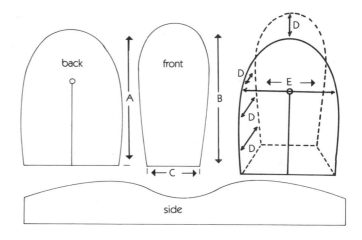

Figure 26–12.
View of a binnacle bag,
also showing winch
covers.

Figure 26–13.
A handsome but more
work-intensive alternative
to the binnacle bag is a
pair of separate covers
for the steering column
and wheel.

double-faced Velcro to fasten flap down

flap to facilitate reading
the sounder with
the cover on

Velcro

elastic with snaps that run under
the sounder

Figure 26–14.
Depthsounder cover.

piece, marking them both to the left and right of the centerline. Connect each point of measurement with a fair curve. Even though a measurement may suggest a sharp corner in the shape of the fabric, make a gradual curve to the next measurement for aesthetic purposes. When you have drawn the outlines of the front and back pieces, use these to check the necessary length of the middle band, and adjust as necessary. Add a 1/2-inch seam allowance to all edges that will be at the sides

and top. Add a 1½-inch hem allowance to the bottom edges, and cut out all of the pieces (Figure 26–11).

Construction

Step 3. Slit the slash for the zipper in the back cloth piece, from the bottom to a point corresponding to the hub of the wheel.

Step 4. Bind the raw edge of this slash with vinyl binding (Figure 15–14).

Figure 26–15.
Air conditioner cover.

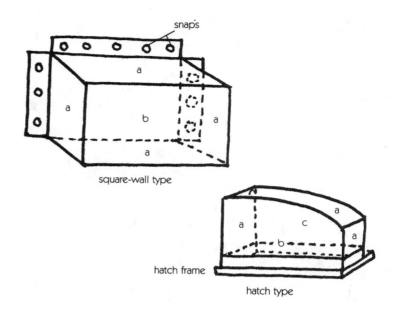

snaps

a
a
b
a
a

square-wall type

a
c
a
a
b

hatch frame

hatch type

Figure 26–16.
Air conditioner cover
fastened with shock cord.

Figure 26–17.
Outboard cover.

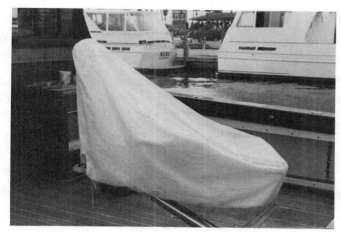

Figure 26–18.
Fishing chair cover.

Place a jacket zipper so that the slider, when in its closed position, is at the bottom edge of the front and stops ¼ inch above the hemline. Topstitch the zipper in place.

Step 5. Beginning at the middle of the top of the bag, pin or staple the center band to the front piece. Begin your stitching at this point, too. Stitch the front to the center band from the middle toward the right-hand bottom. Then come back, and stitch from the same point in the center toward the left-hand bottom. This stitching should be done with the right sides of the fabric together.

Step 6. Starting at the center, with right sides together, stitch the back to the center band.

Step 7. Turn the bag right side out, and hem the bottom edge.

Ideas for Designing Special Equipment Covers

Figure 26–14 shows a depth sounder cover, which is a fairly straightforward box. Like a cigar box, the front swings open to permit the depth sounder to be read without having to remove the entire cover, and this opening flap is held in the closed position with Velcro latches. One method of holding this (bottomless) cover in place is shown. Two elastic straps are sewn to the bottom of one end; when putting on the cover, you slip them under the depth sounder and fasten these straps with snaps or Velcro strips at the bottom of the opposite side.

Figure 26–15 shows two versions of a custom-made cover for an air conditioner. The first is a simple rectangular box for a bulkhead-mounted air conditioner, commonly seen on power yachts, and the second is for a hatch-cover or cabintop installation, more frequently seen on auxiliary sailboats. The power yacht version is made with just two pieces of fabric, the first of which provides three sides and the flaps that hold the snaps to attach the cover to the bulkhead, and the second of which forms the top of the cover. As always, careful measurement should precede the routine assembly job. On the right in the sketch, the sailboat version requires three pieces of fabric: the first piece forms two ends and the top, and pieces b and c, the two sides. This assembly method can be adapted to a number of shapes, as dictated by the item to be covered and the installation site. Snaps, Vel-

*Figure 26–19.
Combination wind
scoop–rain shield
held by halyard and
Velcro tape.*

cro, or turnbuttons will serve as fasteners for the cover.

Studying these plans will allow you to see how you might lay out other custom covers. It is best to keep to a minimum the number of pieces required for any project.

PART THREE

Interior Canvas Work

27
Design and Color Considerations in Interior Fabric Work

The colors and patterns you use below decks will greatly affect your sense of space, comfort, temperature, and motion. Draperies, cushions, and many of the other projects described in the following chapters are important components of your boat's overall interior decor and usually are most successful as part of a coordinated effort, based on an overall design strategy. If your present interior doesn't suit your taste or is in need of replacement because it is worn and damaged, now is a golden opportunity to look at the larger picture. Asking yourself a few questions and then applying a few basic principles of color and pattern will help you design a pleasing interior.

Space

All boats, no matter what their size, are small compared to shoreside standards of living space. Granted, an 80-foot power-boat may seem less small than a 23-foot pocket cruiser, but nearly always in interior boat design the objective is to create a feeling of as much space as possible.

Even before you start thinking about fabric, look at your interior layout and wood surfaces to see how they contribute to a sense of space, or the lack of it. A boat that has many angles, bulkheads, partitions, levels, and small cabins will appear much smaller than a boat that is open. Basically, every time you break a straight line you lessen the appearance of space—although obviously, compromises are continually being made for the sake of utility.

Look at your painted and brightwork surfaces to see how they contribute to a sense of space. For instance, a main saloon that has lots of flat white surfaces will appear much larger than one that is all flat teak. As rich-looking as dark wood may be, you may want to paint over some of it to create a more open look. Shiny varnish will generally give an impression of greater space than mat varnish or oil. You may want to change the Formica on the countertops from a dark to a light color to increase the sense of space. Once you have gone as far as you can toward creating a more spacious interior with the existing hull, bulkheads, and joinery, you can begin to choose fabric that will further enhance your efforts.

145

*Figure 27–1.
Light colors,
even selectively
applied, will
increase the
sense of space
below.*

*Figure 27–2.
Small patterns* (right)
*give a greater impression
of space than large
ones* (opposite).

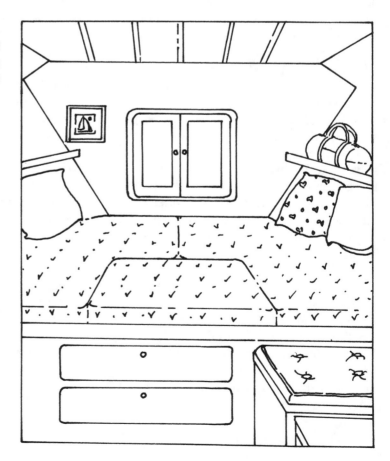

Light colors give a greater impression of space than dark colors. Small patterns give a greater impression of space than large ones, and constantly repeated patterns, whether large or small, give a greater impression of space than intermittent patterns (Figure 27–2). If all the lines on the boat draw your eye fore and aft rather than athwartships and you want the boat to appear wider, use a pattern such as a small stripe that goes inboard to outboard rather than fore and aft. If your boat is very wide and you want to give the impression of length, run the small stripe fore and aft. Obviously, light, solid colors will give the greatest impression of space—as reflected in the traditional practice of decorating yachts in medium blue, green, or red, with the yacht's name or burgee embroidered on the linen and towels as an accent.

Be sure to avoid patterns and fabrics that "move." I once redid a boat's interior and then delivered the boat to the owner, who lived four sailing days away. He had picked a lovely, very expensive fabric that did wonders for the interior of his boat: a navy background with a small, rust-colored dot pattern that resembled a fleur-de-lis. Once out to sea, however, I discovered to my distress that the pattern moved. Of course it didn't really move, but during those four days of tossing around at sea you would have been hard-pressed to convince me otherwise. Since my recovery from that trip, I have noticed that you can tell if a fabric will "move" by standing in front of a piece of it and moving your head from left to right. If you perceive movement in your peripheral field of vision, do not choose that fabric unless you have an ironclad stomach. Generally, the patterns

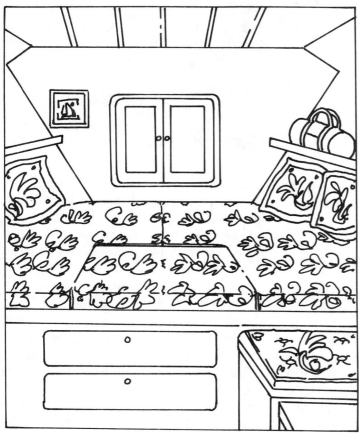

*Figure 27–3.
Light solid colors can be
effectively set off with
decorator accents.*

most likely to move are small geometrics that have very little contrast with the background color.

Warm and Cool Colors and Surfaces

How warm or cool a boat feels to you comes not just from the actual temperature but also from the colors you see and the surfaces you feel. Cool colors like blue and green will give a sense of cooler temperature than hot pink and coral. Even when a color is considered warm, a light shade of that color will generally feel cooler than a dark shade of the same color.

Surfaces contribute to this impression of warmth or coolness as well. A tile sole will feel cooler than a teak one because of conduction. Vinyl flooring is also cooler than teak, tacky as the thought may seem to some of you. Rugs, of course, add a sense of warmth and coziness.

When designing your interior decor, think carefully about the waters you will be sailing in. When I first decorated my 48-foot Atkin ketch *Errant,* I was living aboard in northern Michigan and wanted to create a cozy hearthside atmosphere, centered around the boat's wonderful fireplace with its copper fittings and dark red

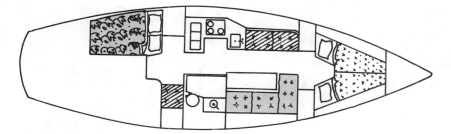

Figure 27–4. If your interior spaces are self-contained, mixing and matching fabrics can be very effective.

tile background. I chose dark burgundy and navy as my colors and put oriental rugs on the cabin sole to keep my feet warm. It was marvelous to come home from a day of skiing to a corner settee next to the warm fire in the fireplace. And it was always nice to come below after a day of sailing and make dinner in the galley without having to wear a sweater. It was not so wonderful, however, when I took *Errant* cruising in the tropics and found that her interior gave no relief from the heat. I was made very conscious of my mistake when I was invited aboard a boat that spends six months a year in the Bahamas. Her settees were covered in a very pale aqua. Her accents were soft yellow and pale green. Her sole was white vinyl and felt wonderfully cool on my bare feet. Compared to my own, this boat was air conditioned!

Mixing and Matching Interior Colors and Fabrics

If your boat is under 25 feet long and its V-berths and settees are all visible to each other, it is probably best to stick with just one fabric. But if your interior spaces are self-contained or at least well defined (as with partial bulkheads, etc.), then mixing and matching fabrics and colors is not only permissible but often delightful. For instance, most modern sailboats 35 feet and longer have an enclosed V-berth forward, with a main saloon amidships and a quarter berth or two aft of the galley. It usually looks very nice to do the V-berth in one fabric, the saloon in another, and, depending on its position relative to the main

saloon, the quarter berth in yet another fabric or the same fabric as the V-berth (Figure 27–4).

I do recommend that you stay with a color scheme when varying the pattern or texture of the fabrics. By color scheme, I mean one to three colors that blend nicely together and, while used differently perhaps in each area of the boat, maintain an overall sense of harmony. Unless you have a large yacht, say, more than 50 feet, changing color schemes does not work well. Usually it breaks the space into small chunks and destroys the lines and space of the boat.

Comfort

The interior of your boat should be a haven from the week's pressures at work, the storm howling outside, or the blazing sun. Although functional design is important, equally important is a sense of comfort—defined in your own terms. A Navy captain may not feel comfortable unless his yacht interior is khaki canvas with brass appointments. The flavor of tradition, function, and "strictly business" may be important to his sense of well-being. A book-lover may want his boat's interior to include walnut paneling, overstuffed chairs, and soft, neutral colors. A Southern belle may find that she cannot feel comfortable unless there are ruffles on the pillows—as well as on the mast sleeve, toilet seat cover, and tool board. I was once aboard a yacht owned by a woman whose tastes ran to the Victorian. Her lovely collection of Victorian figurines had come right along

*Figure 27–5.
Comfort, defined in your own
terms, is one of the most
important ingredients in a
successful interior design.*

to sea with her, through-bolted to countertops and tables.

My recommendation is that you pick a favorite room at home and copy the sense of it. Then carry this sense through when you choose your fabrics. Crisp, "yachty" fabrics such as canvas, Herculon, and nylon may be fine for the Navy captain, but if your tastes run to the softer fabrics—corduroy, cotton, velvet—there is no reason to reject them just because they are not traditionally nautical. Chintz, polished cotton, tapestries, Oriental rugs: why not? If you've never decorated anything so that it gave you a sense of comfort and security, it's high time!

If your tastes are not easily defined, you need to look at enough fabric to see what feels good. I emphasize "feels good" because too often fabric used on boats is chosen only for function when in fact it need not be. In the next chapter we'll see that there are fabrics of all materials, textures, and colors that will offer the yacht owner good durability without sacrificing that all-important dimension of comfort.

Practicality

You know how you want the interior of your boat to feel and the colors that will best suit your needs and increase the impression of spaciousness, but is your plan practical? What an awful question! At least we are asking it last, rather than first, which puts things in proper perspective. Medium colors tend to show less dirt than light ones. Dark colors show more lint. Tweed patterns hide dirt the best, with small geometrics a close second. Some people match the color of their fabric to their pets so that shedding will be less noticeable. That crisp cotton canvas will shrink if it is washed, the lovely handwoven-in-India print will stretch and pull, and those long-wearing nylons and Herculons will stain badly if exposed to any petroleum-based product. Those wonderfully comfortable corduroys, velvets, and ducks may not last as long as a Herculon, even though they feel so much better when you sit on them. Acrylic canvas is very practical, but you may sweat when you sleep on it.

What is a person to do? Go back to your first priorities of space, warmth or coolness, and comfort, and pick something that will give you those qualities. Compromise slightly for practicality if that is one of your major concerns, but realize that whatever fabric you choose for practicality's sake alone will be a compromise at best.

28
Fabrics for Interior Projects

In interior fabric work, the relentless action of the elements—sun, rain, wind, seaspray—is a less important factor, therefore allowing you a wider range of fabric choices. But moisture and stain resistance, as well as general durabilty, are still important concerns. In choosing fabrics, you need to consider what will fit your personal and boating style. If you tend to leave the sparkplug wrench and the fuel filter lying on the quarter berth while lunch is being served, you should choose your fabric accordingly. The following pages will help you weigh your options for functional yet beautiful interior fabrics.

Upholstery Fabrics

Herculon

Herculon is polypropylene fiber woven in a variety of solid, plaid, floral, and tweed patterns. It has a latex coating on the back that makes it water resistant and quite stable. It comes treated with a waterproof coating that usually works for a while and, when new, is also fairly resistant to stain. You'll find it frequently used for interior

cushions on boats and trailers. Herculon is sometimes quite difficult to sew, because its rubber backing can create drag on the machine. A bit of CRC (a silicone lubricant found in most hardware stores) sprayed on the seam line as you sew will not harm or stain the cloth.

The price of Herculon can vary tremendously—from $12 to $40 a yard. Many fabric stores sell Herculon for considerably less than upholsterers do. When making cushions with this fabric, make your cover 1/2 inch smaller than the cushion because the fabric will stretch a bit.

There are a variety of other woven upholstery fabrics on the market that closely resemble Herculon except that their fibers are made of nylon. My observation of these nylon-based fabrics is that they tend to wear better than Herculon, although some colors may fade more easily.

Vinyl

Good vinyl has a heavy but soft and flexible backing that gives it a spongy feeling. Naugahyde vinyl has a reputation as an excel-

Synthetics for Interior Fabric Work
(For a more detailed description of these fabrics, see Appendix 2.)

GENERIC NAME	TRADEMARK NAME	STRENGTH	SHAPE RETENTION	EFFECT OF HEAT
Acetate	Chromespun	Low	Low	Sticks at 350 degrees F
Acrylic	Acrilan Creslan Orlon Zefran	Excellent	Excellent	Sticks at 450 degrees F
Nylon	Anso Antron Enkalure Ultron Zeflon	Excellent	Excellent	Sticks at 445 degrees F
Olefin	Herculon Marvess Vectra	Excellent	Low	Melts at 325 degrees F
Polyester	Dacron, Fortrel, Fortrel Kodel Hollofil Trevira	Excellent	Excellent	Melts at 480 degrees F
Rayon	Fibro Avril	Low	Low	Decomposes at 350° F
Cotton		Medium	Medium	Decomposes at 350° F

lent cloth, and there are other well-made vinyls that you may never have heard of. Beware of vinyl that has a thin, "cheese-cloth" type backing. It will tear easily and will not provide that leatherlike feeling of comfort. Vinyl is often used for interior cushions because it is water resistant and easily cleaned with a wet sponge. Its tendency to stick to the skin after you've sat on it for a while in the heat is a major drawback, but it is still the most mainte-nance-free material for cushions. When sewing vinyl, you must take care not to make too many needle holes, for these will eventually cause the fabric to tear.

Canvas

Canvas has the soft, nonsticky qualities that vinyl and Herculon lack (although acrylic canvas is somewhat stickier than cotton canvas). It is waterproof but not stain resistant. It can be washed and dried easily in the washing maching and dryer, *providing you preshrink the material before sewing.* It is easily handled in the sewing machine and provides a homey atmosphere and an easy change of decor. Canvas cushions will have to be replaced much sooner than Herculon or vinyl ones.

Other Fabrics for Upholstery Work

Corduroy and cotton/polyester blends make attractive upholstery fabrics. Obviously, you must consider the wear and tear they will receive, the water and food stains they may suffer, and the upkeep they will require. Most fabrics can be waterproofed to some extent, but don't forget that old enemy mildew. A damp cushion can make a whole cabin smell musty. Consult the accompanying table for properties of various synthetic blends.

Don't overlook velvet as a good choice for interior upholstery. It wears incredibly well, is fairly resistant to fading, can be washed in cold water and drip dried, and feels nice on the skin in warm or cold climates. There are patterns and prints from the sportiest navy and tan tattersall to shiny crushed velvets for a more formal look.

Knits and other stretch fabrics do not work well for upholstery and draperies. They will stretch, and the threads will pull with the slightest rough treatment or heavy usage. Also unsuitable are the linen-like fabrics with very loose weave. They will stretch in no time and give a very loose, sloppy-looking fit.

Drapery Materials

Any synthetic or synthetic/cotton blend will make good draperies. The more wash-and-wear they are, the better. Definitely line them with a synthetic material if lining is necessary.

29
Interior Cushions

Design Considerations

We are seeing much more of the upholsterer's trade in yacht interiors than ever before. Main saloon settees look more and more like couches, and owner's staterooms often become luxurious suites. You may be feeling bewildered by the profusion of colors and textures available in today's fabrics, so let's look first at cushion styles and what will work in the spaces you have.

The first consideration is how to divide the cushions so that they will be comfortable, complementary to the vessel, and functional in relation to the storage behind or beneath the cushions. In Figure 29-1 you will notice that the cushions are divided in three different ways. The first way requires the fewest number of cushions. Larger cushions may be slightly more difficult to sew because they give you more fabric to handle, but they won't take much more time than small ones. The main consideration in the first example involves the handling of the cushion once it is aboard. The entire cushion will have to be moved to get to the storage behind it, which can be very inconvenient. However,

the lines of the cushion are cleaner and may create a more open feeling than smaller cushions. It also may be more comfortable to lean against one solid cushion than several smaller ones.

The next two examples show the cushions broken into smaller sections to facilitate access to the locker behind or underneath. Smaller cushions allow for softer styling. The smooth, unbroken line, however, is lost. You must decide what the priority is: a more spacious look or easy access to storage? Also, are you willing to take the extra time that the smaller cushions will require during construction? Remember to think about possible locations for backrests, which are rarely provided on production boats. Wouldn't it be nice, for example, to have a backrest for reading at the end of your berth?

Another popular design feature on modern production boats is dinette tables that drop down and join with a settee to make a double bed. Obviously, a cushion must go on the table to complete the mattress. Can one or two of the backrests act as this cushion, or does it have to be an

155

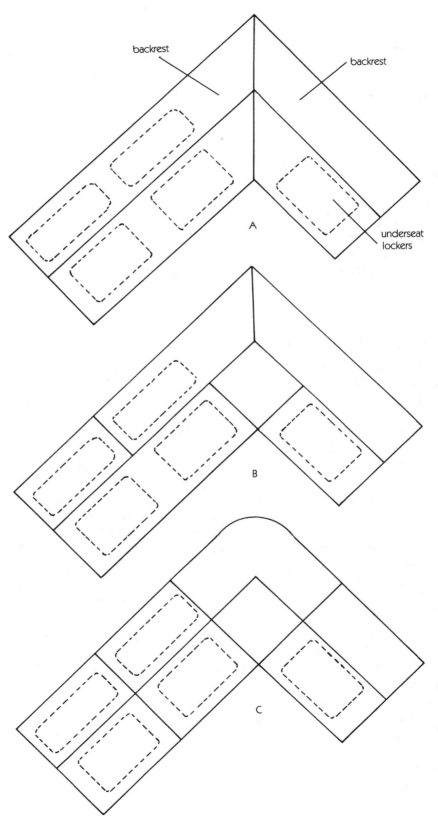

Figure 29–1.
L-shaped settee
divided three
ways.

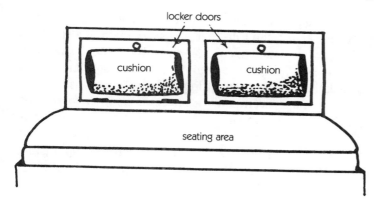

Figure 29–2.
Backrests on locker doors.

Figure 29–3.
A wraparound print can be a
complicated sewing job.

Figure 29–4.
Traditional boxed
cushion.

extra cushion? I don't recommend having an extra cushion if it can be avoided. Where are you going to store it? With careful planning and possibly some unique division of other cushions, you can usually come up with a way to provide a mattress for the table with existing cushions.

Look once again at Figure 29–1 and notice the different ways to treat corners. Think about how you are going to match fabric. The L-shaped settee presents some unique challenges. Should you make the print run fore and aft on all cushions, or should you make a triangular corner cushion and dart the fabric so that the print goes around the corner of the L and on to the next cushion as in the accompanying photo? This is a complicated sewing job, so think twice about it. Remember, too, that the backrests need to match the seats. Be sure you can do that with the number of cushions and the fabric you choose. You will need to buy extra fabric for matching each cushion. How much extra depends on the distance between repeats of the pattern. A plaid that repeats every 4 inches will not require as much extra fabric as a pattern that repeats every 32 inches.

A thought about large mattresses for V-berths, double berths, and queen-size berths. It is always nice to have one solid piece of foam to sleep on. However, most hatches limit the size of the cushion you can get in and out of the boat, and the cushion will have to be split somehow. Give some thought to access to the storage under the berth and to sleeping comfort. If you can split the mattress so that each person can sleep to one side or the other of the split, it should be comfortable. If you can't do that, consider making a mattress pad to cover and pull together all the cushions and smooth out the ridges created by the separations of the cushions. I have even sewn a sheet of 1/2-inch foam to a standard mattress pad to add comfort and camouflage bumps. I recommend a cotton mattress pad to protect the upholstery from staining and to act as a moisture barrier between you and any synthetic fabrics that don't breathe.

Boxed Cushions

Boxed cushions are standard and traditional. They are also easy to make, consisting of a top, a bottom, and a side band, with a concealed zipper at the back or bottom of the cushion. They are called boxed cushions because of their square corners and flat surfaces (Figure 29–4). Should you choose the crisp, clean look of a boxed cushion, decide whether or not you want it corded. Cording, sometimes called piping, is sewn into every seam to protect the stitching against wear and to hide the stitching. It is often made of a contrasting color for decoration. Do not cord cushions made of velvet or corduroy because the nap cannot match and will crush unnaturally.

Bull-Nosed Cushions

Bull-nosed cushions are similar to boxed cushions, except that they have bands only on the sides and back of the cushion rather than on all four sides, and the front of the foam is rounded with batting to give a softer look (Figure 29–5). Bull-nosing can

*Figure 29–5.
Bull-nosed cushion.*

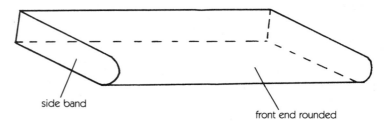

side band

front end rounded

provide softness for a formal or casual fabric. I don't recommend the use of crisp duck or canvas in a bull-nosed style, but it is wonderful for velvet, corduroy, some soft Herculons, and prints. Side cording can be used or not, depending on the fabric you choose.

Before deciding on bull-nosed cushions, know that a high fiddle on the front edge of the settee may interfere with the cushion and cause it to jump out of its space.

Overstuffed Cushions

An overstuffed look can be achieved through a variety of techniques. *Pleating* is one effective method of adding a soft, cushy appearance to a smooth piece of foam. It involves backing the fabric with foam and actually pleating the foam-and-fabric before cutting it for your cushion cover. This treatment will add slightly more than 1/4 inch to the thickness of your cushion, so remember to allow for it (see ahead, to Figure 29–20).

Quilting, similar in many respects to pleating, is discussed in connection with daycovers in Chapter 30. Pleating and quilting can be used with either boxed or bull-nosed cushion covers. Remember that quilting and pleating lines must match in seats and backrests, so don't complicate your life by choosing a print that will have to be matched as well.

Even the crisp styling of a boxed cushion can be softened by gluing a layer of synthetic batting to the foam with 3M Spray Adhesive to add softness to the look and feel of the cover. Usually synthetic batting is about 1 inch thick, more than you need to add softness to a boxed cushion. (If you really want a soft look, pick a softer style.) Split the batting thickness in half by separating the sheet into two layers. You can easily do this with your hands. Don't put cording on an overstuffed boxed cover, because the cording will sharpen the lines you are trying to soften. Usually buttons are used with this style to hold the cover in place and create texture in the cover.

Yet another method of creating an overstuffed look involves *mid-cushion cording.* You've seen thin cushions covered in chintz and corded or ruffled around the middle on old rockers. The corners are gathered or darted, and the top and bottom fabric meet in mid-cushion, requiring no side band. This seam is usually corded (Figure 29–6).

Use a soft-looking fabric, such as velvet or corduroy, cotton prints, or soft-hand Herculons, to complement the softness of an overstuffed cushion.

Materials for Interior Cushions

Fabric

You will need enough fabric to cover the top and bottom and make the side bands for each cushion, plus enough 1 1/2-inch-wide strips to make cording if your design

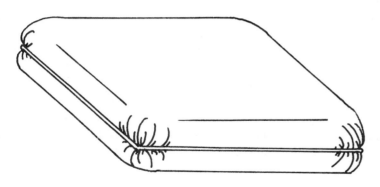

*Figure 29–6.
Mid-cushion cording.*

calls for it. (Both top and bottom edges of the cushion should be corded if they will show or can be flipped over. If there is a retaining fiddle or lip that will hide the bottom edge of the cushion, the bottom edge need not be corded.)

Zippers

Your zippers should be long enough to run along the longest hidden side of each cushion. Delrin zipper tape is the best. Because it is plastic, it will not rust, and even if a few teeth are missing, the zipper will still work. Buy the number of yards needed to do the whole job, and cut each length as you need it. Buy the sliders separately and slip them on yourself. The sides of the fabric are sewn in such a manner as to act as a stop for the zipper (see ahead); you will not need to buy stops. Delrin zipper tape comes in two sizes, 5-D and 10-D. The smaller, 5-D, is adequate for cushions.

Cording String and Thread

Number 4 twine or nylon line is best for cording. Nylon is best for exterior cushions but not absolutely necessary. Buy enough cording to do the whole job. You might want to make up all of it in one session.

Polyester thread with cotton cover works well on all fabrics. Make sure that you are sewing with a long stitch on vinyl, because too many needle holes may cause it to tear.

Foam

As most of you know, poor-quality foam wears out quickly. When foam wears out, it loses its "memory"—its ability to bounce back to its original shape—and low-density foam loses its memory first. Density is created by the number of polyurethane molecules per square inch and is measured by how many pounds of pressure it takes to compress 1 square inch of foam 1 inch. Density can also be achieved by adding

sand, but this "loaded sand" is not recommended. It may take most of a night's sleep before your shoulder and hip sink into the foam, but it will take that long again for the foam to return to its original shape. Loaded foam also tends to be less firm than an all-polyurethane foam of comparable density.

Foam is graded by its chemical composition (the majority of which is polyurethane) and by its density. Ignoring all loaded foam, look for foam rated between 44 and 54 pounds of pressure. This will give you a very good, firm foam that will last a long time. At the Coverloft, we sell 15 grades of foam, but we stock only 2: 44-pound foam and PL 35. The former is a good firm foam that is not significantly more expensive than the soft grade used on most production boats. PL 35, a chemical-combination foam, is the Cadillac of foam. It costs twice as much as 44-pound foam, but it has as much density and more memory, or bounce. Unless price is no object, this foam is usually reserved for the captain's bunk and the corner settee where everyone sits. Don't be afraid to mix foam in this way. Occasionally, for super-soft cushions, you might want to drop down to a 22- or 34-pound foam; jump up to a 74-pound foam for the guy who likes to sleep on the floor. Find out what you're buying before you go to the local foam discount house.

If you're thinking about recovering those old pieces of foam, think carefully. Do not reuse the old foam if it has mildew in it. Mildew is a fungus and will continue to grow right into your new covers until they rot. Also, if the corners of the foam have lost their bounce they will not fill out the shape of your new covers. If you decide to recover the old foam, and you want the covers to be tight, use the old foam as a pattern rather than taking patterns of the space. Be prepared, however, for slightly smaller cushions that won't fit the space.

Buttons and Buttoning

Buttons are often necessary when you are trying to make fabric lie on the inside curve of a corner cushion or a contoured cushion. They are also used to create design, shape, and shadow, and can add the finishing touch to an overstuffed settee. But keep in mind that each time you remove the covers for cleaning, the buttons will have to be removed as well and then sewn back on. The alternative is professional dry cleaning for the entire cushion. Decide on your button pattern carefully by laying out all the cushions that fit together exactly as they will be on your boat. Mark where each button will go. Remember that the arrangement of buttons on seat and backrest cushions must match.

Buttoning requires covered buttons, which you can buy from a sewing or upholstery shop. I recommend that you have your upholsterer make them for you with your fabric, even if he charges you extra. He has a press that will do a better job than you can do with a spool of thread and a hammer.

If you choose to cover your own buttons, button forms for covering can be purchased at most dry goods stores. The better of the two button forms has the attaching ring on the button side rather than on the back. Buttons with the attach-

ing ring on the back tend to pull apart. If you are covering your buttons with vinyl, strip off the laminate from the back if you can. This will reduce thickness and make the button easier to cover.

Sew your buttons on with heavy waxed twine. Otherwise they will separate and pull off constantly. Thread a 20-inch piece of waxed thread through the button. Put this button in the middle of the thread. Thread a long sail needle with both ends of this thread. Insert the needle at the marked position so that it goes through the top fabric, the foam, and the bottom fabric. Pull the thread through, remove the needle, and thread the ends through another button. Pull on these threads evenly until the foam is compressed the way you want it. Wrap the two ends of thread twice, in opposite directions, around the shaft of the bottom button, and tie two square knots. Be sure to be consistent with the tension on each button.

For an alternative installation system, using plastic backing buttons, see page 171.

Fastening Systems

Track for a Hanging Backrest The accompanying photos show backrests hung on aluminum trailer molding so that each cushion is fastened securely but can

Figure 29–7.
Buttoned corduroy interior.
Backrests with tabs to open the upholstered doors.

Figure 29–8. Two views of a hanging backrest system. Three-eighths-inch rope sewn into the tabs along the cushion tops slides within the aluminum track like a sail's bolt rope in a boom or mast groove.

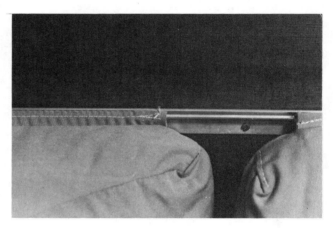

be flipped up easily for access to storage behind it. Tabs are sewn to the cushion where the back meets the top of the cushion. Inside the tab is a piece of ³⁄₈-inch line that slides into the track.

Snap Tabs The same tab arrangement can be used with snaps or turnbuttons. Snaps will not hold as much weight as turnbuttons, so use lots of them to spread out the load. Snaps look more finished however and are not likely to hurt anyone as turnbuttons or Lift-the-Dots do.

Velcro Velcro is the most popular method of fastening cushions to the vessel. It is an excellent system for interior cushions, except for those that are reversible: If you put Velcro on the back of a reversible

cushion, it is obviously no longer reversible. Remember to sew the Velcro to the back piece of the cushion before stitching the cushion together. If you can staple the other half to the boat with bronze or Monel staples, great! If not, buy Velcro with an adhesive back even though it costs an arm and a leg. It will save hours of regluing later.

Patterning and Construction

The first three steps are the same for all cushions, regardless of the style you choose:

Step 1. Use brown wrapping paper to pattern the spaces where you will put cushions. Be sure to mark the pattern so that you know where the zipper goes, and

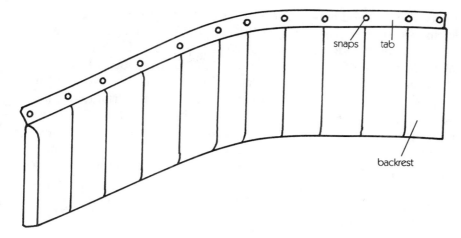

*Figure 29–9.
Pleated backrest
fastened with
snaps.*

snaps tab

backrest

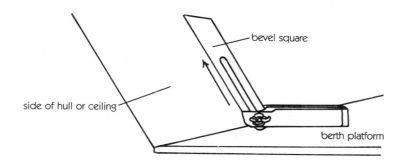

*Figure 29–10.
Measuring the
bevel for the
outboard edge
of a cushion.*

bevel square

side of hull or ceiling

berth platform

designate the cushion's place, for instance "port settee." If the outboard edge of the cushion needs a bevel to follow the curve of the hull, measure the bevel with a bevel square and trace it on the pattern in the correct location. This will tell you how wide the outboard edge must be, and also how much wider the top must be than the bottom. Be sure to note on the pattern if the bevel stops in the middle of a side. If the backrest and seat must match, mark the position of the backrest in relation to the seat cushion on the seat cushion pattern.

Step 2. Use this pattern to cut both foam and fabric, because it is constant. Do not cut the foam and then use the foam as a pattern. Foam density varies with quality. Depending on the density of your foam, add up to ½ inch all the way around the pattern when you use it to cut the foam, so that the foam is actually larger than the pattern. This will ensure a tightly fitting cover. Use a felt-tip pen when marking the foam for cutting. Mark carefully, and be sure to measure twice before you cut!

If you are not using foam already cut to size or you cannot get the dealer to cut it for you, a serrated knife, electric carving knife, or handsaw will cut the foam easily. With the serrated knife, use a lot of sawing action and very little pressure. Slow, smooth strokes make a clean cut.

Step 3. Cut your fabric as necessary for the style of the cushion you are making, using the following general points:

• Roll the fabric out on a large flat surface. Arrange to cut the tops and bottoms along one edge of the piece of fabric and leave the remaining edge for the long side pieces.

- Mark and label all pieces before cutting. Write only in the seam allowances, or use pencil or tailor's chalk. (Felt-tip pen will eventually bleed through the fabric.)

- In general, cut the tops and bottoms to the pattern size, then stitch *inside* the pattern line. This will make the cover a bit smaller than the pattern and allow for the gradual stretching of all fabric.

- It's a good idea to cut your side bands slightly shorter than the height of the foam. This will help ensure a tight cover and prevent the cover from rolling on the foam. Be sure to allow for adequate (1/2-inch) seam allowances, however.

- The zippered side of the cushion should have its own band. Cut the zipper band wider by 1 inch to allow for the fabric you will fold under next to each side of the zipper.

- *Planning extra ties or snap tabs:* If a cushion needs to be snapped to a bulkhead or seat, or to be tied around a chair, plan for snap tab locations first. Measure how long

they should be, and label the edge of the material to which they will be sewn. A snap tab will usually need to be 1½ inches wide, so cut a strip 3½ inches wide and the required length, hem the ends of the strip, fold it in half, and stitch it together. There is no need to finish the raw edges because they will be inside the cushion seam. When you stitch the side piece to the bottom of the cushion, be sure to insert this tab into the proper seam and stitch through all thicknesses. Ties should be made the same way.

- Arrange all the pieces for each cushion in piles to keep the pieces organized. Don't forget extra ties and tabs if they are to be used.

Boxed Cushions

Construction

Steps 1–3.   Follow the patterning and cutting instructions outlined above.

Step 4. Side Band: If you have had to cut separate pieces to form your side band, stitch them end-to-end to get the proper length. (Do not include the zipper band yet.)

Step 5. Cording: Mark off enough

Figure 29–11.
Inserting the snap tab.

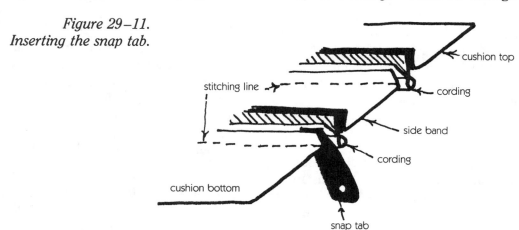

cushion top

stitching line

cording

side band

cording

cushion bottom

snap tab

1½-inch cording strips to do all of your cording. Cording strips cut from woven fabrics without backing should first be cut on the bias, then sewn together to produce the required length. Place the ends of the strips right sides together and sew a ¼-inch seam, cutting away the triangular excess from each strip end. Vinyl and backed fabrics will not ravel, and strips made of these fabrics need not be stitched to the required length beforehand. Pieces can be added as the cord is sewn into the strips.

Step 6. Zipper: Stitch the zipper in the zipper band by cutting the band in half lengthwise and stitching first one side and then the other to the zipper. Stitch the end opposite the slides to one end of the side band.

Step 7. The cording string can be sewn into the cording strips as they are being sewn onto the side and zipper bands. Take a cording strip and fold it over the

cording so that the edges of the strip match up.

Match the edges of the cording strip with the edge of the side and zipper bands. This should give you a ½-inch seam allowance if you sew through the strip right up against the cord. Using the zipper foot in your machine, sew both the top and bottom cording onto the bands. Leave the last few inches of cording strip and side and zipper bands unstitched for overlapping later.

Step 8. Sewing the Side Band to the Top: Place the right side of the zipper band next to the right side of the top along the edge to be zippered (usually the outboard edge). Line up the edges and begin stitching 3 inches in from the free end of the band. Stitch the zipper and side band to the top all the way around, staying tight against the cording with the zipper foot. When you reach the end of the side band,

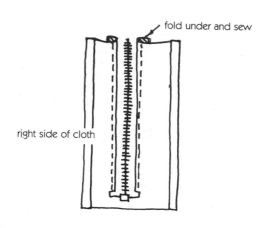

fold under and sew

right side of cloth

Figure 29–12.
Installing the zipper.

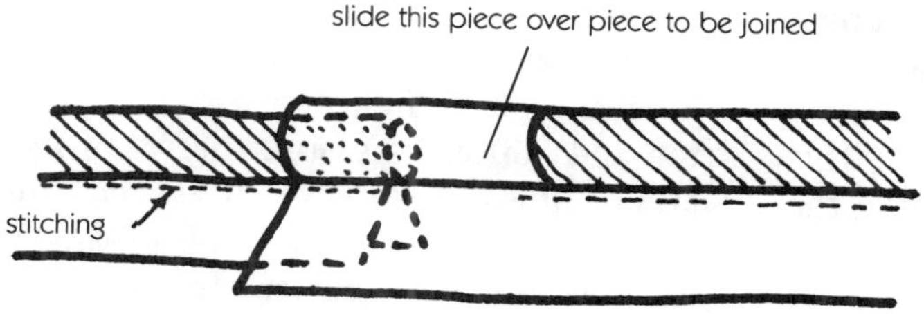

slide this piece over piece to be joined

stitching

Figure 29–13.
Joining cording strips.

*Figure 29–14.
Sewing the cording to the
side band.*

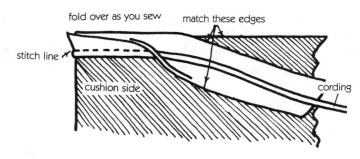

*Figure 29–15.
Finishing the end of the
side band (inside out
view).*

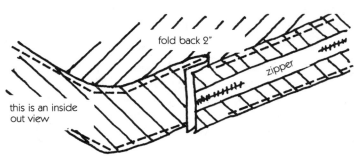

cut the excess away, but leave enough to
fold under 2 inches of the end to finish the
raw edge (Figure 29–15). Tuck this folded
edge under the end of the zipper band. Cut
out 1/2 inch of cord from the free end of the
side band, and cut away 1/2 inch of cording-
strip fabric from the free end of the zipper
band. Lap the cordless end of the cording
strip over the other end of the cording and
stitch through all thicknesses. (Refer to
Chapter 3 for making cushion corners.) If
your machine can't handle this much
thickness at once, sew the last few inches
by hand (Figure 29–16).

Stitch the end edges of the side and
zipper bands together, incorporating the
tucked edge (Figure 29–17) and overlapping the bottom cording as you did on the
top.

Step 9. Sewing in the Bottom: Unzip
the zipper halfway. Make small slashes in
the bottom edge of the side band directly
above the corners made in the top. This
will show you exactly where to make the
bottom corners. Stitch the bottom onto
the side band, right sides together, just as
you did the top. Remember to sew in the

tabs and ties where needed (Figure 29–11).
As you sew, make sure that all corners are
strong and that you are consistently close
to the cording. Go back and restitch any
places that don't look just right. Turn the
cushion right side out. Put the foam carefully into the cover, working it into the far
corners, and zip it up. Small corners of the
cover that are slightly too large can be
stuffed with shredded foam or batting. The
next cushion you make will be easier.

Bull-nosed Cushions

Bull-nosed cushions also consist of a top
and bottom but have bands only on two
sides and the back of the cushion (Figure
29–5). Notice that the top piece wraps
around the front of the cushion and covers
part of the bottom. The side bands are cut
with the front edge curved and the back
beveled if necessary. The zipper band
should be cut wide enough to cover the
beveled edge. To figure the exact length of
top and bottom, measure the side bands
around the outside edge. If any cushion
edge is beveled to fit the hull or angled
joinery, you must increase the height of
the band. For instance, the bevel on a 4-

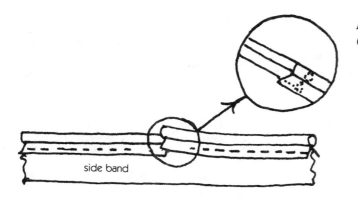

Figure 29–16.
Overlapping the cording.

side band

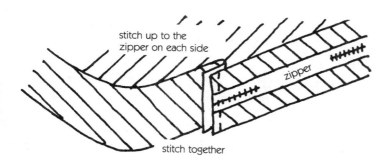

Figure 29–17.
Stitching the ends of the side band.

stitch up to the zipper on each side

zipper

stitch together

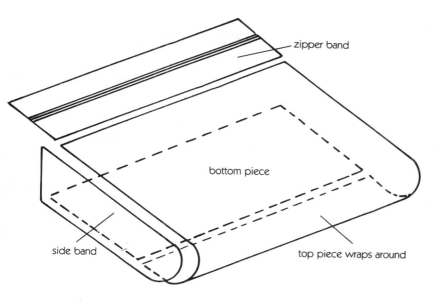

Figure 29–18.
Component pieces of a bull-nosed cushion.

zipper band

bottom piece

side band

top piece wraps around

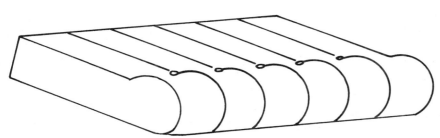

Figure 29–19.
Bull-nosed cushion with pleats, built up under knees.

inch-thick cushion may require a 4³/₄-inch band.

The bottom piece is shorter than the bottom of the cushion because the top piece will cover part of it. Cut cording for the side pieces if you're using it. The width of a cording strip should be 1¹/₂ inches, and it should be long enough to wrap around the side band edge, with a little extra at both ends to tuck inside the cushion at the top and bottom outboard corners.

Materials

In addition to the materials described earlier in this chapter, you will need a layer of synthetic batting, to be glued to the foam.

Construction

Steps 1–3. Follow the patterning and cutting instructions outlined above.

Step 4. Stitch the cording to the side bands. These cushions look best without cording on the zipper band. Do not stitch the zipper band to the side bands yet.

Step 5. Stitch the bottom to the top where they join, right sides together.

Step 6. Stitch the zipper band to the top and bottom, right sides together. Melt the teeth of the zipper chain together with a match or hot knife so that the slider can't come off.

Step 7. Stitch the side bands into the cushion cover, right sides together.

Step 8. Stitch the zipper band to the side bands along their overlaps at the outboard corners, right sides together.

Step 9. Unzip the zipper and turn the cover right side out.

Step 10. Stuffing: Wrap the foam in batting. Often you need only wrap the top, front, and part of the bottom to take the corners of the foam off. Note that you aren't cutting the foam rounded, it is up to the cover and the batting to compress the square corners. It is helpful to glue the batting to the foam with 3M Spray Adhesive or something similar before stuffing the foam into the cushion cover.

Step 11. Insert the foam into the cover. Button it if you like.

Figure 29–20.
Pleating foam and fabric.

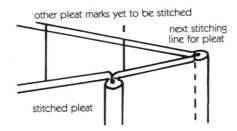

other pleat marks yet to be stitched

next stitching line for pleat

stitched pleat

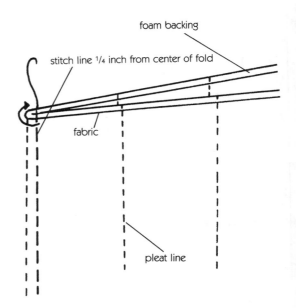

foam backing

stitch line ¹/₄ inch from center of fold

fabric

pleat line

Bull-nosed Cushion with Raised Edge

You may wish to imitate the styling used on some modern production boats. The edge of the cushion that fits under your knees on a seat or behind your neck on a backrest will have an added piece of foam an inch or two thick that is also rounded out by batting. To accomplish this you must first glue the added piece of foam to the main piece of foam with contact cement. Then wrap the foam as in the bull-nosed cushion. Cut the side bands to reflect the new shape and add length to the top fabric piece. Otherwise the procedure is the same as for a bull-nosed cushion. You must use buttons placed just at the inside edge of the added foam to hold the fabric tight to this inside curve.

Be careful where you use the raised-edge cushion. I do not recommend using it if you expect people to sleep on these cushions.

Quilted Cushions

Make all quilted cushions according to the style you prefer. Refer to Chapter 30 for quilting instructions. Be sure to quilt the fabric before you cut it to size, because it will take up—i.e., grow smaller—during quilting.

Pleated Cushions

Materials

In addition to the materials described earlier in this chapter, you will need one or more pieces of 1/4-inch foam to back the fabric.

Construction

Step 1–3. Follow the patterning and cutting instructions on pages 162–164. Cut all pieces of fabric to the pattern except the top. Cut this piece longer to account for the 1/4-inch take-up of each pleat.

Step 4. Mark the pleat lines on the right side of the fabric with chalk so that your pleats are evenly spaced. They can be anywhere from 1 to 4 inches apart. Using your top pattern, cut out a piece of 1/4-inch foam for backing and stitch it to the top piece all around the outside edge, or staple or pin the foam to the fabric.

Step 5. Fold the fabric-and-foam combination on the first pleat line, and stitch 1/4 inch away from the axis of the fold (Figure 29–20). Repeat for each pleat. Then cut the pleated fabric and foam to the pattern.

Step 6. Batting is not necessary because the foam and pleats add the softness.

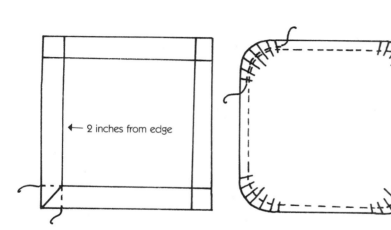

← 2 inches from edge

Figure 29–21. Making corner darts in a cushion with no side bands.

Stitch the cover according to the directions for the style of cushion you choose.

Mid-Cushion Cording

Materials

In addition to the materials detailed earlier in this chapter, you will need a layer of synthetic batting, to be glued to the foam.

Construction

Steps 1–3. Follow the patterning and cutting instructions on pages 162–164. Notice, however, that this cushion has only a top and bottom and cording. There are no side bands. To measure this type of cushion, add half the cushion height to all sides of the top and bottom. For instance, if the cushion is 24 by 24 by 4 inches, the top and bottom pieces will be cut 28 by 28 inches.

Step 4. If you want to dart the corners, mark a line half the height of the cushion (2 inches) all around the outside edge on the wrong side of the top and bottom pieces of fabric. Make a dart in each corner where these lines cross (Figure 29–21). If you want to gather the corner, put a basting stitch around the top and bottom pieces, and gather the corners until you have the exact length that you need. Staystitch each corner.

Step 5. Stitch the cording to the top of the cushion.

Step 6. Stitch the zipper to the hidden side of the cushion so that the cording hides it.

Step 7. Stitch the top to the bottom, right sides together. Open the zipper, and turn the cover right side out.

Step 8. Wrap the entire piece of foam with batting and insert it in the cover.

Covering a Settee Back

If you have the type of settee with a plywood back, you can recover it easily.

It is often advisable to button cushions that are used as backrests. This will keep the material from sagging downward when people slouch against the cushions, and also give the cushions a bit of an overstuffed look.

Materials

- fabric of choice
- bronze or Monel staples

For buttons (optional):

- covered buttons
- plastic backing buttons
- strong marline or Dacron cord (waxed)

Step 1. Remove the back from the settee and remove any staples or buttons. Cut a piece of fabric that will cover the back generously. If the back is curved, note how the darts were made in the old cover and duplicate them in the new piece of cloth.

Step 2. Using bronze or Monel staples (because they don't rust), stretch the new piece of cloth over the foam and around to the back side of the plywood. Begin at the top edge. Staple from the middle toward the outside edges, making sure to pull the material snug. Then do the bottom edge, again starting at the center and pulling the material down and out toward the ends. The side edges are the most difficult. Make neatly pleated corners, and stretch the fabric tightly over the ends, but do not depress the foam any more in one spot than you have elsewhere.

Step 3. Buttons: Buy covered buttons, or cover them yourself. Refer to page 161.

Step 4. Mark the positions of the

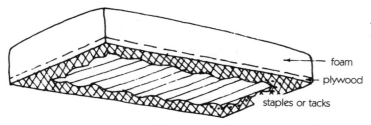

Figure 29–22.
Covering a settee back.

foam

plywood

staples or tacks

Figure 29–23.
Buttoning.

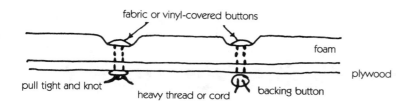

fabric or vinyl-covered buttons

foam

plywood

pull tight and knot

heavy thread or cord   backing button

buttons on the back of the cushion or ply-wood. Drill a small hole for each button in the plywood.

Step 5.   With a 2-foot length of heavy waxed cord, thread a long sail needle. Put the needle through one side of the plastic backing button, then through the back of the cushion. Compress the foam until you can reach the needle. Pull the thread through until you have 2 to 3 inches left below the backing button. Feed the needle through the covered button and back through the cushion and backing button. Pull the threads so that the covered button compresses the foam, and tie a good square knot on top of the backing button.

Continue this procedure with all of the buttons, being careful in each case to be consistent with the tension on each button.

I have just one more remark to make about stitching cushions: it takes patience. If your corners don't come out according to plan, turn the cushion around and stitch the other way. When you get back to the corner, start ripping out stitches until you get back to the problem. Remember that fabrics stretch; watch for it to happen so that you don't get into trouble trying to make the next corner line up. Have fun with it, and don't try to do it all tonight.

30
Sheets and Quilts Versus
Expensive Upholstery

Let's look at the creature comforts that fitted sheets provide to see if they are for you.

Usually we find boat interiors that consist of cushions covered with fabric that hopefully enhances the overall appearance of the inside of the boat. We then use sleeping bags or various sheets and blankets to turn these perfectly upholstered cushions into beds, or berths, as they are called aboard. In the morning we must strip the cushions of these sheets and blankets, find a locker to stow them in, and return our vessel to its proper condition. Of course, the next evening those same sheets and blankets must come out of hiding and be made up into berths again. And so it goes, night after night.

If you spend only an occasional night aboard, this isn't really a problem, unless you have a shortage of space in which to stow those sheets. So let's assume that you would rather have that locker space for flashlights and running rigging. Let's assume that you are basically lazy or just have better things to do with your time than make and unmake beds. Let's also assume that leaving the pink blanket on one cushion when all the rest of the cushions are covered in turquoise plaid Herculon doesn't fit your concept of a tidy ship. If all of the above is true about you, perhaps you should consider making fitted sheets with interior matching quilts or daycovers as a means of achieving both your goals: comfortable beds to sleep in and a tidy and good-looking interior.

Once you have decided that storing bedding in lockers is not for you, you can move on to designing an interior with daycovers to match your interior cushions. Better yet, you can start from the beginning and design an entire interior with fitted sheets and daycovers for the V-berths, owners' stateroom, and pilot berths.

Fitted Sheets and Bedspreads

All that is required to make fitted sheets is a bit of elastic, some thread, and sheets to cut down—either sheets you already own or new ones. If you buy new sheets, consider using the large king- and queen-size sheets as well as those closest to the size of

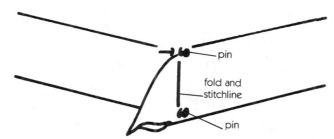

Figure 30–1.
Pinning the dart.

your berth. Sometimes it is possible and economical to get two boat sheets out of one large sheet, with little waste. Don't throw away any scraps; at the very least, they make good rags, and I have even been able occasionally to make draperies or pillowcases from leftover scraps.

Materials

- sheets to be cut down for each berth
- 48 inches of ¼-inch flat elastic to sew around the corners of each sheet

Construction

Step 1. Bottom Sheets: Lay the sheet, right side up, over the mattress to be fitted. With a pin mark the place where the mattress's upper corners hit the sheet.

Step 2. At each corner pin in the dart that will be made (Figure 30–1). For outside corners greater than 90 degrees, make darts as marked, or simply cut a curve around the corner, and the elastic will take up the slack (Figure 30–2). For an inside corner, leave enough slack mate-

rial for the sheet to cover it. An inside corner will take more cloth than an outside corner (Figure 30–3).

Step 3. Cut off the excess material. Be sure to leave enough material to cover the sides of the mattress, plus 2 inches (Figure 30–4).

Step 4. Stitch the darts and cut off the excess material. Hem the outside edges you have cut, using a small, rolled hem.

Step 5. Cut pieces of elastic 12 inches long to sew to each corner. If one end of the sheet is only 20 inches or so long, cut one piece of elastic to sew around the entire end.

Step 6. Pin one end of the elastic 10 inches away from the corner along the end edge, and the other end of the elastic 10 inches away from the corner along the side edge.

Step 7. Begin sewing at one end, stretching the elastic as you sew. The elastic should stretch enough so that the sheet remains flat until after the presser foot has passed over it. Then the elastic will relax

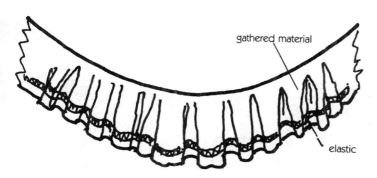

Figure 30–2.
Making an outside corner greater than 90 degrees.

*Figure 30–3.
Making an inside
corner.*

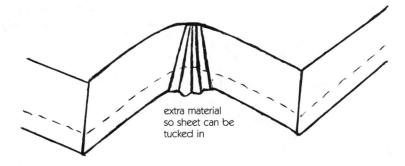

extra material
so sheet can be
tucked in

*Figure 30–4.
Leave enough material
to cover the sides of the
mattress, plus an
additional 2 inches.*

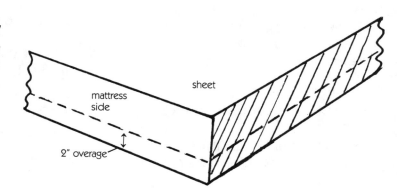

sheet

mattress
side

2" overage

*Figure 30–5.
Stitching the elastic.*

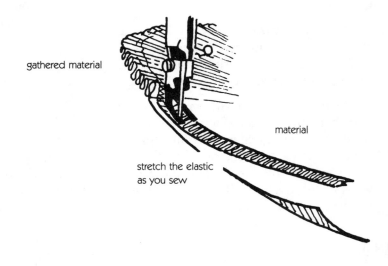

gathered material

material

stretch the elastic
as you sew

*Figure 30–6.
Blanket binding.*

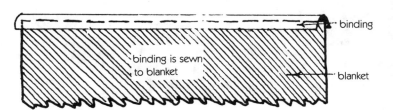

binding

binding is sewn
to blanket

blanket

and gather the sheet (Figure 30–5).

Step 8.   Repeat steps 6 and 7 for all corners.

Top Sheets and Blankets

Measure top sheets and blankets the same way you measured the bottom sheet, but make corners at the foot only. The sides of the top sheets and blankets should be left at least 8 inches wider than the mattress on both sides to allow a person to roll over and still be covered. Hem the sides, and make the corners at the foot of the sheets as you did for the bottom sheets. The head of the sheet will have been hemmed by the factory.

Blankets can be cut and fitted at the bottom exactly like sheets. Blanket-binding tape to bind the edges can be purchased from any fabric store. Fold this binding over the raw edge of the blanket, and stitch through all three thicknesses at once (Figure 30–6).

Bedspreads

Quilts or heavy-fabric spreads can also be fitted. It is often desirable to allow a spread to hang slightly over the edge of the berth (Figure 30–7). In this case, take very small darts at the foot of the spread and cut the extra overhang from that point. Half-inch elastic might be preferable for the corners of very heavy material.

A V-berth can be finished nicely with one spread for both berths. Place the spread you are cutting down or adequate cloth over the V-berth cushions. Mark the outside corners at the foot of the berth and make darts. Place elastic around the entire end. Put the spread back on the cushions and mark the inboard, outboard, and head edges of the spread. Allow for the side edge and a 2-inch overlap, as you did with the sheets. Cut the cloth and hem all around the edges. Finish the inside edge with blanket binding or bias tape of a matching or contrasting color.

Pillowcases and Bolster Covers

Pillowcases or bolster covers that match or complement your upholstery or bedspread make an attractive addition to your vessel's interior. A pillowcase also allows you to use a sleeping pillow for lounging without soiling the pillow, and because it fits in with your decor, it eliminates the need to stow the sleeping pillow in a locker during the day.

The simplest pillowcase to make is a

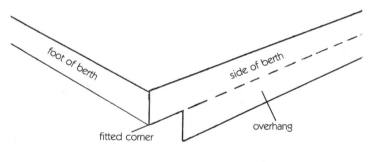

*Figure 30–7A.
Spread overhang.*

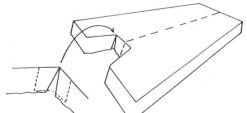

*Figure 30–7B.
Measuring for a V-berth
spread.*

Figure 30–8.
Case-type cover with Velcro.

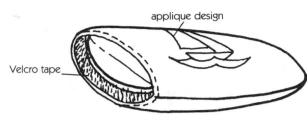

applique design

Velcro tape

Figure 30–9.
Overlapping pillow cover.
When the long edges are sewn
together, the pillowcase is
turned right side out through
the opening.

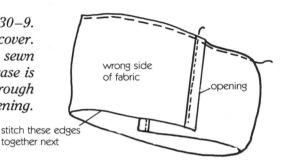

wrong side
of fabric

opening

stitch these edges
together next

Figure 30–10.
Bolster pillow cover with
zipper.

Figure 30–11A.
Quilted boxed daycover.

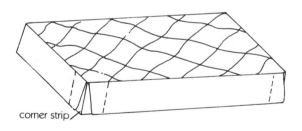

corner strip

copy of a regular pillowcase, made of matching or contrasting fabric and fastened with snaps or Velcro tape at the open end. A pattern can be taken from a regular pillowcase. Appliqués, embroidery, needlepoint, and monogramming can be used to dress up the pillowcase, if desired.

Another method of making a pillowcase requires no fastening. This type of pillowcase has overlap edges and works best with small prints or plain material that doesn't require matching. First, cut a piece of fabric long enough and wide enough to fit the pillow with the overlap. If

the pillow is 24 inches long (as measured with a string laid over the pillow) and 16 inches wide, make the fabric 32 inches long and 17 inches wide. Hem both ends with a narrow hem. Fold the cloth wrong side out so that it matches the size of the pillow and overlaps on one side, and pin. Sew the pillowcase up both long edges with the right sides together. Turn it right side out.

A bolster-type pillowcase is another nice way to stow extra pillows that are used only when guests are aboard. Such bolsters can also be used to stow bedding that

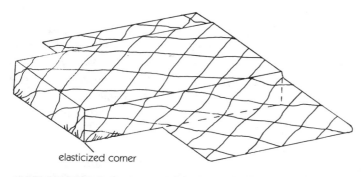

Figure 30–11B.
Tucked-in quilt (top), *and a fitted comforter with barrel quilting pattern and matching shams.*

elasticized corner

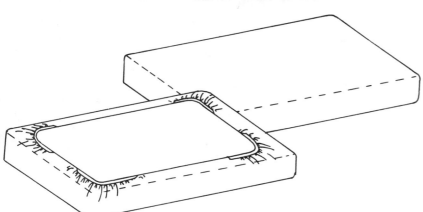

Figure 30–12. This darted day-cover, with all four corners elasticized, would be removed for sleeping.

is not needed often and is difficult to stow. A round bolster is constructed exactly like a duffel bag, but without handles. For more complete instructions, refer to Chapter 7. To make a simple bolster, roll up the pillow or bedding the way you would like it to be in its finished shape.

Measure the diameter, circumference, and overall length of the roll. Cut two circles to match the diameter, one for each end, and one length of cloth to match the circumference and the overall length of the main piece. Remember to add seam allowances and hems. Put in the zipper as Chapter 7 describes—a long dressmaker's dress zipper will usually do—and stitch in the end pieces. Turn the bolster right side out, and there you have a wonderful bolster for your weary back and stowage for your pillows or bedding.

Daycovers

There are different types of daycovers that will look like upholstered cushions when they are made up, including the boxed cover, the tucked-in cover, and the darted cover. A boxed cover is actually a flat piece of fabric with a skirt that goes around three sides of the cushion (Figure 30–11). Note that the sides of the boxed daycover are only as long as the cushion is deep. For this reason, you would not be able to sleep under it for warmth; it would have to be removed for sleeping or at least rolled down to the foot of the berth. A fitted blanket could be used under the daycover for warmth; the alternative is to make a tucked-in cover—a fitted daycover with extra width along the sides to allow the sleeper to lie on his side and still be covered. These sides are tucked under the cushion during the daytime for a fitted look.

Decide what type of cover will work best for you. If appearance is the most important feature, choose a boxed or darted cover (Figure 30–12) because it will look the most finished. If you want to use the daycover for warmth while you sleep and possibly eliminate the need for a blanket, choose the tucked-in cover. Whichever design you choose, I recommend that the daycover stop at the head of the berth rather than having an additional overlap that needs to be tucked in. The less bulk you have, the easier the berth will be to make and the fewer lumps and bumps you will have to sleep with. (A darted cover, obviously, will have to go over the head of the cushion to stay in place.)

Fabric Choices

Most daycovers are made of medium-weight cotton or cotton-polyester-blend fabrics. I like to choose a fabric with dense thread count so that it feels smooth and cool to the touch, much like a sheet. For ease in making up the bed each day, though, the daycover must have some weight to it. If the fabric is too light, it will wrinkle and look unkempt. For this reason you often find that daycovers are made of quilted fabric. The extra body that the batting and lining add to the cover will allow the fabric to lie smooth and handle easily. And a quilted fabric will also provide some warmth.

Velvet also makes a nice daycover, but the daycover must be of the sort that tucks under the cushion like a blanket. Quilted

*Figure 30–13.
Measuring the
fabric right on
the cushion.*

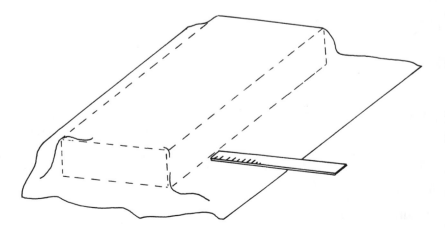

velvet doesn't work well because the nap of the fabric will crush unnaturally. By tucking a velvet cover under the cushion, you can pull the wrinkles out; the fabric has enough body of its own to resist the small wrinkles of very light cotton.

I do not recommend making daycovers out of Herculon-type fabrics, because they will not be comfortable to sleep under. If you do not plan to sleep under it and you want to match the main saloon fabric, you can make a darted daycover, with all four corners elasticized, that you would remove entirely for sleeping (Figure 30–12). You may find that Herculon-type daycovers will not fold up very tightly because the latex backing used in making this sort of fabric adds bulk.

Quilting

If you want your daycover to be quilted, there are two ways to go about it. The first is the easiest and often the least expensive. Sheet manufacturers often make quilts to match their sheets. If you can find a print or color that is compatible with your interior decor, you can buy ready-made quilts of a size that will fit the berth you wish to cover.

If you have ordered fabric by the yard, you can also inquire if the mill will quilt it for you. Most distributors of fabric have facilities for quilting most of their quilt-able fabric. It will probably add about $10 per yard to the cost of the fabric. If you want to quilt the fabric yourself, you will need lots of pins.

Buy enough fabric to do the job. Also buy enough lining—usually a cotton or cotton-polyester blend—to back the quilt with. The width of the lining may be different from the width of the quilt material, but that will not matter if the berth is narrower than the narrowest fabric. If the berth is wider than either fabric, you will have to buy enough to sew panels together to get the width you need.

Materials
- fabric of choice

For quilted covers:
- fabric for lining
- synthetic batting

For boxed covers:
- buckram

For darted and tucked-in covers:
- medium- to heavy-weight elastic

Construction

Step 1. Measure the cushion for the cover type you have chosen.

Darted Cover: A darted cover is made exactly like a bottom fitted sheet. Measure the top of the berth, add the height of the

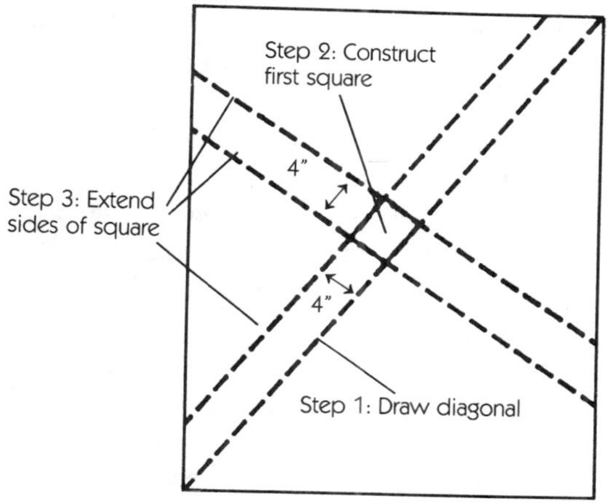

Figure 30–14. Drawing a pattern of diamonds on a quilt. After Step 3, rule off parallel lines at 4-inch intervals in both directions until the pattern is complete.

sides of the cushion, and add 2½ inches for the fabric to tuck under the bottom of the cushion.

Boxed Cover: Measure the top of the cushion and the height of the sides.

Tucked-in Cover: Measure the length and width of the cushion and the side height of the cushion at the foot end of the berth. Add 12 inches to the height of the cushion on both sides of the cover to accommodate a person's shoulders.

Step 2. Create a piece of fabric wide enough to do the job. Don't forget to add seam allowance where necessary. For instance, if the berth cushion measures 49 inches across at the head and your fabric is only 36 inches wide, you will need to sew two panels together to obtain the necessary width, no matter what type of daycover you are making. The easiest way to measure the cushion and cut the fabric is to create a wide enough piece of fabric and lay it over the top of the cushion it is intended to fit (Figure 30–13).

If you are making a darted cover, you can pin or mark the darts right on the cushion. If you are making a tucked-in cover, you can pin the darts at the foot of the cushion, using the cushion as a form, and then measure 12 inches out from the edge of the cushion as it lies on the floor to mark the cutting line. If you will be quilting your fabric, be sure to cut it 3 inches bigger than the measurements call for— the quilting will cause the fabric to take up, or shrink.

Step 3. Quilting (optional): If you decide to quilt your fabric, you must first choose a quilting pattern. The easiest patterns are diamonds, squares, and lines. The most time-consuming pattern is the one that follows the fabric print. To decide which pattern will look best on your fabric, look at the print on the fabric. If there are lines, squares, or diamonds on the print,

simply stitch on those lines. If the fabric is a floral print that lends itself to one of the above patterns, choose the one that fits the layout of the flowers best. If you have trouble visualizing the patterns on your fabric, get come correction tape in an office supply store, and tape the proposed lines on your fabric. If none of the geometric patterns work, you have to quilt the print itself. Usually this is done by choosing the dominant flower or shape in the print. The problem is trying to connect your stitching line from one shape to the next. If you can determine a quilting pattern that will allow you to stitch from one shape to another, great. If not, you will have to cut your thread between each shape that you want quilted.

Let's assume that the fabric you have chosen looks nice with a 4-inch diamond pattern but does not have diamonds in the print. Lay the fabric out flat. Using a water-soluble chalk pencil, create one diamond by first drawing a diagonal line between opposite corners of the fabric. With a carpenter's square, draw a 4-inch square that lies diagonally on the fabric, using the first line you drew as one of the sides of the diamond. Once you have created your first diamond, you can take all the rest of your lines from it. Extend each line until you run out of fabric. Measure 4 inches away from the first lines in both directions in several places along the line, and draw another line. Continue in this fashion until the entire piece of fabric has been lined (Figure 30–14).

On a flat surface, first lay out the lining fabric that will form the backing of the quilt. On top of that, lay a piece of batting material. If you need more than one width of batting, stitch two panels together with an overhand stitch. Lay your cover fabric on top of the batting. Make sure that all these layers are smooth and as wrinkle-free as possible. Place pins approximately every 6 to 8 inches all over the cover fabric so that all of the layers are securely pinned together. Don't place a pin on a stitching line. If you are trying to match two covers, as for a V-berth, you must be sure to match your quilting lines as well as the fabric pattern.

Stitch through all layers of the quilt using a fairly long stitch. If your stitch-length dial gives you a choice of 1 through 5, use a 4 setting. Be sure to hold all the layers of fabric tight and flat so that you don't create wrinkles to stitch over. If your fabric starts to get out of line with the pins you placed, re-pin the whole quilt, or rip out what you have done and start over. You will not be able to get rid of the excess fabric otherwise, and you'll probably end up with a pleat in the middle of the piece if you don't.

Step 4. Cutting: Lay the fabric on the cushion. Be sure to align the fabric with the fore-and-aft line of the boat.

Darted Cover: If you are going to make two daycovers for two cushions that are mirror images of each other, you can turn the fabric upside down so that the lining is facing up. Pin the darts or mark them with chalk. Hold the fabric so that it molds to the cushion and drapes down to the work surface. Measure out from the edge of the cushion 2½ inches, and mark the cutting line all around the cushion. Cut on this line. If you are making only one cover of a particular shape, lay the fabric on the cushion right side up and measure for the cutting line (Figure 30–15).

Tucked-in Cover: Again, lay the fabric

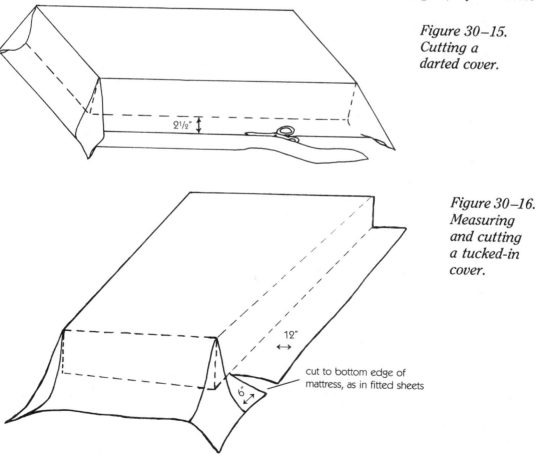

*Figure 30–15.
Cutting a
darted cover.*

2½"

*Figure 30–16.
Measuring
and cutting
a tucked-in
cover.*

12"

6"

cut to bottom edge of
mattress, as in fitted sheets

Figure 30–17A. Measuring and cutting a boxed cover.

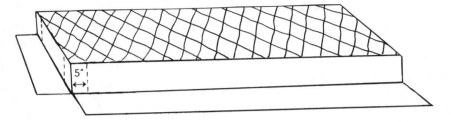

Figure 30–17B. Component pieces for boxed daycover.

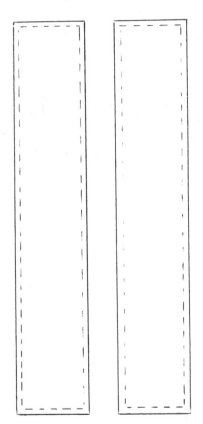

side skirts

top piece

corner strips

foot skirt

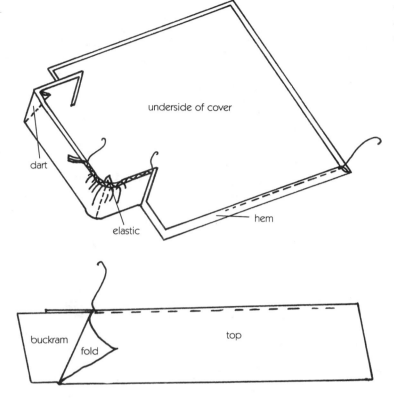

*Figure 30–18.
Hemming a tucked-in
cover.*

*Figure 30–19.
Placing buckram in
skirt strips for a
boxed cover.*

on the cushion, and line up the print with the fore-and-aft line of the boat. Fit the cover around the two corners of the foot of the cushion, just as you did the darted cover. Measure 6 inches toward the head of the cushion from the foot, then measure out 12 inches from the bottom edge of the cushion. Carry this measurement up both sides of the cushion, staying always 12 inches away from the edge of the cushion. That way, if your cushion gets progressively wider as you move toward the head (and most berth cushions do), your cover will get wider too (Figure 30–16).

Boxed Cover: If you are using quilted fabric, use it only on the top of the cushion. The same fabric, unquilted, should be used on the sides to reduce bulk. Again, lay the fabric on the top of the cushion, and mark the outside edge of the top of the cushion. Cut ¹/₂ inch away from this line.

Measure the height of the cushion, and cut three strips of fabric, whose length equals that of the right side, left side, and foot of the cushion respectively, and whose width equals twice the height measurement plus 1 inch (Figure 30–17). Also, cut corner strips to mask the corners of the cushions. These strips should be the same width as the side and foot skirts but only 10 inches long. You will also need strips of buckram (available at your local sewing store) which will stiffen the skirt, to match the length of each skirt. The buckram should be as wide as the finished length of the skirt plus ¹/₂ inch.

Step 5. Stitching:

Darted Cover: Refer to the beginning of this chapter for instructions on how to stitch a fitted sheet. The darted cover is made exactly the same way. Use ¹/₂-inch

Figure 30–20. Placing the corner strips in a boxed cover.

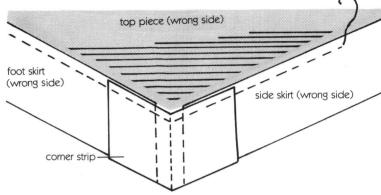

Figure 30–21. Sewing bias tape to the raw edge of the seam allowance.

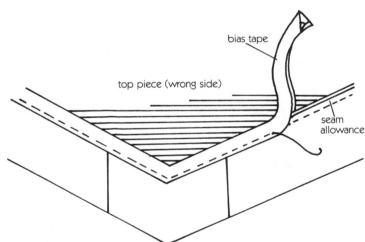

elastic of medium to heavy weight if you are using medium to heavy fabric.

Tucked-in Cover: Stitch the darts at the foot end of the cover. Cut away the excess fabric. Hem the outside edge of the entire cover. Stitch elastic in the two darted corners (Figure 30–18).

Boxed Cover: Stitch a narrow rolled hem at the head of the cover. Take each strip of fabric that you cut for a skirt, and press it in half, right side out. Place a strip of buckram the width of the skirt inside this folded strip. Baste it along the bottom edge if you don't feel you can keep the fabric flat while you stitch the top edge. Stitch the top edge of each strip (Figure 30–19). When you finish stitching the strips, pin them to the appropriate edges of the cover top. Pin the corner strips over the top of the side and end strips so that they overlap (Figure 30–20). Stitch the skirt to the top. For a finished look on the inside of the cover, fold bias tape over the raw edge of the seam allowance, and stitch in place (Figure 30–21).

31
Curtains

Curtains aboard any vessel should be functional, practical, and attractive. Whether you are closing out the night and the people in the next slip, or dividing the forward head from the forward cabin, a curtain does not provide privacy if you can see through, under, or around it. Nor is it desirable for the curtain to float on the wind from an open port or sway in and out with the motion of the boat. It is necessary, therefore, to design boat curtains that are securely fastened and easy to open and close. It is equally important to make them of a material that washes well, resists water staining and mildew, and retains its shape. The hardware used to hang and fasten the curtains should be rustproof: brass, stainless steel, plastic, or aluminum.

Fabric

Most synthetic fabrics such as nylon, polyester (including Dacron), and fiberglass wear well aboard boats. Before buying material, be sure to check the fabric for washing instructions. Because most curtains aboard will often be wet or damp, it is impractical to have to dry clean them.

Polyester and cotton blends are excellent for the hardiest curtains but may limit your choice of pattern and texture.

Unless you are an experienced seamster, choose a pattern or texture that does not have to be matched. A plaid pattern or a horizontal stripe will need to be matched from one curtain to the next. You will need about one-third more cloth if you choose a pattern that must be matched.

Lining Fabric

Woven cloth that looks the same or nearly the same on both sides may not have to be lined. If lining isn't necessary to darken the curtained area, this type of fabric is a wonderful choice, since lining curtains is difficult and expensive. However, if your chosen material rots in sunlight, you may save money in the long run by lining the curtains with a sun-resistant fabric. There are some synthetic linings that are coated with a rubbery latex to keep water from reaching the drapery fabric and also to act as a total sunscreen. For large saloon windows this lining is probably a good investment. If your curtain fabric is washable

*Figure 31–1.
Pleated drapes, fastened
top and bottom.*

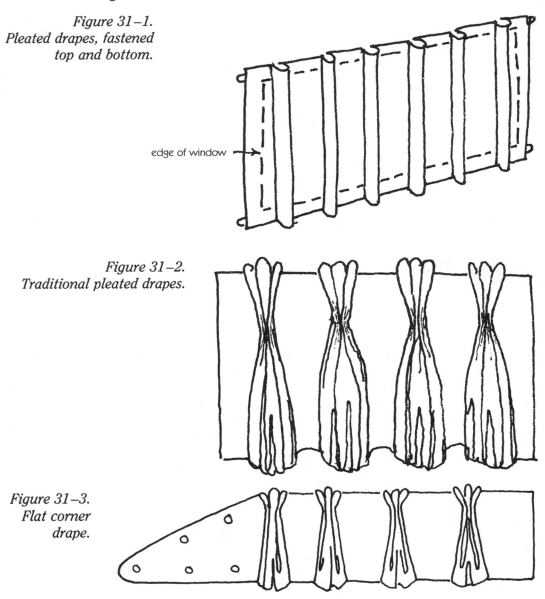

edge of window →

*Figure 31–2.
Traditional pleated drapes.*

*Figure 31–3.
Flat corner
drape.*

and preshrunk, your lining fabric should be as well.

Shape

Shape, as well as color and texture, should be carefully considered before buying fabric. Large saloon windows in power yachts can be curtained in many ways but the most functional style is the pleated drape that follows the window shape and fastens at the top and bottom of the window.

If the boat is rarely used in rough seas, a traditional pleated drape can be used without being fastened to the bottom of the window (Figure 31–2).

Beware of large windows. They may seem to be parallel to the cabin sole or overhead but often are not. Careful measuring will be necessary to achieve an even hem.

Corner windows on power yachts are

often covered with a flat drape. A more attractive drape can be made by pleating the angle as well (Figures 31–3, 31–4).

Shirred (gathered) drapes can be used to cover the forward windows of the saloon.

Round or oval ports can be covered with a "showercap"-type of curtain. This can be slipped over the port when privacy is desired and easily stowed when not needed (Figure 31–5).

Cabin sides with a row of ports that open can be curtained with traditional casing curtains. They can be closed when the port is closed or slid to the side when the ports are open. These curtains can have rods at the top and bottom (Figures 31–6, 31–7).

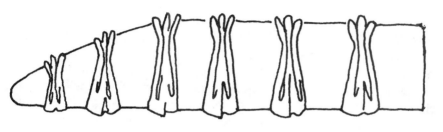

Figure 31–4.
Pleated corner
drape.

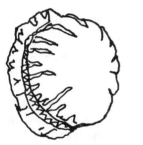 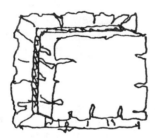

Figure 31–5.
"Showercap" curtains.

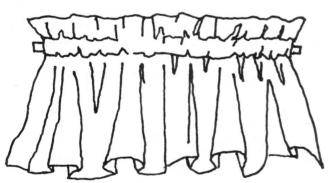

Figure 31–6.
Casing curtain over forward
windows.

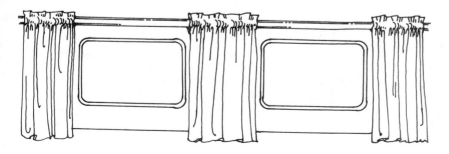

Figure 31–7.
Casing
curtains in the
saloon.

Variations on the casing curtain can be used to cover lockers, doorways, and hatches.

Tiebacks

Tiebacks should be used whenever a curtain is longer than 15 inches and is not fastened at the bottom. The tiebacks will restrict the motion of the curtain and keep it shipshape.

Fastenings and Hardware

When you are choosing hardware for your curtains, take into consideration the type of drape you are hanging, where the curtains will fall, and where you must fasten the hardware. A simple drape that does not have to be pleated or full may be easily attached to a bulkhead with Velcro tape. Use contact cement to hold the softer strip to the bulkhead and sew the prickly side of the Velcro tape to the top of the curtain. This type of drape can be removed when not in use. Café curtain rods for casing curtains can be used on the top and bottom of a curtain, or you can make your own rods out of wooden blocks and dowels.

Whatever you use, don't buy hardware made of metal (ferrous) that will rust. Check it with a magnet if in doubt. Stick to brass, aluminum, plastic, or stainless steel, or your curtains will be rust-stained in no time, especially in a saltwater environment.

There are several different brands of hardware for hanging pleated drapes. Kirsch of Sturgis, Michigan, manufactures the Marinetrac system most often installed in production boats, but there are many others that are similar. Basically the system consists of a slotted track that is mounted on the overhead or the top of a window casement. Several different types of tabs are offered for attaching the drape to the track.

The snap carrier is used in combination with snap-on tape. This tape is used in the same manner as pleater tape and often has the pleat marks already stamped on the tape. If you wish to cut down on costs, use sew-on tabs. They are easily stitched to the top of the drape and don't tear easily. Be careful to place all the tabs at exactly the same level or your hemline will be thrown off.

When you buy Kirsch hardware, you get a table of measurements for making curtains with 60 percent fullness using the Kirsch snap-tape system. This table will work with the sew-on tabs, too, and you can increase the fullness if you wish.

Another type of curtain hardware that I have had good results with is called Aqua

Figure 31–8. Marinetrac hardware for hanging pleated drapes.

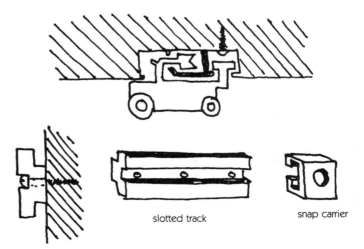

slotted track   snap carrier

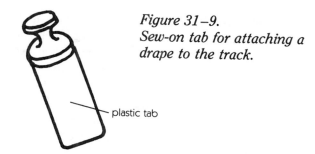

Figure 31–9.
Sew-on tab for attaching a
drape to the track.

plastic tab

Glide and can be found at most good chandleries. Figure 31–10 shows the many cross sections of track available. Obviously you will use one section for overhead mounting, one section for cabin-side mounting, and one section for shower curtains. You will need the appropriate end stops and mounting hardware for each section of track. The plastic tabs are sewn directly to the curtain with your sewing machine. These tabs slide fairly easily and are incorporated into many styles of curtains. I think you will find Aqua Glide a workable system for many applications.

When planning your curtains, be sure to consider the safety aspect of their positioning. Power yachts with flying bridges often have curtains over the forward windows of the saloon because the owners never plan to use the inside steering station. However, the first squall that forces them below often makes them curse drapes that won't open easily. Remember that curtains near stoves, navigation instruments, or engine controls can pose a hazard. Consider also that curtains that

are not firmly fastened may interfere with safe handling of the vessel.

Preparing the Fabric

The secret to well-made drapes that do not sag or hang unevenly is cutting the panels exactly "on grain." There are two sets of threads that make up a woven fabric: the warp that runs lengthwise and the weft that runs crosswise. The warp threads should parallel the selvage of the fabric. These threads are usually stronger than the weft threads, and so most curtain panels are cut along the lengthwise grain. Be sure that all the warp and weft threads in your fabric run at right angles to each other or your curtains will sag. If a fabric is treated with a soil-release or permanent-press finish, you will not be able to straighten the grain of the fabric. In this case, be sure that the pattern is printed "on grain" before buying the fabric. An off-grain pattern cannot be matched.

If the fabric is not labeled "preshrunk," clean the fabric before you cut it, in exactly the way you intend to clean it in the fu-

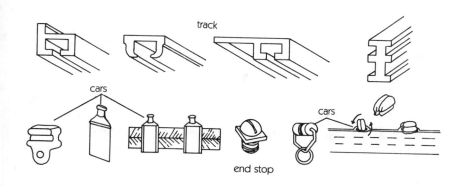

track

cars

end stop

cars

Figure 31–10.
Aqua Glide
curtain
hardware.

ture, i.e., wash it in warm water and tumble dry. This should ensure that any shrinking will take place before the curtains are cut.

Finding the grain is the next step. If the fabric can be torn without pulling the threads off grain, snip the selvage about 1 inch deep, and tear the fabric with a quick pull right across to the opposite selvage edge. If the cloth will not tear, snip the selvage edge until you can pick up one or two crosswise threads, and pull these threads gently until you create a line to the opposite selvage edge. Then cut along this thread line from selvage to selvage. Plaids can be straightened by cutting across the material on the edge of a bold crosswise stripe. If none of the above methods will work, ravel the edge of the cloth until one thread can be pulled all the way out. One of these methods will give you the first straight edge for cutting the panels of the curtains. Careful measurement from this first straight edge should keep you "on grain" for the rest of the panels. If you're not sure, rip another straight grain thread before you cut each panel.

Lining

Prepare the lining fabric the same way you prepare the curtain fabric. Be sure to find the straight of the grain before cutting any panels.

Measurements

Length

Measure each window or port that you are going to curtain. They may look alike but often are not. (Right angles on boats are hard to find.) Where do you want the curtain to stop—just above the covering board, just below the sill? What will your fasteners do to the length of the curtain? If they will lower it, be sure to take that into account when figuring length. Pleater hooks raise the curtain, so be sure to add

extra length if you are going to use them. Casement curtains will rise a bit when the rod is inserted, so remember to make them a little longer than the measurement indicates. A standard hem for casing curtains is 2 to 3 inches, and 3- or 4-inch hems are usually used on pleated drapes. When cutting your fabric, add enough to fold over along the desired hem with an extra 1/2 inch to be tucked under to finish the raw edge. Also be sure to add enough fabric to finish the top edge of the curtain. An example of a casing curtain layout would be:

- the space you want to cover = 11 inches
- you want a casing of 1 inch to accommodate rod = 1 inch
- you want a 1/2-inch ruffled header at the top (add 1 inch here to achieve 1/2-inch header front and back) = 1 inch
- you want 1/2 inch to turn under to finish edge = 1/2 inch
- you want a 2-inch hem on the bottom = 2 1/2 inches
- total length to cut = 16 inches

A pleated curtain will need enough fabric on the top to cover the width of buckram you are using and enough extra fabric for the hem. For instance:

- the space you want to cover = 36 inches
- you are using 4-inch buckram to stiffen top edge = 4 1/2 inches
- you want a 4-inch hem = 4 1/2 inches
- total length to cut = 45 inches

Width

Casing curtains or café curtains should be at least half again as wide as the area that they are to cover. An attractive curtain will result if the curtain panel is twice as wide as the window or port. Pleated curtains traditionally use fabric panels three times the width of the window, but they will also be attractive at just twice the width. Try to plan the panels of wide drapes so that they are somewhat symmetrical. A ½-inch seam is enough between panels, and 1 or 2 inches should be allowed for side hems.

Ironing

When making any type of curtain, use a steam iron before you stitch anything. Careful measurement as you press in hems and seams will give you perfect curtains. For instance, after the panels have been sewn together, press the seam allowances open and flat. Then press in the top-edge hem. If you want a 2-inch hem, measure exactly 2½ inches all the way along the top, fold over that amount, and press. Then do the bottom edge the same way. Check the overall length of the curtain. Finally, press the side hems, and then begin stitching. The same procedure should be followed with the lining of each curtain.

Casing Curtains

Casing curtains are the easiest to make and often the most practical choice aboard ship.

Materials Needed

- fabric of choice
- lining (optional)

Construction

Step 1. After preparing the fabric and cutting the necessary panels, sew the panels for each curtain together with a ½-inch seam. If you are using lining, prepare the lining in the same way.

Step 2. Place the curtain and lining panels right sides together, and stitch across the tops and sides. Turn right side out and press the panels flat.

Step 3. Hem the side edges with a 1-inch hem.

Step 4. Turn the top edge under enough to allow for the diameter of your curtain rod, plus ½ inch for hemming. Either stitch the hem exactly the width necessary to fit the curtain rod, or, if you wish to have a heading, hem the top so that the hem stitching forms the top of the casing and a second line of stitching forms the bottom (Figure 31–11).

Step 5. Finish the raw edge of the bottom by folding over a ½-inch hem on both the curtain and the lining. Stitch these edges together. If you wish to have rods in the bottom of the curtain, too, make another line of stitching, the width of the rod, above the first line of stitching for the bottom casing. Careful measurement of the length will be needed to achieve a tight-fitting curtain.

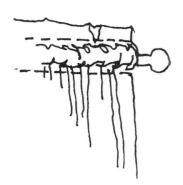
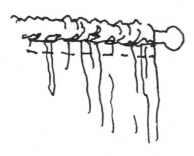

Figure 31–11.
Casing curtain
hems.

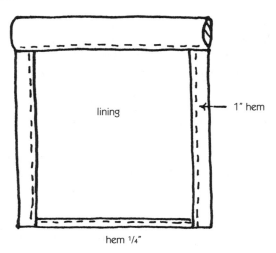

Figure 31–12.
Lining a casing curtain.

lining

1" hem

hem ¼"

Showercap Curtains

Showercap curtains are simple to make if
you make a paper pattern first.

Materials Needed

- fabric of choice
- elastic

Construction

Step 1. Hold a piece of heavy paper
up to the port you want to cover. With a
pencil, trace the outside edge of the port.
Add to the paper pattern the depth of the
port, from outside edge to cabin side. For
instance, if the port protrudes 2 inches out
from the cabin side, extend the outline on
the paper pattern 2 inches all around. Add
1 inch more with which to make an outside ruffle (if desired) and ½ inch for the
hem. (With a 2-inch port depth you would
add a total of 3½ inches to the original
pattern outline.)

Step 2. Cut two pieces of fabric to fit
the extended paper pattern. You can make
the curtain reversible if you use a different
fabric for each side.

Step 3. Place these two pieces right
sides together. Allowing a ½-inch seam
allowance, stitch around the outside, leaving the last inch open. Turn showercap
curtain right side out through the opening
left in the seam.

Step 4. To make the outside ruffle,
measure in 1 inch from the outside edge,
and mark with a row of small dots all the
way around the edge. Stitch along these
dots, through both thicknesses, all the way
around, leaving a small opening above the
lower opening. Stitch again through both
thicknesses, ⅜ inch inside the first stitching line all the way around. If you have not
added the extra inch for a ruffled edge,
make only one line of stitching ⅜ inch in
from the outside edge.

Step 5. Measure and cut a length of
¼-inch elastic to fit snugly around the
port. Allow an extra inch for sewing the
ends together. Fasten a safety pin through
the end of the elastic, thread the elastic up
through the opening (or openings for a
curtain with a ruffle) and into the casing.
Pull both ends out of the openings, overlap
them 1 inch and stitch them together.
Work the elastic around the casing so it is
evenly distributed.

Step 6. Complete the outside casing
stitching and close the hem opening.
Stretch the elastic and place the showercap over the port when privacy is desired.

Pleated Curtains

Materials Needed

- fabric of choice
- lining (optional)
- buckram for stiffener

Pinch, Box, and Cartridge Pleats

Pinch pleats, box pleats, and cartridge pleats differ only in the manner in which they are folded. The pleats are marked off on the fabric after the side and bottom edges of a curtain have been hemmed. A stiffener is required in the top hem to make the pleats stand stiff and straight. This stiffener, or buckram, can be purchased by the yard in different widths at most fabric stores. It is usually 4 inches wide, which is fine for long drapes. Short pleat drapes, however, look better with a short pleat. If you cannot find the width

you need, cut the 4-inch buckram down to the desired width.

Pleater tape makes it easy to achieve uniform pinch pleats in a hurry. It will not always work on boats, because boats often do not have the space between the top of the window and the overhead to accommodate the hardware needed to hang the drapes. Instructions are usually included with the tape, so I will not discuss it further here.

Step 1. Measure the area to be covered, as described on page 190. Use either a 3:1 or a 2:1 ratio to determine the width of the fabric panels for your flat curtains.

Step 2. Lay the buckram over the top of the curtain's wrong side; stitch one edge of the buckram close to the top edge of the curtain. Turn the buckram to the wrong side of the curtain and then fold the

Figure 31–13.
Sewing in the buckram.

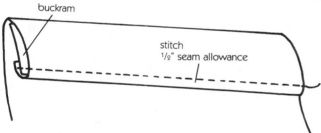

buckram

stitch
1/2" seam allowance

Figure 31–14.
Lining a pleated drape.

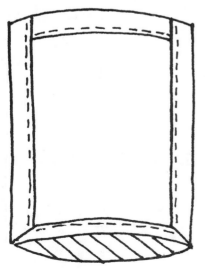

top of the curtain down so that the buckram is totally encased in fabric. Press this fold.

Step 3.   If no lining is to be used, press and hem the bottom and side edges of the curtain, then go to step 7. If the curtain is to be lined, follow steps 4–6.

Step 4.   After properly preparing the lining fabric, cut the panels needed.

Step 5.   Press and stitch the side seams and bottom hem in both the lining and the curtain. Place the lining and the curtain wrong sides together so that the top of the lining tucks under the buckram by ½ inch. Stitch the bottom edge of the covered buckram down so that the lining is stitched to the curtain at the top.

Step 6.   Stitch the side edges of the liner to the curtain. Press flat (Figure 31–14). The lining and the curtain should hang free of each other, with the lining approximately ¼ inch shorter than the curtain.

Step 7.   Box pleats and pinch pleats need from 3 to 5 inches to be effective. Cartridge pleats usually use 2½ inches of cloth. To determine how much cloth can be taken out with pleats, subtract the space measurement from the flat curtain measurement. Then divide this number by the width of each pleat or pleat allowance to determine how many pleats you need to make. For example, if you have made a 60-inch flat curtain for 20-inch window space, your calculations are as follows: The width of the curtain panel will be three times the width of the window (20 inches × 3 = 60 inches). Subtract 20 inches, the width of the window, from 60 inches, the width of your curtain panel, to determine how much fabric you have to pleat (60 − 20 = 40 inches). If you are using a 5-inch pleat, divide the 40 inches by 5 to obtain the number of pleats that will use up the excess fabric (40 ÷ by 5 = 8 pleats). If 8 pleats are required, there will be 9 spaces between them. Divide the planned curtain width by 9 in order to calculate the correct spacing between pleats (20 inches ÷ 9 = approximately 2¼ inches between pleats). Mark the top of the drape on the stiffener with small dots to tell you where to make the pleats (Figure 31–15).

Step 10.   Match the pleat dots on the stiffener and make a fold at the center of the pleat allowance. Stitch from the top of

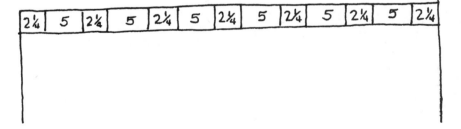

Figure 31–15 Marking the pleats.

Figure 31–16. Stitching the seam allowance.

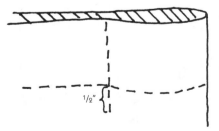

the curtain to about ½ inch below the stiffener. Backstitch both ends of this stitching line. Do this to all of the pleat allowances (Figure 31–16).

Step 11. Pinch pleats are made by folding the pleat allowances in thirds and hand-tacking or machine-stitching the pleats together (Figure 31–17).

Box pleats are made by folding the pleat allowance flat against the pleat seam so that the folds are equidistant from the middle of the pleat and hand-stitching

both pleats ½ inch above the lower edge of the buckram (Figure 31–18).

Cartridge pleats are made by stuffing the pleat allowance with a rolled piece of stiffener or cotton batting (Figure 31–19).

Pleats with Fasteners

Curtains that are fastened at the top and bottom with plastic slides can be pleated with the fastener.

Step 1. Prepare the curtain as you would a pleated drape, but put 4 inches of

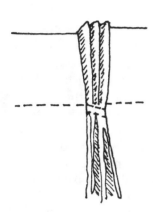

Figure 31–17.
Stitching a pinch pleat.

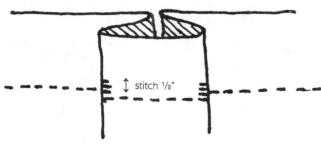

Figure 31–18.
Stitching a box pleat.

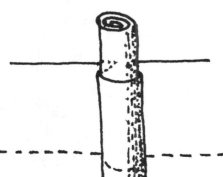

Figure 31–19.
Stuffing a cartridge pleat.

Figure 31–20.
Pleating with fasteners.

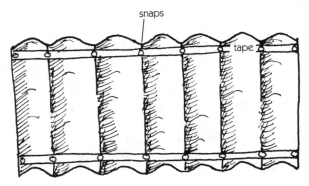

stiffener in the bottom as well as the top.

Step 2. Calculate the spacing of the plastic sliders so they will pleat attractively when the curtains are closed without looking too bulky when open. Mark the placement of the fasteners, being careful to keep the fasteners perfectly in line from top to bottom.

Step 3. Measure the exact distance between rods and transfer that distance to the curtain. Draw two lines, one across the top and the other across the bottom, to indicate the exact placement of each fastener. Measure the exact width you want the curtain to be when closed. Cut pieces

of bias twill tape exactly that length for both the top and bottom of the curtain.

Step 4. Pin the bias tape to the curtain at the spots you have marked for fasteners. Begin by pinning each end of the tape to the side edges of the curtain. Next pin the middle of the tape to the middle-fastener spot. Then divide the right section in half and pin the fasteners in that section. Continue pinning the tape to the fastener locations in this manner until you have all the pleats equally folded with pins. Tack the fastener and the tape to the curtain as you have pinned them. *Note:* The tape is sewn to the curtain under each fastener only.

Figure 31–21.
Setting the pleats.

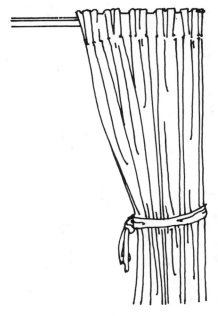

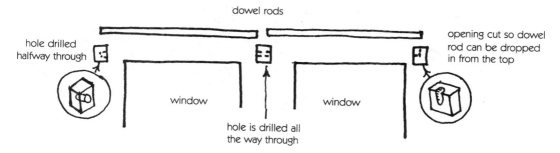

dowel rods

hole drilled
halfway through

opening cut so dowel
rod can be dropped
in from the top

window

window

hole is drilled all
the way through

Figure 31–22.
Wooden curtain rods.

Step 5. Hang the curtains by attaching first a top fastener, then a bottom one, until the entire curtain is hung. Pleat the drape as it should be, and tie it open for a few days to set the pleats.

Hanging the Curtains

All curtains look better after they have been hanging for a few days. You can help the curtains hang well if you will spend a few minutes gathering each curtain on the rod and arranging the pleats or the folds. Once you are satisfied that they are hanging correctly, tie each panel to set the pleats (Figure 31–21).

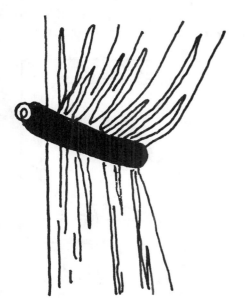

Tiebacks

To make a tieback out of the same material as the drapes, measure the circumference of the drape as it hangs in its open position. Cut a length of cloth 1 inch longer than this measurement and 1 inch wider than you want the tieback to be. Fold the strip of cloth in half, right sides together, and stitch one end and the open side edge. Turn the strip right side out, and hem the open end. Press. Decorative cording can be stitched on the right side of the tieback if desired. Attach the tieback to the bulkhead or window casing with a male snap that is screwed through one end of the tieback

Figure 31–23.
Tiebacks.

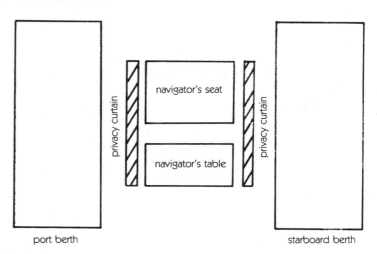

Figure 31–24. Privacy curtains for navigator's station and two quarter berths (top view).

and then into the window casing, and a female snap that is attached to the other end.

Tiebacks can also be made with spliced line, ribbon, or trim braid.

Privacy Curtains

Another type of curtain frequently needed aboard is a privacy curtain, used to create temporary partitions between open areas below decks. Usually such a curtain is fixed on three or four sides and does not move with the motion of the vessel. A good example of how well this kind of curtain can function was provided by a racing

yacht turned-cruiser-for-a-weekend-or-two, owned by an acquaintance of mine. Like many no-compromise racing boats, this one had an open interior, with very little in the way of accommodations. To accommodate a mixed crew, the owner installed a curtain around the head area to give a modicum of privacy. The two main sleeping berths were directly outboard of the navigator's station, which was set in the middle of the boat under the cockpit. From either berth the navigator's station and the opposite berth were clearly visible. No privacy. However, the navigator's station provided some joinery on which to fasten privacy curtains that would still al-

Figure 31–25. Hems and tabling on privacy curtains.

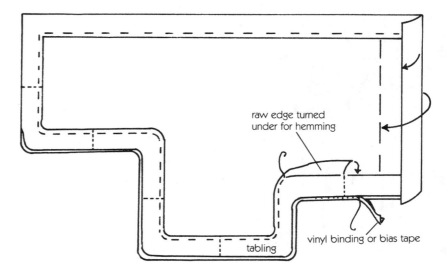

low the navigator to function while the crew slept (Figure 31–24). Two flat pieces of canvas joined with snaps to the woodwork around the navigator's station created three separate "staterooms"—easily removable when the boat returned to its racing mode.

Materials Needed

- canvas (cotton or acrylic), medium-to-heavy weight
- vinyl binding
- snaps

Step 1. Cutting: After taking accurate measurements of the space you want to enclose and determining where the snaps can fasten to the joinery, cut your piece of canvas to fit the space. If all the edges are straight, allow a 2½-inch hem all around the piece. If there are any curved sides, cut the fabric to fit the shape exactly.

Step 2. Tabling and Hemming: For straight edges, fold the fabric twice so that there is a double layer of fabric for the hem, and stitch once on the outside edge of the hem and once on the inside edge of the hem.

For curved edges, cut a piece of fabric that is 1½ inches wide and the exact shape of the curved edge. Lay this piece on the wrong side of the privacy curtain, and hem the inside edge by turning under ½ inch and stitching. Bind the outside edge in vinyl binding or bias tape so that raw edges are covered (Figure 31–25). Refer to Figure 15–14 for instructions on stitching vinyl binding.

Step 3. Installation: After you are certain that the curtain fits the space, ascertain that your snaps will all line up with the corresponding points on the joinery before you install any snaps. The simplest and surest way to align snaps is with the drill that you use to make the hole for the male half of the snap. Do the top two corners first. Position the curtain correctly. Drill through the fabric and into the wood or glass exactly where you want the snap to be. Install the female half of the snap in the curtain through the hole you made with the drill. Install the male half of the snap in the hole you made in the wood. Once the top two corners are installed, you can hang the curtain up and drill for the remaining top snaps. After the top is complete, install the bottom corners and then the remaining side snaps. If you need snaps along the bottom edge, install them last (Figure 31–26).

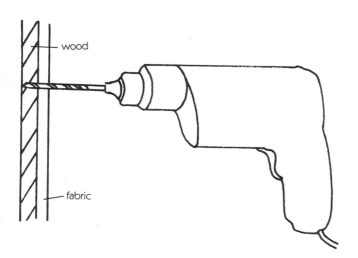

Figure 31–26.
Installing snaps with drill alignment.

wood

fabric

Figure 31–27.
Cutting darts in a shower
curtain track.

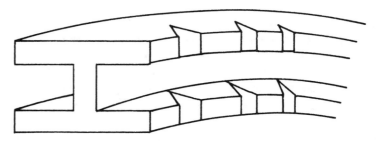

Shower Curtains

Shower curtains aboard can be fancy or plain. The important thing is obviously that they keep the shower water from damaging the joinery in the head. The easiest and most effective way to create a shower curtain is to buy a premade shower curtain and cut and hem it to fit your needs. The little wheeled cars that go with Aqua Glide shower curtain track can easily be fixed into the premade holes, and most shower curtains are light enough to be kept out of the way with a tieback.

Other options for shower curtains are cotton canvas because it is waterproof and nylon spinnaker cloth because it is light. Plastic or vinyl shower curtains need not be hemmed because they will not ravel. The new, woven synthetic shower curtains that need no liner are probably the most attractive shower curtain on the market.

Installing the shower curtain track is a simple matter if you follow instructions and if you only need a straight piece of track. If you need a curved piece of track, however, you will need a hacksaw or some sharp tinsnips to cut small wedges in the track so that you can bend it to the desired curve. If you go slowly and cut enough "darts," you can bend fairly tight curves (Figure 31–27).

32
Locker-Mounted Laundry Bag

Stowing dirty laundry can be a problem aboard many cruising boats. If you have a locker that is suitable for a laundry bin, consider designing a custom-fitted laundry bag. The bottom of a hanging locker will work well, since it has an opening large enough to allow the bag to be pulled out when full. Top-loading lockers will also work well if the opening is nearly as large as the locker itself. Deep lockers with small side or front openings may allow you to hang a bag, but once the bag is full you will not be able to remove it from the locker. (Even this may be preferable to allowing the dirty clothes to collect on the cabin floor; you'll simply have to reach in and empty the bag before you can remove it.) It is a nice touch if you can design this bag so that it will double as a carrying bag for the trip to the laundromat.

Materials Needed

- acrylic canvas,—10- to 13- ounce weight
- Dacron tabling for tabs
- fastenings: turnbuttons, snaps, or Lift-the-Dots

handle (optional)

- 2-inch webbing
- clips or snaphooks (if detachable)

drawstring (optional)

- piece of line (number 4 Dacron recommended)
- 2 grommets

Designing a Bag

If you want the maximum possible space in the bag, design it with square corners, a drawstring, and tabs for fastening it to the overhead of a top-loading locker or to the sides of a hanging locker (Figure 32–1). If you want to get really fancy, design a small pocket on the side somewhere for quarters. A bag that will double as a carrying bag should have a sturdy, 2-inch-webbing handle (the type used on duffel bags) that is stitched all the way around the bag to spread the load over the canvas (Figure 32–2). If space in the locker is a problem, this handle can be detachable, but in this case be sure to use strong hardware.

If the bag will always stay in the locker, or if space in the locker is extremely lim-

*Figure 32–1.
Laundry bag in top-
loading locker.*

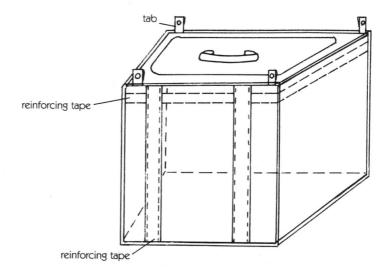

*Figure 32–2.
Portable laundry bag with
webbing handle and
drawstring.*

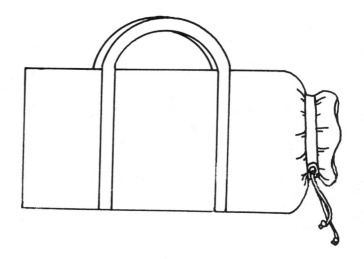

*Figure 32–3.
Laundry bags can be
patterned to conform to the
shape of your locker.*

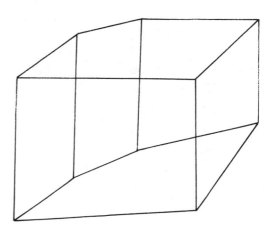

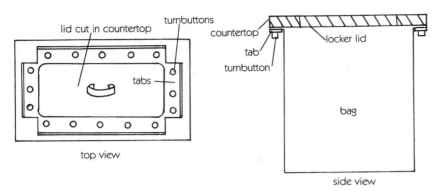

Figure 32–4. A laundry bag in a dry locker with a lifting lid.

ited, design the bag so that its shape exactly duplicates that of the locker. For instance, if the locker is on the outside edge of the boat and the bottom of the locker conforms to the boat's hull, you might have a bag similar to the one in Figure 32–3.

Determine how the bag will fasten to the locker. A top-, front-, or side-loading locker will probably need tabs on all four sides to fasten the bag to either the top or the side of the locker. A hanging locker will usually need tabs on three sides, leaving the door side to the locker unfastened (Figure 32–4). Choose strong fastenings that won't break when the bag is fully loaded. I recommend that you use twist fasteners because they do not pull loose easily and are simple to install.

Measuring

Measure the height, width, and depth of the space to be filled with the bag. If the shape is complicated (say, for example, there is a double angle in the bottom of your locker as in Figure 32–3), you can use a piece of paper or cardboard to pattern the space. Put the paper in the locker and trace the shape on the paper to determine what the bottom of the bag should look like.

Construction

Step 1. Cut all the necessary pieces with 1/2-inch seam allowances and 2 1/2-inch hems.

Step 2. If you want a drawstring in the top, mark its position on each piece before stitching the sides together. Be sure to place the drawstring at least 1 inch below the tabs.

Step 3. Stitch the sides together first, right sides together. Finish with a flat-felled seam. (*Note:* If your design includes a pocket for change, stitch it on before putting the sides together.)

Step 4. Stitch the handle in place, making sure that its webbing encircles the bag (Figure 32–2). If you chose to make part of the handle detachable, stitch the appropriate clips or snaphooks to the webbing at this time.

Step 5. Stitch the bottom into the bag, right sides together.

Step 6. Stitch a strip of fabric 2 inches wide to the inside of the bag at the positions marked for the drawstring. Stitch the side closest to the bottom of the bag first, turning under 1/4 inch as you go. Set two grommets in the outside layer of the bag where you want the drawstring to exit. (Backing squares may be desirable unless you are using 13-ounce canvas.) Lay the line inside the cloth strip, and run it out of each grommet before you stitch

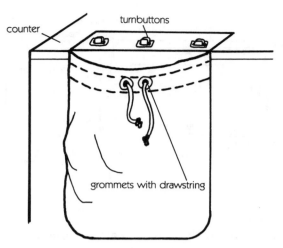

Figure 32–5. Grommets for drawstring with top of strip stitched.

the top side of this strip to the bag (Figure 32–5).

Step 7. Construct the tabs, making sure that they are heavily reinforced. I recommend that you use Dacron tabling for this task, sandwiching several layers of heavy Dacron in the middle for strength. After stitching each tab, stitch the tabs to the bag on their respective sides.

Step 8. Set the fastenings in the tabs, and attach the male end of the twist fasteners to the locker.

33
Galley and Navigator's Strap

Those of you who make ocean passages or sail in rough waters will need some way of holding yourselves in position while cooking or navigating (Figure 33–1). A galley or navigator's strap needs to be very strong and securely fastened to the boat. It should have non-loosening snapshackles at either end; these should fasten to padeyes or ring bolts that are through-bolted to something strong.

The idea behind such a strap is to be able to rest your weight against it when the boat heels in one direction and against the boat when the boat heels the opposite way. For this reason, the position of the strap is critical. If your galley is three-sided, it will be simple to "close the box" with a galley strap. But if your galley runs along one side of the boat and is not bracketed by bulkheads, it may be necessary to build something structurally sound to attach the strap to (Figure 33–2).

Since a galley strap is often stored away, it should be made of something mildew-resistant. I recommend one of the acrylic canvases, strengthened with an inner layer of 5-ounce Dacron. Nylon or Dacron webbing should be used for strapping. One-inch webbing is more than adequate for strength and will fit easily through the eye of most shackles.

I don't recommend that the strap be adjustable, because buckle systems usually depend on constant tension to work. With the boat bouncing around, you will be continually putting your weight on and off the strap, and a strong jolt could make the buckle slide and send you flying. If more than one person needs to use the strap and the size of each person is significantly different, I would suggest having a strap for each person, made to exactly the proper length.

Materials Needed

- 1 yard acrylic canvas
- ½ yard 5-ounce Dacron
- nylon or Dacron webbing
- 2 snapshackles
- 2 padeyes or ring bolts with nuts and washers
- vinyl binding (optional)

*Figure 33–1.
Galley strap.*

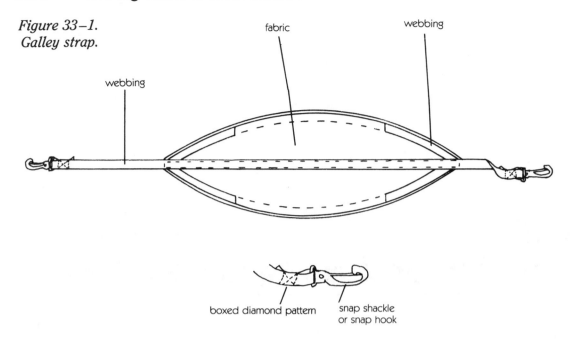

*Figure 33–2.
A three-sided
galley makes
positioning the
strap easy.*

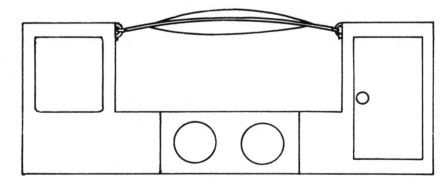

Construction

Step 1. Measure the maximum distance the galley strap will extend from padeye to padeye. My suggestion would be to make the fabric part of the strap between 30 and 36 inches long; the rest of the distance can be taken up by webbing. If your space is smaller than that, you must obviously make the cloth fit inside the padeye—*just* inside if necessary. Remember that your shackles will also take up a portion of the total distance.

Step 2. To draw the shape of the fabric portion of the strap, start by measuring out its length and maximum width on the canvas. Let's assume this portion of the strap is to be 30 inches long and a maximum of 14 inches wide. Locate the center of the strap by finding the center of the length (15 inches) and the center of the

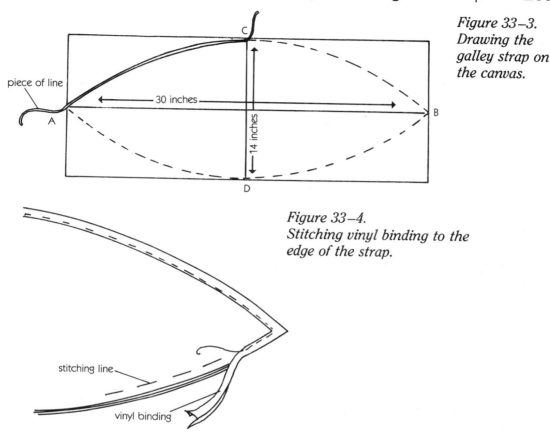

Figure 33–3. Drawing the galley strap on the canvas.

Figure 33–4. Stitching vinyl binding to the edge of the strap.

width (7 inches); then mark the four end points (A and B on the length lines; C and D on the width line). Picking any adjacent pair of points (say A and C) lay out a fair curve between them, using a thin batten or piece of line (Figure 33–3). Cut on this line just between these two points. Fold the fabric in half on the center length line, and draw this curve on the opposite side. Cut at this point. Fold the fabric on the center width line, and trace the two curves on the remaining half of the fabric.

Step 3. Cut one more piece of canvas and one piece of Dacron to match this piece.

Step 4. Pin all three layers of fabric together, with the Dacron in the middle. Stitch all around the fabric, through all the layers, 1/4 inch from the edge. For a sturdy finish, stitch vinyl binding all around the edge (Figure 33–4).

Step 5. Slide the shackles onto both ends of the webbing, and stitch the ends to the desired length, using a boxed diamond pattern (Figure 33–1). Stitch the webbing to the middle of the fabric portion of the strap. Reinforce the webbing by sewing 6 inches of webbing around the ends of the strap, as depicted in Figure 33–1.

Step 6. Install your padeyes or ring bolts in the boat, and check your measurements. Adjustments can be made by restitching the position of the shackles. Bear in mind that the weakest point of this system is usually where the padeyes are mounted. Use backing plates, if necessary, to ensure that the padeye's mounting point can withstand lots of pressure.

34
Lee Cloths

We've discussed the whys and wherefores of anchoring the cook and navigator during rough weather. Next, let's talk about anchoring sleeping crewmembers. If the crew can navigate, eat, and sleep, the passage should be a success.

Lee cloths and/or lee boards are used to keep sleeping crewmembers in their bunks. Some boats are equipped with 8-inch-wide or 10-inch-wide lee boards that drop into slots at either end of the bunks. I prefer lee cloths because they are softer to lean against. You might think about putting lee cloths on all possible berths (including pilot berths and settee berths) to offer your crew the greatest amount of comfort for the weather and the tack.

The length of the lee cloth should allow 12 to 18 inches of room between the bulkhead at the head of the berth and the leading edge of the cloth, to provide open air space for the sleeper's head. If possible, an air space should be left at the foot of the berth as well. For instance, a 6-foot berth should have a lee cloth 4 feet long, with 1 foot of air space at either end. The height should be approximately 18 inches, so that

a person sleeping on his or her side and leaning on the cloth will get plenty of support. Note that you can also use lee cloths to keep a small baby or toddler in a bunk. These cloths should be higher than adult-size cloths; in fact, they probably should enclose the entire opening so that the child cannot crawl out.

The simplest system is usually the best, no matter what you are trying to accomplish. The fastening system for lee cloths requires a piece of line tied to a grommet in each upper corner of the cloth and a ring bolt or padeye placed optimally fore or aft of the appropriate grommet and slightly inboard from the edge of the berth (Figure 34–1). This should allow each person to get into his or her bunk and still be able to tie up the lines. The bottom edge of the cloth is permanently secured to the berth by a batten installed beneath the cushion.

As with the navigator's and galley strap, the weakest link in the system will be where the lee cloth is tied to the vessel. Use a through-bolt if at all possible; otherwise use a number 10 screw and be certain

208

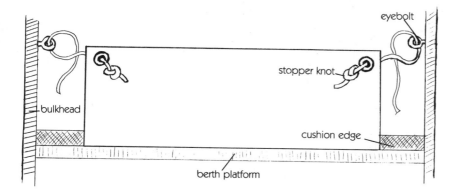

Figure 34–1A. Lee cloth configuration (bunk edge fiddle not shown).

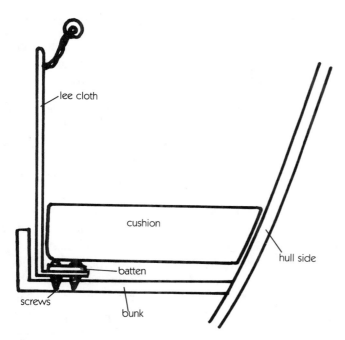

Figure 34–1B. Schematic section of lee cloth installation.

that it is securely fastened. The weight of a 200-pound man against the lee cloth will surely test a weak fastening.

Do not be tempted to attach snap-hooks to the end of the line that secures to the ring. If you have the snap positioned where it will stretch the fabric tight, you will not be able to hook it up. If you have the snap positioned so that you can hook it up, it will not create enough tension on the fabric to hold the sleeper securely.

The layout of each berth and the joinery surrounding it will determine the dimensions of the lee cloth for that bunk. Some situations are difficult and do not allow you to follow optimum rules. However, some protection is better than none.

Materials Needed

- canvas or Textilene (see below)
- Dacron tabling
- 2 grommets
- 2 ring bolts or padeyes
- lacing line
- aluminum or wood battens, the length of the lee cloth

I normally recommend that lee cloths be made of acrylic canvas because they are

Figure 34–2.
Hems and grommets.

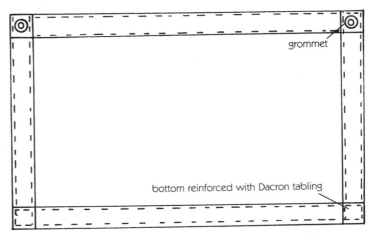

grommet

bottom reinforced with Dacron tabling

stowed most of the time under a synthetic foam berth cushion that doesn't allow much air to circulate. This is a prime place for mildew, and acrylic is very resistant to it.

If you are enclosing an area for a child (or if ventilation is a primary concern), consider using Textilene. Textilene is a screenlike material that comes in a variety of colors and will allow air to circulate better than acrylic. It will not provide privacy, and it may leave a screen pattern on your back if you lie against it for long, but the temporary tattoo is a small price to pay for good ventilation.

Construction

Step 1. Measure each berth; then cut out each individual lee cloth, adding 2½ inches on all sides to be hemmed, and an extra inch of height to fold under the batten. Cut each cloth so that the bottom edge is on the selvage edge of the fabric. (The bottom edge wants to be as free from bulk as possible.) The measured width of fabric for an 18-inch-high lee cloth should be 21½ inches.

Step 2. Hem the sides and top of each cloth with a double-rubbed hem; i.e.,

fold the fabric over twice and stitch once near the outside edge of the hem and once near the inside edge of the hem.

Step 3. Stitch Dacron tabling over the bottom edge of the cloth to reinforce it without adding much bulk.

Step 4. Install two grommets, one in each upper corner (Figure 34–2).

Installation

Position the cloth so that the Dacron bottom edge is lying on the wood or glass at the inboard edge of the berth cushion. Place a wood or aluminum batten over the Dacron tabling and drill through the batten and cloth, and into the wood or glass. Use short (number 8 or 10) screws no more than 6 inches apart to hold the batten and cloth to the berth support, and secure the eye rings or padeyes in a position that will allow the cloth to be drawn tight. Be sure that the person sleeping in that bunk can reach the ring, so that he or she need not call for help to get in and out of the berth. Attach lines of suitable length to the grommets, and stow the cloth under the cushion when not in use. Sleep well!

35
Creating Storage out of Open Shelving

Almost inevitably, production cruising boats come equipped with above-berth shelves mounted on the hull. Usually these shelves have only a 2-inch fiddle as a retainer, which will not keep much from falling off when you are underway in any sort of a breeze. A ship's carpenter could probably build some fancy retaining rods or cabinets using the existing shelf as the support mechanism. A simpler option is to sew some canvas "walls" to retain the clothing, books, or gear that you would like to stow in these shelves.

Designing the Storage Unit

Decide what you would most like to store on a particular shelf. Will a front retaining wall do the trick, or would you like to divide the length of the shelf into several sections? Should the front retaining wall go all the way to the overhead or just halfway? Once you know how you would like to use the available space, draw it to scale and be sure that what you intend to store there will fit and be accessible with the retaining wall you have designed. You will find several design suggestions in Fig-

ure 35–1 that may help you to solve your own particular storage problems. Sewing a curved zipper into your canvas wall is a nice touch—very practical as well.

To secure the fabric to the shelf and overhead, use a wood or aluminum batten wherever possible. This will put a line of tension on the fabric rather than points of tension only where there are fastenings. Figure 35–2 shows details.

Measuring

Once you have designed the space, measure the length of each section and/or the entire shelf. Take height measurements at different stations along the shelf because they may differ. If you are making dividing walls, measure the depth of the shelf and the inboard and outboard height. There may be an angle where the shelf meets the hull so be sure to measure carefully when planning the dividing walls.

Transfer all your measurements to the drawing you have made, and add the following allowances for fastening the fabric to the shelf and overhead and hemming: 1) Allow for an extra inch of fabric both top

211

Figure 35–1.
Design ideas
for canvas
"walls."

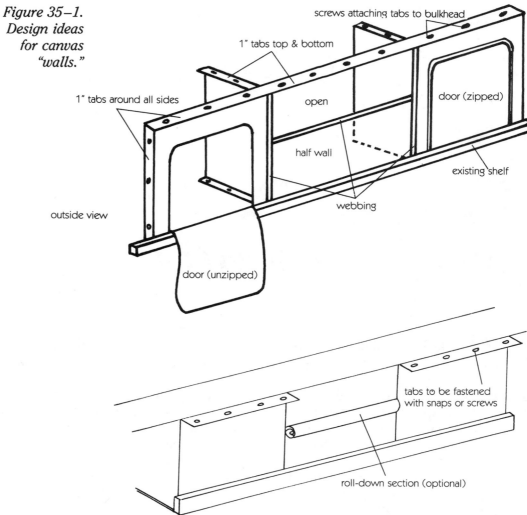

screws attaching tabs to bulkhead

1" tabs top & bottom

1" tabs around all sides

open

door (zipped)

half wall

existing shelf

webbing

outside view

door (unzipped)

tabs to be fastened
with snaps or screws

roll-down section (optional)

batten

Figure 35–2.
Mounting the
retaining wall
with battens.

1" tabs around all sides

screws attaching batten to bulkhead

webbing

batten

add Velcro to these edges

looking from inside

1" tabs top and bottom

zippered doors

Figure 35–3.
Stiffening for
half-wall
section.

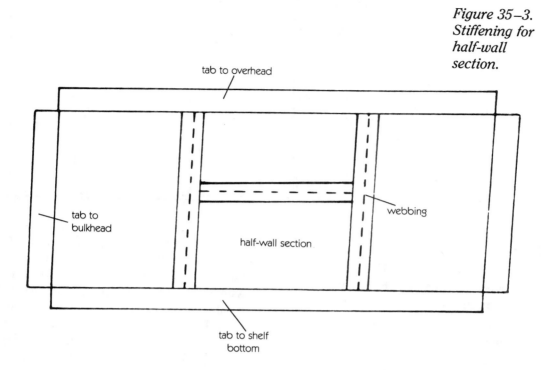

tab to overhead

tab to
bulkhead

webbing

half-wall section

tab to shelf
bottom

and bottom as tabs to fold between the batten and the shelf or overhead. For instance, if your wall needs to be 12 inches high, measure 14 inches, including 1 inch for the bottom batten and 1 inch for the top batten. 2) Add ½ inch for the top hem and ½ inch for the bottom hem. If you can use the selvage edge of the fabric on the bottom, you will not need to add anything there for hemming. 3) Often the shelf will butt into a bulkhead at one or both ends. In this case, add a ½-inch seam allowance to the end, because later you will stitch on a canvas tab that will mount on the bulkhead. If the end of the wall is freestanding, leave ½ inch for hemming. 4) If you choose to put a curved zipper in the wall

(which, when opened, allows a flap of the wall fabric to fold over, giving you access to the shelf contents), remember that in the process of stitching the zipper to the fabric you may cause the fabric to take up a bit. It's a good idea to leave an added inch of height in your fabric until you have stitched the zipper into the piece, to be sure that you have enough height. 5) If you wish to use a design similar to the one in Figure 35–1A, you will need stiffening on all sides of the half-wall cutout in the center compartment. Add ½ inch to the edges of the cutout so that you can turn them under and stitch a strip of webbing or a double layer of matching fabric tabling to them (Figure 35–3).

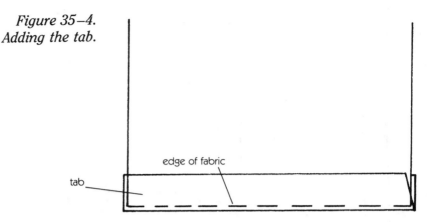

Figure 35–4.
Adding the tab.

edge of fabric

tab

Materials Needed

- acrylic or cotton canvas (decorator fabrics can be used but may not wear so well)
- number 5 Delrin zipper tape (optional)
- strip of webbing or fabric for stiffening (half walls only)
- wood or aluminum battens for mounting.

Construction

Step 1. Once you are sure that you have planned out all the edges of the fabric and have added the appropriate amount for hemming, stiffening, and tabs, cut the fabric into the required pieces.

Step 2. If your design calls for zippers, stitch them in now. Do not make such tight curves that the zipper slider cannot travel over the teeth of the zipper chain. Use number 5 Delrin zipper tape, if possible; it is more flexible than number 10. If you need to cut slashes in the tape that will be on the outside of the curve, be sure to melt the cut edges by passing them quickly through the flame of a candle or by using a hot knife. Be careful not to melt the teeth of the zipper. Stitch the zipper to the fabric before cutting the fabric open. Do this by laying the zipper in its desired

position, but on the wrong side of the fabric. Stitch one side of the tape and then the other as far away from the zipper teeth as possible. Turning the piece right side up, carefully cut the fabric on a line that will expose the teeth of the zipper. Turn under the raw edge of fabric and stitch both sides of the zipper again, this time on the right side of the fabric, using a zipper foot.

Step 3. Add the stiffening and hems that you need.

Step 4. Add the tabs.

Installation

Position the retaining wall on the shelf as you designed it, and determine that everything fits correctly. Make whatever alterations may be necessary. Begin at the bottom, which will probably be the most difficult to work. Lay a batten over the bottom tab and drive screws through the batten and fabric into the shelf. Work in sections or you will not be able to get to the top. For example, install the bottom batten for the first two feet and then install the top of the same two feet of shelf. This will also make it easier to get the proper amount of tension on the fabric. The last few screws may be difficult, but your opening should allow you enough room to get your hands in behind the retaining wall and drive them in.

If you use dividing walls, install them first. Install the tab that goes on the hull liner, then the bottom, and then the top.

The most difficult part of installing a retaining wall on a shelf is getting enough tension on the fabric so that it is crisp and taut. If your shelf is made of wood, it may be helpful to drive a couple of staples through the fabric into the wood to allow you to pre-position the fabric.

36
Protective Carpet Runners

On the most expensive yachts, you will find expensive carpeting or beautiful teak and holly floors protected with carpet runners made of cotton canvas—removed, of course, for company. Those of us with smaller pocketbooks may have other priorities, but we can still consider making such runners ourselves in order to save a beautiful floor or the new carpeting.

Basically, a protective carpet runner duplicates the shape of your floor and is snapped or tied down to padeyes so that it will not slip (Figure 36–1). It is made of cotton canvas because cotton takes the chafe and abuse better than acrylic canvas and comes in heavier weight cloth than acrylic. The runner's edges are well reinforced to take the strain of the fastening

Figure 36–1.
Carpet runner.

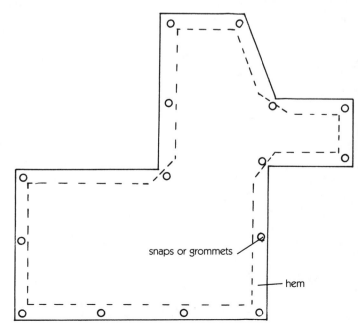

snaps or grommets

hem

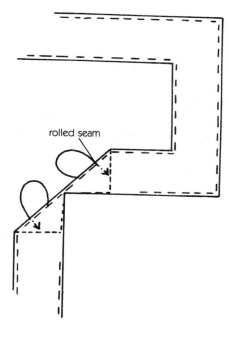

Figure 36–2.
Inside corner hem.

rolled seam

system, and the fabric is washed before it is cut so that any shrinkage occurs before you make the runners. This is very important if you expect the runners to fit—don't forget to do it. *Note:* When washing these runners, use cold water whenever possible and drip dry. This is the best way to prevent further shrinkage.

Materials Needed

- 13-ounce Vivatex or Permasol cotton canvas
- grommets and small padeyes or snaps
- vinyl binding (optional)

Designing the Runner

To pattern your floor space, use brown wrapping paper to make a pattern of the floor. Of course, if you plan to do only a straight hallway or a rectangle to put on the floor next to the engine hatches, a pattern isn't necessary. But if the space has angles or extensions, a pattern is a must. Lay the paper on the floor and cut it so that it will lie exactly the way you want the runner to lie on the floor. Mark on the

pattern each fastening location and be sure to mark the right side of the pattern. Too often a pattern is flipped over when the fabric is cut and you end up with a mirror image of what you wanted.

Construction

Step 1. Lay the pattern on the fabric with the wrong side of the pattern to the right side of the fabric. With Permasol or Vivatex, you must arbitrarily choose the right side, so be sure to mark it as such. Draw a line around the outside edge of the pattern. If the pattern requires more width than the fabric allows, stitch pieces of fabric together with an overlap seam, before transferring the pattern shape to the fabric. Remember, an overlap seam can be used only with selvage edges. This type of seam will not add much bulk to the runner where you are likely to be walking.

Step 2. Once the pattern shape has been established, add 2½ inches to each edge for a double-rubbed hem.

Step 3. Cut out the runner on this line.

Step 4.   Fold the double-rubbed hem to the bottom side of the runner, and stitch once on the fold line and once on the outside edge. Whenever you come to an inside corner, slash the hem allowance to the exact corner and finish the end of the hem with a narrow rolled seam (Figure 36–2). If this will be a point of strain, reinforce it with vinyl binding.

Step 5.   Set the grommets or snaps in the hem where appropriate, and install the padeyes or male snaps in the boat.

Remember to remove your runners when company comes. But be sure to put them back again before the grease monkeys in your crew decide the fuel filter needs changing or the head needs rebuilding. You might even make a drop cloth for the quarter berth or settee where greasy work is likely to take place. Consider making one small enough to fit in the toolbox. If it's handy, maybe someone will use it.

37
Fitted Toilet Seat Cover

If you're in the mood to cheer up the head, or if you are tired of the feeling of cold porcelain on the back of your knees while you're brushing your teeth, it's time to make a fitted toilet seat cover. It's a simple project that really adds a touch of class to any vessel, large or small. It will take only an hour or two once you have collected your materials.

Materials

Your materials will consist of the fabric you choose, some wide elastic, and some thread. I recommend that you make this cover out of synthetic fiber as it will tend to resist mildew better than cotton. Terrycloth might be the one exception. It tends to mildew more quickly than a synthetic, but because of its absorbency and washability it usually makes a nice cover. Other fabrics I recommend are the fake fur-pile fabrics that commercial toilet seat covers are generally made of, cotton-polyester-blend fabrics of medium to heavy weight, acrylic canvas, and medium-to-heavy-weight synthetic ducks.

The elastic should be 1 inch wide so that you can fold it over the raw edge of the cover and stitch it easily. Do this with a zigzag stitch so that the thread will not break when the elastic is stretched out. If you do not have a zigzag machine, make a small drawstring casing around the edge of the cover to cinch the cover around the lid of the toilet.

Before you choose a fabric, consider doing some sort of appliqué or needlework on the cover. Your personal burgee symbol or a favorite design or logo might be appropriate. If you plan to add a design, your fabric should be a solid color that will complement your design. You can work the design directly on the cover, or work it on another piece of fabric and then stitch it to the cover. Either way works, but be aware of the fact that a large piece of fabric stitched on top of the cover may shift a bit as people sit on it. This type of strain on the fabric will probably cause it to rip. If the logo is large, it's best to work it directly on the cover fabric.

If you want to use your curtain fabric for the toilet seat cover but the fabric is not suitable, you can back the curtain fabric

Figure 37–1.
Toilet seat cover with
decorative appliqué.

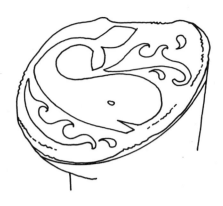

Figure 37–2.
Pattern with darts.

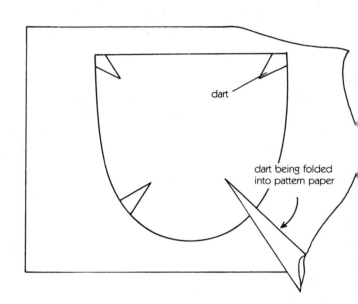

dart

dart being folded
into pattern paper

Figure 37–3.
Stitching the elastic into
the cover.

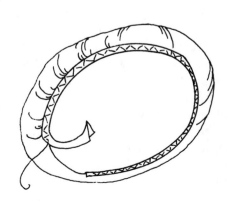

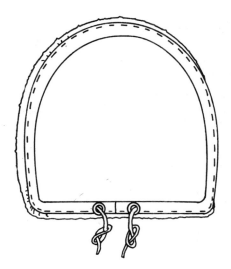

Figure 37–4.
Threading the drawstring
through the casing.

with a synthetic canvas or duck to add strength to the lighter-weight cloth. You might want to use just a stripe or flower from the curtain fabric. If so, appliqué it to the cover as if it were a logo.

Construction

Step 1.   To measure the toilet seat lid, place a piece of brown paper over the lid and trace its shape onto the paper. If there is a significant convex curve to the lid and your fabric has no nap to hide the slight wrinkles this curve will cause in the fit, mark two or four darts in the cover. Be sure to place them symmetrically. You can mark these darts temporarily in the paper by folding the paper in the shape of the darts and taping the folds down to retain them while you trace the toilet seat (Figure 37–2). You may have trouble getting the darts accurately symmetrical at this point, but you can even them up later before you cut the fabric. A napped fabric such as fake fur or heavy cotton terry will not need these darts because the nap will camouflage the wrinkles.

Step 2.   Before cutting your fabric,

preshrink it by washing it and drying it the way you intend to launder it in the future.

Step 3.   Once you have the paper pattern drawn and your darts measured so that they are symmetrical, add 2 inches to the pattern on the front and sides of the lid. Because of the hinge on the back of the lid the cover usually cannot tuck under here. Add only 1 inch to the back edge of the cover. Trace around this expanded pattern on the fabric you've chosen, and cut on this line if you are using elastic. If you are using a casing and drawstring, cut ½ inch outside this line.

Step 4.   Stitch any necessary darts. If you are using a logo or design, place it on the cover now.

Step 5. Elasticized Cover: Beginning at the back edge of the cover, fold 1-inch elastic over the raw edge of the fabric. Using a wide zigzag stitch, stitch the elastic all the way around the cover and overlap the ends at the back edge (Figure 37–3). Be sure to stretch the elastic as you are stitching so that when it relaxes it will gather the fabric and fit snugly on the toilet lid.

Drawstring Cover: Since most suitable fabrics for toilet seat covers will be too heavy to gather nicely, you will need to make the casing out of something lighter. Lining fabric or scraps of dress-weight material might do the trick. Or buy bias tape with one edge folded that matches your fabric. The bias tape is the easiest to work with. Stitch the unfolded edge of the tape, right sides together, to the cover. Fold the tape to the wrong side of the cover and stitch the folded edge to the wrong side of the fabric. Set small rivets or grommets in the bias tape for the drawstring to exit to the outside of the casing. With a small safety pin, thread a light piece of line through the casing and knot both ends so that they will not slip back through the grommets (Figure 37–4).

Step 6. Install the cover by slipping it over the lid.

38
Tablecloth, Napkins, and Placemats to Fit Your Table

For an added touch of class in your main saloon, make tablecloths, napkins, and placemats that complement your interior decor or carry out your personal logo. If you've ever been to a boat show or dined on a classy yacht, you know how lovely most boats look when every detail has been attended to and coordinated in appearance. At home, I would set a beautiful table for company; on board I like to pay the same kind of attention to detail. In fact, I think it may be more important on board, because of a boat's limited space and the sense most of us have that sailing is really a form of "roughing it." Well, let's rough it in style and have some table linens.

Tablecloths

A tablecloth can be made of any fabric that will hang nicely over the edge of the table. A very lightweight fabric will not have enough body and will wrinkle too easily to look nice. Very heavy fabrics will not hang nicely either. It is best to stay with a medium-weight cotton-polyester blend that will work well for tablecloths, napkins, and placemats. If your interior fabric is of medium weight, you may want to carry it over in your table linens, or perhaps you have throw pillows or shams of a suitable fabric. Think about how this fabric could be used as trim or appliquéd to the center or corners of the cloth. You can have too much of a good thing, so don't overdo any single fabric. A combination that I always find pleasing is a solid color for the table-cloth and napkins that complements the interior cushions, and a print that matches the throw pillows for placemats. For the second set of napkins I would use the placemat fabric.

If your table has permanently fitted fiddles, it may not be practical to use a tablecloth unless you make it to fit inside the fiddles. This type of cloth may not look the way you think a tablecloth is supposed to, but it is a good way to dress up the table. If your table has removable fiddles, you can always use a tablecloth when the fiddles have been removed. Or if you really want to get fussy, make machine button-holes for each fiddle pin. This will allow the tablecloth to lie under the fiddles and hang over the table (Figure 38–2).

Construction

Step 1. If the table is rectangular or round, you can make a tablecloth by measuring the table and adding 4 inches of overhang and ½ inch for a rolled hem. If the table is any other shape, it is best to pattern it with paper. Lay the paper on the table and trace its outer edge on the pattern. After the shape of the table has been patterned, add 4½ inches to the outside of the line for overhang.

Step 2. Cut the cloth as you have measured it, remembering that you need ½ inch for the rolled hem. If you are going to appliqué or trim the cloth, do it now.

Step 3. Sew the rolled hem, using a rolled-hem foot if possible. This specialized foot will roll the fabric in a tight hem just before the needle stitches it. Beginning at the corner of the cloth, cut a diagonal slash the depth of your ½-inch hem allowance and start the fabric in the rolled-hem foot. If you don't have a rolled-hem foot and can't buy one for your machine, roll the hem yourself. This will take a bit of patience, and your hem will end up being wider than one that a rolled-hem foot would create. You may in fact want to leave yourself a ¾-inch hem allowance if you must roll the hem by hand. When hemming along the bias of the cloth, be sure not to stretch the fabric or your hem will be crooked. If you have fairly stretchy fabric, you may want to stitch all the way

Figure 38–1.
Placemats can be designed to the shape of your table.

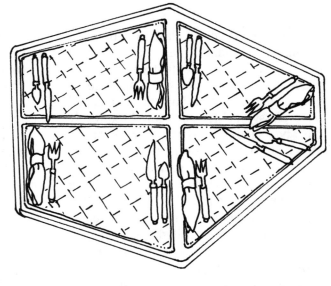

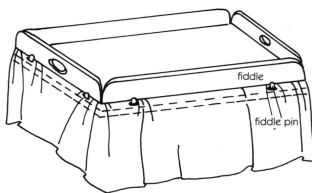

Figure 38–2.
Tablecloth with buttonholes for each fiddle pin.

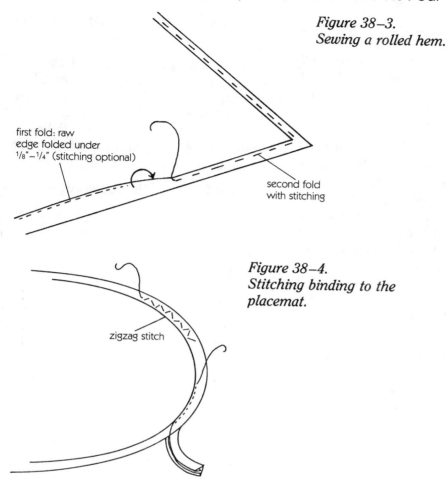

Figure 38–3.
Sewing a rolled hem.

first fold: raw
edge folded under
1/8"–1/4" (stitching optional)

second fold
with stitching

Figure 38–4.
Stitching binding to the
placemat.

zigzag stitch

around the cloth with a stay stitch to eliminate stretching before you hem the piece.
Press the hem flat with a steam iron if
possible (Figure 38–3).

Napkins

Construction

Step 1. Most napkins are 10, 12, or
14 inches square. Determine the desired
finished size of your napkins, and cut them
1 inch bigger all the way around. For instance, a 12-inch napkin should be cut 13
by 13 inches.

Step 2. Cut the cloth as measured.
Hem the napkins either by hand or on the

sewing machine, as described in Step 3 for
the tablecloth.

Placemats

Oval or square placemats may work well
on your table. If not, design a shape that
will allow you to use the number of mats
you will normally need on your table. Usually, such mats will be wider on the bottom
than on the top.

The edges of each mat are finished
with binding. It will be much easier to
make attractive placemats if you buy selvage edge or prefolded binding. The knit
type is difficult to work with because it will
stretch, creating uneven widths. When

you buy the binding, check its color carefully against your mat fabric in natural daylight because the fluorescent lighting in most stores can deceive your eye and leave you with a mismatch.

Construction

Step 1.   Cut the placemats to their exact finished size and shape. No hem allowance is necessary. If you want your placemats to be quilted, refer to the quilting instructions in Chapter 30 and quilt all the fabric before you cut the mats. I recommend that you split the batting thickness in half, because the full thickness will be too much for a placemat.

Step 2.   Stitch binding all the way around the placemats. You will have a better chance of catching both sides of the binding if you use a zigzag stitch the width of the binding. If you are very skilled, a straight stitch close to the inside edge of the binding will look best (Figure 38–4).

Step 3.   Press the bound edges flat.

39
Canvas Insert for Pipe Berths

I know that we don't find the traditional pipe berth on many yachts today unless they are older models or racing boats. However, if you have a pipe berth on board and the fabric rots or if you want to use a tried-and-true method of creating an extra bunk, knowing how to make the cloth insert will be helpful. I might add that pipe berths are quite comfortable to sleep on and provide a bunk that doesn't have to be set up at all times. They lend flexibility to a layout and allow one space to be used for several purposes.

Materials Needed

- Vivatex or Permasol cotton canvas or acrylic canvas
- grommets
- vinyl binding
- number 4 Dacron line

Construction

Step 1. Remove the pipe berth frame from the boat and place it on a piece of paper larger than the frame. Do not use the old cloth for a pattern because it has probably shrunk or stretched out of shape. Trace around the inside of the frame on the paper and use this template for your pattern.

Step 2. Most pipe berths have rounded corners because of the nature of bending pipe. Because of these curves, the edge of your canvas should be tabled rather than hemmed. Make the fabric insert slightly smaller than the frame so that you will be able to stretch the fabric tightly. Draw a line 1/2 inch inside the pattern line, and cut the paper pattern on this inside line.

Step 3. Cut one piece of canvas to match the pattern. Cut tabling strips 2 1/2 inches wide to match the outside edge of the pattern. Be sure to duplicate the curves exactly.

Step 4. Add Dacron tape to all pipe berth inserts except those made of 13-ounce cotton canvas. If you use 10-ounce cotton or acrylic canvas without reinforcements, the strain on the grommets may cause the fabric to rip. Stitch the tabling to

*Figure 39–1.
Lacing the fabric to
the frame.*

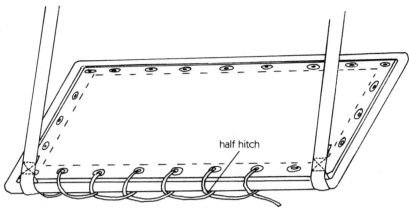

half hitch

the wrong side of the berth canvas at the outside edge. As you stitch place two layers of Dacron between the tabling and the berth piece. Fold under the remaining edge of the tabling, enclosing the Dacron tape within the hem, and stitch the inside edge of the tabling to the berth. Refer to Figure 39–1.

Step 5.   Bind the outside raw edge with vinyl binding.

Step 6.   Set grommets every 3 inches all the way around the berth within the hem. By using this many grommets, you distribute the weight evenly around the fabric.

Step 7.   Lace the fabric to the frame, using half hitches as shown in Figure 39–1. I suggest tying all four corners with short pieces of line first to center the cloth in the frame. Then, with one continuous piece of number 4 Dacron line, lace the fabric to the frame, being sure to pull the line snug. Once you have all of the grommets laced, you may have to start at the beginning and tighten each hitch to make sure the fabric is taut on the frame.

Note: Remember to wash cotton canvas in cold water and drip dry before making the berth to keep shrinkage to a minimum.

40
Screens

If you sail in warm weather, chances are good that pesky flies and mosquitoes will put a damper on your fun. The charter boat companies we work with at the Coverloft have a list of options for boat owners to choose from when outfitting their boats for charter. Several items on the list are marked with an asterisk, indicating a "must have" for successful chartering. There are two asterisks next to screens. Screens are unfortunately expensive, because they are time-consuming to make. They are not very difficult to make, however, so they are a perfect project for those of you able to do them yourselves.

Materials Needed

- fiberglass screening
- Dacron tabling, 3 inches wide
- Velcro
- snaps

Construction

Step 1. If the hatches are square with square corners, a screen can be cut from measurements. If the corners are rounded, make a template of the curve. Companionway screens can also be made from measurements, as long as you take stations for your width dimensions (Figure 40–1). If there is teak or mahogany trim around the inside edge of the hatch, measure the screen so that the outside edge of the screen meets the outside edge of the trim perfectly. If there is no trim on the inside of the hatch, you must determine how far in to take the screen, depending on what sort of fastening surface you have. The important thing when there is no trim to use for a guideline is to be consistent.

Step 2. Cut the screens to your exact measurements with no hem allowance.

Step 3. Fold a strip of 3-inch-wide Dacron tape in half to make tabling. Stitch this tabling around the entire edge of the screen, sandwiching the screening between the two halves of the Dacron (Figure 40–2).

Step 4. The best fastening system I know of is a combination of snaps and Velcro. Velcro alone would be nice, but you

229

*Figure 40–1.
Measuring for a
companionway screen.*

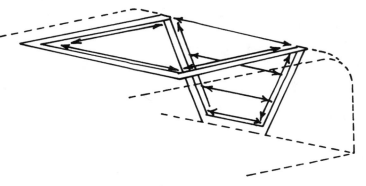

*Figure 40–1.
Measuring for a
companionway screen.*

*Figure 40–2.
Sewing tabling to the screen.*

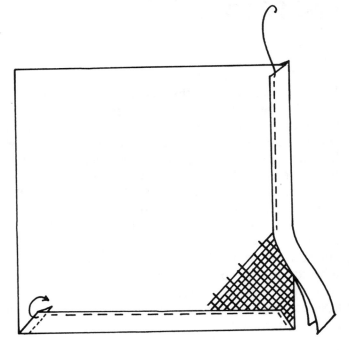

*Figure 40–3.
Positioning the snaps.*

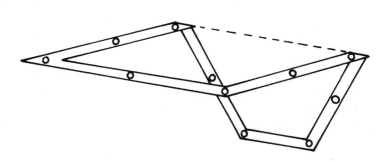

may have trouble getting Velcro adhesive to stay put after repeated removal of the screens because of the dampness of the environment. If there is a wooden surface, the Velcro can be glued and stapled to it, but it sometimes stretches and sags with repeated pulling. What I have devised consists of a piece of fuzzy-sided Velcro sewn to the screen to act as a forest for bugs to crawl through before they can get in between the snaps. Then I attach snaps to the corners and possibly the mid-sides of the screen, and these actually hold the screen to the boat. The male half of the snap is installed in the wood or glass so that the screen fastens in the proper position under the hatch (Figure 40–3).

Install the snaps as described in Chapter 31 in the section on privacy curtains. If you have more than one hatch of the same size, drill the holes in all the screens at the same time to ensure that the snaps are installed in exactly the same place on all identical hatches. If you do not do this, you will waste a lot of time trying to figure out which screen goes to what hatch. You can mark the screens with appropriate names and label the aft edge, but the label looks a bit tacky on the ceiling once the screen is installed. For further protection from bugs, spray the Velcro with bug repellent just before putting the screens up for the evening. This combination is very successful and guarantees that your sea stories will not revolve around the bugs you had to endure during your trip.

Appendix 1
Care and Cleaning of
Clear Vinyl and Acrylic Canvas

Taking Care of Vinyl

Regardless of how well clear vinyl is cared for, it will eventually turn color. When vinyl is made, a softener, called a plasticizer, is added to keep the vinyl supple. Eventually this plasticizer will evaporate or leach out, causing the vinyl to become stiff and brittle and to change color. The plasticizer leaches out more quickly in a clear vinyl than in a colored one. This process is accelerated by the ultraviolet rays of the sun, salt water, constant flexing, and extreme cold temperatures. To slow the degradation caused by the sunlight, manufacturers add ultraviolet inhibitors to all clear vinyls. You can also slow this process by cleaning your vinyl properly and not exposing it to the sun except when necessary.

Clear vinyl can be cleaned with fresh water and a mild soap such as Ivory. Even if the vinyl is not cleaned, it should be rinsed frequently with clean fresh water to remove any accumulation of salt spray.

Commercially available vinyl cleaners with preservatives and softeners, such as #990 Spray-way Vinyl Cleaner (available from most canvas shops and some chandleries), will often do a better job than soap and water.

Another method, recommended by an old-timer, for preserving and keeping the vinyl clean is spraying a very fine layer of furniture polish on the vinyl. Although I have not scientifically tested furniture polish, there are some logical reasons why it should work.

Washing Acrylic

First soak the fabric (with occasional agitation) in a solution with the following proportions of liquid bleach and soap flakes:

1/2 cup (4 ounces) bleach

1/2 cup (4 ounces) soap flakes

1 gallon lukewarm water

The fabric should remain in this solution for 20 minutes, or until most of the stains disappear.

The fabric may be washed in an automatic washer on the *cold* cycle, using 2 cups (16 ounces) of bleach and one cup (8 ounces) of soap flakes. Under no circumstances should acrylics be put in hot water, or run through the hot cycle of an automatic dryer. Nor should they be steam-pressed at a dry cleaner. The fabric should be line-dried.

If your acrylic canvas leaks after washing, this may be the result of insufficient rinsing. If the fabric continues to leak after a very thorough rinsing, it may be necessary to apply a coat of silicone air-drying water repellent. This should be done on a warm, sunny day. Be sure to give the application sufficient time to dry completely. Some of the silicone water repellents available are Scotchgard™ or products of the 3M Company.

Appendix 2
Glossary of
Interior Fabric Terms

In an effort to resolve some of the confusion that most of us feel when reading fabric sample books, I have included here a list of fabric characteristics and definitions. It is by no means a complete course in textiles; however, I have tried to include the terms that you are likely to find while choosing fabrics for your boat.

Batik. A Javanese method of resist-dyeing, employing wax as the resist. The pattern is covered with wax and the fabric is then dyed, producing a white design on a dyed ground. The waxed patterns will not take the dye; the wax is removed after dyeing. The process is repeated to obtain multicolored designs. The effect is sometimes imitated in machine prints.

Blend. The combination of two or more types of staple fibers and/or colors in one yarn. Blends are sometimes so intimate that it is difficult to distinguish component fibers in yarn or fabric. A highly sophisticated textile art, blending today is creating new fabric types, performance characteristics, and dyeing and finishing effects.

Block printing. The printing of fabrics by hand, using a design applied by means of a carved wooden block or linoleum-faced wood block. A slower process than roller printing or screen printing.

Calico. A plain, closely woven, lightweight printed cloth of East Indian origin. In England it is considered to be a plain woven, bleached cotton fabric heavier than muslin. Until the end of the seventeenth century, all cotton goods were called calicos.

Carded and combed cotton. Cotton yarn, whose fibers are separated and aligned in a thin web, then condensed into a continuous, untwisted strand called a sliver, has been carded. Carding removes most of the impurities of the fiber. Cheaper cottons are simply carded. More expensive ones go through an additional cleaning and combing process called combing.

Cationic. Cationic dyeable fiber is the newest tool in the fashion designer's kit. It's a dye technique that allows certain fibers (such as nylon or polyester) to take deep and brilliant colors. When cationic fiber is fixed with conventional fiber, various multicolors and cross-dye effects can be achieved from a single dye bath.

Challis. Various soft, supple, very lightweight, plain weave fabrics, often printed in small floral, Persian, or cravat effects. The word derives from an Indian term "shallee," meaning "soft".

Chenille fabric. A fabric woven with chenille yarns, which have a pile effect similar to velvet. When woven through various warps, the chenille yarns can create a pile-like velvet, or if woven on a jacquard loom, they can look like a cut velvet.

Chevron. Broken twill or herringbone weave giving a chevron effect, creating a design of wide V's across the width of the fabric.

Chintz. A plain, tightly woven cotton fabric processed with a glazed finish. Chintz can be either plain dyed or printed. The term is sometimes used for unglazed, fine-count cottons.

Corduroy. A pile fabric with the pile usually cut into ridges. The fabric was developed in France and for years was a specialty of royalty, thus its name meaning "cord of the king."

Crocking. Rubbing off of color from woven or printed fabrics.

Direct print. Pattern and ground color printed on fabric in the colors desired, as opposed to extract printing done on a dyed cloth. Cretonne is an example of a direct print.

Dobby. Fabric with geometric figures woven in a set pattern. Similar to, but more limited, more quickly woven, and cheaper than jacquards, which require elaborate procedures to form patterns.

Dyeing of textiles. The coloring of unbleached, undyed goods or fibers with either natural or synthetic dyes. This may be done in many different ways depending on the type of fabric (or fiber), the type of dye, and the desired result. Some of the more common methods are: *Continuous* — Fabric is continuously dyed. Dye lots may run to 30,000 yards per color. *Jet* — Used for dyeing polyester. Pressure kettles take dyes up to extremely high temperature and force dye into the fiber. *Millitron* — Developed by Milliken and Co. for continuous pattern dyeing. *Piece* — Fabric is passed through the dye solution for a specified length of time. *Printing* — A term referring to methods of applying designs to unbleached, undyed goods. Some types of printing are roller printing, screen printing, and hand-blocked printing. *Solution* — A solution of dye is added to a liquid synthetic before spinning it into a yarn. *Vat* — An insoluble dye rendered soluble and applied to the fiber, and then oxidized to the original insoluble form. Average dye lot is 700 yards. *Yarn* — Yarn is dyed before it is woven into fabric.

Fiber. Any tough substance, natural or man-made, composed of threadlike tissue capable of being made into yarn.

Fiber base. Most man-made fibers are formed by forcing a syrupy substance (about the consistency of honey) through the tiny holes of a device called a spinneret. In their original state, the fiber-forming substances exist as solids and therefore must first be converted into a liquid state for extrusion. This is achieved by dissolving them in a solvent or melting them with heat. If they cannot be dissolved or melted directly, they must be converted chemically into soluble derivatives. The basic substance for the three cellulosic fibers (acetate, rayon, and triacetate) is cellulose, which comes from purified wood pulp. It can be dissolved for extrusion into fibers. The substances used in the production of the non-cellulosic fibers generally are melted or chemically converted into a liquid state.

Fiber content. The makeup of the yarn content of any given fabric (ie., 60 percent cotton and 40 percent rayon). By regulation of the Federal Trade Commission, this information must be provided in all price lists.

Fiber types. Natural fibers: cotton, wool, silk, linen, hemp. Man-made fibers: (generic definitions) acetate, acrylic, fiberglass, modacrylic, nylon, olefin, polyester, rayon, sara, spandex, vinyl.

Fibers (generic definitions). *Acetate*— An economical, man-made fiber with a luxurious feel, that dyes in brilliant colors. It offers only low resistance to wear and only fair resistance to sunlight. When blended with other fibers, it can add beauty and luster to a fabric. Acetate is seldom used in today's fabrics. *Acrylic*— A man-made fiber with a soft feel, outstanding durability, and excellent resistance to sunlight. It has excellent cleaning characteristics and takes vivid color well. Acrylic is normally used to create velvet and plush looks in fabrics and carpets. *Cotton*— Vegetable fiber, perhaps man's oldest. Cotton has fair resistance to wear and sunlight, a soft feel, and poor resistance to soil unless treated; dyes well. *Nylon*— A man-made fiber, considered the strongest synthetic for upholstery fabrics, offering the best resistance to abrasion and soil; offers a cool, soft feel. Good cleaning characteristics. *Olefin*— Another strong, man-made fiber giving resistance to abrasion and stain. Good resistance to fading when solution-dyed, very sensitive to heat. *Polyester*— A man-made fiber, crisp and strong. Excellent resistance to wear and sunlight. Most like natural cotton in its appearance and physical properties. *Rayon*— An economical, man-made fiber with a soft feel and fair resistance to wear and sunlight; dyes well. *Fiberglass*— Fibers and yarns produced from glass and woven into flexible fabrics. Noted for their fireproof qualities.

Gingham. Yarn-dyed, combed or carded cotton fabric woven in checks, stripes, and plaids of two or more colors.

Glazed. Cotton fabrics such as chintz or tarlatan treated with starch, glue, paraffin, or shellac, and run through a hot friction roller to give a high polish. These finishes are not durable in washing. Newer, more durable methods use synthetic resins that withstand laundering.

Heat-transfer printing. The technique of printing fabrics by transferring a printed design from paper to fabric via heat and pressure. Derived from the art of decalcomania, which is the process of transferring pictures or designs from specially prepared paper to other materials such as glass. Transfer printing is used mainly on fine knit fabrics and lightweight fabrics and is rapidly gaining in importance in textile circles. Also being used by apparel makers on parts of garments to enhance their fashion appeal.

Jacquard. A method for producing elaborately patterned weaves on a mechanical loom. Named for the Frenchman who invented a loom that operates somewhat like the roller on a player piano. Instead of notes, it gives instructions to the machine on how to create the design.

Knitting. Process of making fabric by interlocking series of loops of one or more yarns.

Linen. Flax is the plant; linen is the product from flax. The term *linen* cannot be used except for natural-fiber flax.

Velour. A term loosely applied to all types of fabrics with a nap or cut pile on one side. Specifically, velour is a cut-pile fabric similar to regular velvet but with a higher pile.

Velvet. A pile fabric with a clipped nap. Before clipping, the nap is a loop as found in frieze or bouclé. Velvet was introduced during the Renaissance in Italy and Spain and later moved to France. Designs can be woven into it or made by cutting the velvet nap into different lengths or by cutting different lengths over a pattern.

Vinyl upholstery. A polyvinyl chloride film with a fabric backing.

Appendix 3
Sources

The following suppliers will ship directly to you. Some may refer you to local dealers in their network. Most prefer to deal with individuals on a C.O.D. or cash in advance basis. Local sailmakers are another, often invaluable source of information and sometimes supplies. Don't overlook canvas specialty stores, marine supply stores, and the marine supply discount catalog houses.

THE ASTRUP CO., 945 W. Flagler St., Miami, FL 33130, 305-591-8147. *Industrial canvas, thread, grommets, etc.*

THE CANVAS CO., 6319 Seaview Ave. NW, Seattle, WA 98107, 206-782-6667. *Custom marine boat canvas and hardware, raw materials, and finished products.*

H.L.S., 2120 W. Lafayette, Baltimore, MD 21217, 301-362-6622. *Foam only.*

McWILLIAMS AND LIPE, LTD., 330 Second Street, Annapolis, MD 21403, 301-269-5900. *Canvas, hardware, grommets, etc., raw materials, and finished products; also, materials for boat interiors.*

SAILRITE KITS, Route 9, Columbia City, IN 46725, 800-348-2769. *Marine canvas, all related hardware, grommets, thread, deck fasteners, etc. Send $2.00 for catalog.*

SEATTLE FABRIC, 3876 Bridge Way N., Seattle, WA 98103, 206-632-6022. *Marine fabrics, zippers, grommets, fasteners, treated cotton canvas, vinyl marine boat toppings.*

TEXTILE COMMISSION, INC., 217 Chestnut St., Phila, PA 19106. 800-523-4946 outside PA; 215-923-7440 in PA. *Marine canvas, all related hardware, grommets, thread, deck fasteners, etc.*

Index